21.⁰⁰

INSTITUTIONAL ECONOMICS
Contributions
to the Development
of Holistic Economics

Essays in Honor of
ALLAN G. GRUCHY

JOHN ADAMS
Editor
University of Maryland

Martinus Nijhoff Publishing
Boston / The Hague / London

Distributors for North America:
Martinus Nijhoff Publishing
Kluwer Boston, Inc.
160 Old Derby Street
Hingham, Massachusetts 02043

Distributors outside North America:
Kluwer Academic Publishers Group
Distribution Centre
P.O. Box 322
3300 AH Dordrecht, The Netherlands

Library of Congress Cataloging in Publication Data

Main entry under title:

Institutional economics.

    1.   Institutional economics—Addresses, essays,
lectures. 2. Economic policy—Addresses, essays,
lectures. 3. Underdeveloped areas—Addresses, essays,
lectures. 4. Gruchy, Allan Garfield, 1906–
I. Gruchy, Allan Garfield, 1906–   II. Adams,
John, 1938–
HB99.5.I57   330.15   79-13203
ISBN 0-89838-022-7

Printed in the United States of America.

CONTENTS

PREFACE

Allan Garfield Gruchy, now Professor Emeritus at The University of Maryland, retired in 1977 from full-time duty. That he continued to teach his graduate seminar in institutional economics and simply accelerated work on a major study of planning in world economies is only more evidence of the energy and concern he has brought to his teaching and writing throughout his career. His undergraduate classes in comparative economic systems and modern economic thought, and his two graduate courses on institutionalism, were always among the most popular in the department. They were firmly grounded in a perspective that opened the minds of hundreds of students to new avenues of thought and to different modes of economic organization. Returning students who report they quickly forgot the arid intricacies of intermediate theory courses nonetheless recall Allan's verbal thrusts at orthodox positions and at the shortcomings of American economic institutions. Allan worked for many years with Dudley Dillard to construct Maryland's present department and served ably as acting chairman in 1976–77 after Dudley relinquished the chairmanship. His impatient wit enlivened faculty meetings and rendered them expeditious in the extreme, and it was welcomed by all except those with a penchant for pontification.

Allan is best known among economists for his elucidation of institutional and neoinstitutional thought and for his comparative analysis of planning and growth. His *Modern Economic Thought* (1947/1967) and *Contemporary Economic Thought* (1972) have long been touchstones for those seeking expositions of heterodox thought. Likewise, his *Comparative Economic Systems* (Second Edition, 1977) has been a standard text for over a decade. Allan's professional impact has not been limited, however, to the written word. He was the early moving force behind The Association for Evolutionary Economics and was that group's president in 1968.

This book honors Allan Gruchy and his career. To many of its contributors he has been a stimulus, friend, and ally. It would be remiss not to report, as editor, the enthusiasm that the sixteen authors expressed for this project. Respect and affection motivated them to write essays of the first quality and made the task of editing remarkably easy.

The contributions are grouped into four sections. The first is devoted to Allan's writings and professional activities. The other three contain clusters of papers touching on each of the themes that run with enormous consistency right through the whole of his lifetime work as an economist: the evolution of institutionalist ideas, planning in modern industrial economies, and planning and growth in the developing world. They are all written from what Allan calls the *holistic* viewpoint; that is, they treat economic ideas and problems as part of a process in which social, political, and economic factors intermingle in an interdependent fashion.

The collection as a whole also embodies one of Allan's major precepts: that we must always be concerned with where we are going—in our thought and in our actions. It is often said by those who should know better that institutionalism is dead or dying or that its ideas have been absorbed into the mainstream. None of the authors in this volume thinks of himself as dead or as having been absorbed. Rather, they regard themselves as very much alive and still ready to fight. They all understand where they are going and the tasks that lie just ahead. There is a living institutional tradition, and that tradition is healthy, vigorous, and perhaps even expanding. There are institutionalists who are writing of the same problems about which the orthodox are writing, but from their own vantage point. The papers assembled in the book attest to these things, and they indicate that institutionalism—holistic economics—has a future and that institutionalists have contributions to make to the solutions of today's economic problems.

Dudley Dillard and Wendell Gordon were extremely helpful in the initial phases of this undertaking. The contributors were all cooperative in meeting their deadlines and otherwise making the editorial job a pleasure. My thanks to all. Mrs. Edith Van Ness assisted most helpfully with correspondence and with preparation of copy. My thanks to her.

John Adams

ALLAN G. GRUCHY
Man and Ideas

1 THE WRITINGS OF ALLAN G. GRUCHY

John Adams

It is rare that one sits down to read the entire range of another's work. I have done this twice, or two-and-a-half times, with Jane Austen, once plus odds and ends with Hemingway, Henry James (with some cheating), and a few other serious writers, and with a legion of authors of mysteries, thrillers, romances, and what Graham Green called entertainments. The only economist whose writings I have read all of in a deliberate, concentrated way is Allan Gruchy. I recommend the exercise, at least in this case, because I have come away with enormous respect for the continuity and unity of his writing and for the consistency with which he has held to and argued for a set of profoundly important ideas in the fields of economic thought, economic systems, and national planning. It is obvious that Gruchy seized in the late 1930s upon two giant ideas, one stemming from the horrors of the Great Depression and the other from the strong contemporaneous intellectual current favoring active government. The first was that modern capitalist economies had ceased to function — if they ever had — in the automatic self-adjusting fashion described by the orthodox tradition of economics. The second was a perception of an underlying unity in the writings of the major American institutionalists. Both realizations — one about the nature of the economy, the other about the character of economic thought — made it possible to build chains of argument leading ineluctably to one conclusion: the need for national economic planning. The evolution of the economic system and the evolution of ideas pointed in an identical direction.

To date, the systematic development and presentation of these two ideas and the conclusion to which they lead has generated two books on institutional thought and one in the field of comparative economic systems. *Modern Economic Thought* appeared in 1947 and was reprinted in 1967, *Contemporary Economic Thought* was published in 1974 and editions of *Comparative Economic Systems* came out in 1966 an 1977.[1]

Further, the early study of banking in Virginia (1937) stands as a monographic effort to examine relations between the state government and a part of the economy everywhere congenitally unable to manage itself.[2] With the stream of related journal articles and book reviews, the total number of pages Gruchy has in print amounts to over 2,500, not counting separate editions. A study of national planning — another book — will soon appear and a new book on institutional economics is also planned. Gruchy has thus comprehensively surveyed institutional thought, examined national economic performances in a comparative perspective, and, so to speak, will close the cycle of his argument with a volume on national planning. Over four decades have been devoted to this task: to elaborate the vision that was there in more or less full form by the end of the decade of the 1930s. Vogues have come and gone — even Keynesian thought is being redefined and merged into older convention—but Gruchy has continued to argue with patient consistency that contemporary national economies cannot be left to manage themselves, or measures of their performance — growth rates, inflation, unemployment, and others — will prove popularly unacceptable. Also, he has made explicit the links of a second generation of institutionalists — the neoinstitutionalists — to the earlier group. Thus, remarkable continuity and coherency mark Gruchy's career as an economist and distinguish it from those of economists who bounce opportunistically from fad to fad, from topical issue to topical issue, and from one palliative to the next.

I have no intention of undertaking a full review and assessment of Gruchy's writings. Most of those who will read these remarks are at least as familiar with them as am I, and have been for a longer time. For the uninitiated his works speak for themselves: they are not arcane and they are not plagued with the abstruseness of much modern technical economics. The references I list can be pursued as one's interests dictate. The scope of this essay is deliberately limited: it is not supposed to serve as a comprehensive survey and assessment of Gruchy's whole corpus of work; rather, what I will do is review the handling of certain key themes and introduce the contributions that constitute this collection. I am thus not essaying to do a "Gruchy" on Gruchy, to add an eleventh review of an institutionalist's thought to his ten. (Or perhaps one could say a twelfth, if Millar's contributed essay on Copeland is numbered eleven.) It is significant that Gruchy does not need a Gruchy to be understood. Commons without a crutch (or a Liebhafsky lighting a fire under one) is not easily grasped by the neophyte; Veblen can go out of his way to say what he does not mean (the best example perhaps is "instinct," and there are paragraphs and pages, too); reading Ayres without coming into contact with someone in the oral tradition does not seem to do much for people. But Gruchy's strategy of argumentation — and it is clearly conscious — is to be plain and direct and to work out the lines of reasoning as unambiguously as possible. He needs no pulling guard, no explicator.

Gruchy introduced the term "holistic" to describe one of the unique and contrasting features of institutionalism: its striving to look at all aspects of reality — not just at the narrowly economic — and to see them as an interrelated whole. It is worth saying, before going on to deal with the various facets of Gruchy's writings, that his body of work is itself holistic. To look at the work on institutional thought apart from the comparative systems book is to miss a portion of the argument. His writings are also unified over time. *Modern Economic Thought,* which covers the older generation of institutionalists (Veblen, Commons, Mitchell, Clark, Tugwell, Means), and *Contemporary Economic Thought,* which reviews largely postwar developments in neoinstitutionalist thought (Ayres, Galbraith, Myrdal, Colm), constitute, in effect, a two-volume set, separated by twenty-seven years. An early important paper, which appeared in the *Southern Economic Journal* of 1939, lays out the consensus in much institutional thought in favor of planning.[3] This precursive article forms a tandem with "Institutionalism, Planning, and the Current Crisis," which came out in the *Journal of Economic Issues* in 1977, thirty-eight years afterwards.[4]

Those who bounce from problem to problem in economics — who dabble here and there — might wonder at the discipline and concentration required by Gruchy's holistic consistency. I believe it is important that this be perceived as a chosen path, reflecting an obviously early and deep-seated judgment about the ultimate valuation of one's career as an economist. As might be expected, Gruchy is sparing of his criticisms of institutionalist writers. Of our great god Veblen, however, he says:

No careful reader of Veblen's essays and treatises can lay them down without feeling that there are certain very grave deficiencies in his work. The elements of his system of economic thought for the interpretation of twentieth-century economic enterprise are scattered over many essays and volumes. . . . If he had shown a greater willingness to organize his ideas within a shorter compass, the nature and significance of his institutional economics would have been made available to a wider public. . . .

Furthermore, Veblen displays a lamentable unwillingness to pursue new insights until they have been drained of their final unit of significance. Frequently he has come upon a new field of thought but has failed to explore it fully.[5]

It is thus clear from these passages what Gruchy believes should form a research career: the production of a unified body of work in which the main themes are developed to the fullest possible extent.

Two stylistic features of Gruchy's writings merit explicit recognition. He rejects the agressive confrontationism of the Veblen-Ayres tradition, preferring instead more measured language and a degree of toleration. Not to be found are the vigorous demeanings of orthodox thought; the posture is rather that there are some uses of orthodoxy albeit with narrow latitude. He says of Ayres:

When he emphasizes the limitations of standard economics he gives some of his readers (judging by the reactions of his critics) the false impression that all standard economics is 'bad' economics, and that he would dispense with it as a body of tools or concepts used for analytical purposes. A reading of Ayres's writings very quickly shows that he makes much use of the analytical tools of micro-economics and macro-economics. More detailed statements by Ayres with regard to this matter would have prevented much of this misinterpretation on the part of his readers and critics.[6]

The second attribute of Gruchy's writings is their lack of stylistic egocentricity. I can find only rare conversational instances where the first person singular pronoun is used. In textual use, he never says "I think" or "I believe" or "I recommend." Yet, at the end of an essay or book we do know what Gruchy thinks. The legerdemainic device that permits this is perhaps most accurately described as "writing through the words of others." (Liebhafsky also remarks on this trait in his contribution to this collection.) Gruchy marshalls his institutionalist troops as a screen for his own argumentation, not to disguise but to reveal his own position. He does this by highlighting their proplanning stances, by extracting and brushing off chosen aspects of their pennings. When he wishes to move past the constraints of others' published thoughts, he resorts to phrases such as "The neo-institutionalists assert," "The institutionalist position is," or "Many critics say."[7] This is an effective — and admirably modest and restrained — technique. It does, however, make it easy for the careless peruser to read Gruchy's books and essays at a superficial level, to see them only as rehashes or syntheses of others' writings. To do this is to make a grave mistake and to undervalue by a large margin the originality of

Gruchy's conceptions. (One might contrast Gruchy with Galbraith in these matters, but I will refrain from so doing.)

In the following sections I will do the following: in the first, explore Gruchy's views on the scope and interests of economic science; in the second, comment on his thoughts on the nature of the economy, its relation to politics and society, and its direction of movement; in the third, describe his synthesis and elucidation of institutional thought; in the next, discuss his commitment to planning. The final section introduces the contributed papers.

THE SCOPE OF INTEREST OF ECONOMICS

Institutionalists part company with orthodox economists at a very early stage of debate. There is fundamental disagreement between them over what economists ought primarily to be interested in studying. The old definition about economics being what economists do is true, but it requires extension by adding "what economists do is what they see." What I mean by this is that what economists do is defined by what they see as "economic," by how they identify economic behavior. In dealing with market-type economies orthodox economists are content to study the allocational efficiency of the pricing system, while institutionalists see the market system — the forces of supply and demand — as being part of, and dependent upon, an evolving social and political order. Gruchy writes:

> The neoinstitutionalists define economics to be the study of the evolving pattern of human relationships which is concerned with the disposal of scarce resources for the satisfaction of personal and collective wants. What the neoinstitutionalists do is place economizing or economic decision-making within the framework of the evolving economic system.[8]
>
> When the economist makes his science a cultural rather than a formal science, he seeks to provide for his science a larger setting than that provided by more formal economists. . . . The cultural scientist seeks to achieve the aim of a broader and more realistic science by systematizing his thought within a new conceptual scheme which is broad enough to make room for the recent contributions of cultural anthropology, sociology, and social psychology. The new holistic or overall conceptual scheme of the cultural economist centers in the concept of the economy as a going system or process rather than as a stable mechanism. Economic society as a "connected system" is a cultural pattern or complex with a past, present, and future.[9]

Perhaps the most serious error made by the orthodox economists, according to Gruchy, is that they take wants or ends as given and thus do not try to answer how such wants and ends come into being and change over time. In doing so, they neglect to ask how human values emerge. "The main issue today in the field of economics, in the opinion of the neoinstitutionalists, is not 'efficiency,' but rather it is wants, goals, or values. . . . To the social scientist people are goal-creating, goal-possessing, and goal-achieving individuals, and the social sciences, including economics, are properly concerned with the goals or wants of people."[10]

What economists, at least institutionalists, are concerned with is human welfare, and human welfare is enhanced to the extent that the existing institutions permit the economy to help people satisfy private and collective wants and attain their goals. The performance of the economic system is determined by its ability to enable all people to meet their variety of wants.[11] Wants and goals change over time as the industrial system evolves, but are subject to misinformation, pressures from business interests, and limited recognition of the externalities of consumption and production.[12]

Gruchy adopts the practice, for mnemonic and pedagogical purposes, of using adjectival epithets to epitomize the economics of the various institutionalists and neoinstitutionalists he reviews. We thus have chapters entitled "The Collective Economics of John R. Commons" and "The Instrumental Economics of Clarence E. Ayres."[13] A fair question is what title a chapter on Gruchy and his economics should bear. The obvious is to elect "The Holistic Economics of Allan Gruchy." This suffers from the fact that all institutionalism is supposed to be holistic and Gruchy is thus not unique in this regard. I would prefer "The Futuristic Economics of Allan G. Gruchy" for the following reasons. Gruchy differs from many institutionalists in his construal of what one does with the core concept of economic evolution in evolutionary economics. He agrees completely that the economic system is evolving, but he is not concerned with where the system has been — what it has looked like — in the past. Ayres, Veblen, Polanyi, and Commons spring to mind at once as institutionalists who were deeply interested in historical analysis. Yet Gruchy spends little or no time in any of his writings on the past. He is not even especially concerned with the details of present economic organization. But he is vitally interested in where the economic system is going — and to a proportionate degree that differentiates him from other institutionalists and sharply divides him from the formalists:

> Although the cultural economist cannot predict in a scientific fashion what the future course of economic development will actually be, he is in a position to draw attention to the alternative courses of development. Furthermore, he can emphasize the point that it is possible to make some useful generalizations about the nature and direction of evolution. As we have seen, the futuristic aspects of the thought of the cultural economists is not to be found in the work of the formalistic economists.[14]

Secondly, it is not only the future of the economic system that absorbs Gruchy, but the future of economics. He believes firmly that this future favors the upsurgence of the institutional viewpoint. "The holistic economists are convinced that impending events will favor a wider acceptance of their manner of interpreting the realities of the twentieth century American economic world"[15] The institutionalists are on the right track, are gaining greater analytical leverage, and will ultimately come to the fore, just as the movement of social, political, and economic forces will eventually lead to a democratically controlled planned economic system. Thus, virtually everything that Gruchy has written has a futurity to it and bespeaks of events and ideas to come. Hence, justifiably I believe, I propose "The Futuristic Economics of Allan G. Gruchy."

THE NATURE OF THE ECONOMY

The keystone of Gruchy's vision of American capitalism since the early 1930s is that the free enterprise system, with its more-or-less self-regulating market economy that had existed since the late eighteenth century, has ceased to be automatic and self-righting in crisis.

> The price system is no longer the smoothly functioning, coordinating mechanism that the late nineteenth- and early twentieth-century orthodox economists took it to be. The capacity of the price system to allocate resources in a balanced, efficient manner, to distribute the national income widely over many classes in the community, and to maintain high levels of general economic activity has been seriously impaired by the changes which have occured in recent decades in the structure and functioning of the American economy.[16]

The reasons for the loss of automaticity are complex, but standing forth as the most critical is the movement from a generally small-scale competitive industrial sector to a dualistic economy with a core of large, powerful monopolizing firms and a competitive periphery of smaller ones. Prices become rigid, entry is barred, a full-employment equilibrium becomes less probable, the business cycle is exacerbated, inflation becomes chronic, consumer wants are artificially created and not merely satisfied, and the pattern of consumption and investment is distorted.[17] Thus, the major problems of orthodox economists become epiphenomena of a deeper cause. Similarly, their policy solutions are fundamentally useless placeboes, perhaps capable of occasional symptomatic relief but not of anything more. The American economy has become an economy of affluence because of its splendid technological vitality, and "scarcity" is no longer a crucial issue. The modern tragedy is our inability to change the economic structure—to alter the institutions of the economy—so that people may all share in this abundance, to the enhancement of the general welfare.[18]

In common with most institutionalists, Gruchy's explanation of the process of economic change is in accord with the Veblen-Ayres theory. Technology is the most important dynamic force in modern industrial economies, although this does not mean that it is the only factor. A technological determinism is not espoused. Changes in institutions are also important in determining how technologies are utilized and diffused.[19] Gruchy says that social and political factors cannot be ignored, but the major active factors that give momentum to the economic process are the changing and proliferating industrial technology and the progress of science.

In his synthesizing interpretations of institutional and neoinstitutional thought, Gruchy's comments about economic structure and change are largely confined to this country's economy. Most of his subjects — an obvious exception is Myrdal — were almost exclusively writings about the economic system of the United States. Gruchy is noteworthy, however, in wanting to put the experience of the United States in a comparative perspective, or to look more broadly at variations in structure, performance, and rate of change across a sample of major North Atlantic economies, the Soviet Union, China, and India. He is not unique in this, since a number of institutionalists have also found comparative economic systems and comparative studies a congenial field. What I find exceptional about Gruchy's detailed study of capitalist, democratic socialist, communist, and Third World economies is his emphasis on the motif of planning. In the final chapter of *Comparative Economic Systems* he summarizes the chief lesson of his comparative research: "As economic systems undergo changes in the crucible of world developments, they will all face a number of challenging economic, social, and political problems. . . . In the Western nations, we are seeing the end of an era — the era of the essentially directionless welfare mixed society — and the emergence of a new, guided or directed mixed economy.[20] He returns to the futurity theme: "In this emerging era, society is more future oriented and anticipatory in its outlook on economic and social problems."[21]

SYNTHESIS AND ELUCIDATION OF INSTITUTIONAL THOUGHT

Beyond doubt Gruchy is best recognized for his two surveys of institutional thought. I doubt that there is a single institutional economist — a questing beginner or established practitioner — who has not pulled one or both of these off the library shelf for use as guidebooks. They are helpful for those who seek to enter the temple and for those who want to recall what paths they traversed some time long past. One can always brush a Baedeker aside, of course, but he is then exposed to the risks of not knowing what he is seeing, or of missing an out-of-the-way monument or vista. Certainly there are those inveterate tourists who will quibble that the guide has missed a charming side street in Port Ayres, or not recommended the view from the north side of Mount Commons, but all this seems beside the point. A travel guide is not intended to be a substitute for the actual excursion, but only a stimulus to the appetite, a map of the terrain, a whetter of the imagination.

In *Modern Economic Thought* Gruchy begins with Veblen and, in total, reviews the writings of six institutionalist economists. The roster constitutes a roll of honor of the early giants: Veblen, Commons, Mitchell, Clark, Tugwell, and Means. Four neoinstitutionalists — Ayres, Galbraith, Myrdal, and Colm — are examined in *Contemporary Economic Thought*. The early institutionalists, as typified by Veblen, and the later neoinstitutionalists differ in several ways, although they have a good deal more in common. Neoinstitutionalists, as a group, are more willing to borrow some of the language and concepts of orthodoxy and have toned down the overheated criticism of Veblen. They also differ from Veblen, in particular, in rejecting an "untenable technological determinism."[22] Veblen thought the government had a minor role in the economy and was the tool of the industrial interests, but the neoinstitutionalists think that government can be an instrument of the common purpose.[23]

I will not conduct a reprise of the content of the chapters devoted to each of these makers of the holistic tradition. Rather I want to describe the format used to review the thought of each and comment on one or two traits of institutionalism that Gruchy distills from their work. Gruchy typically begins by reviewing the intellectual and personal influences that helped shape the economist's mind. He notes the special contributions each has made, but he also recognizes what is shared in common: the emphasis on holism, the recognition of the evolutionary economic process, the concern with values, the differences with orthodoxy, and, most of all, the conviction that conscious economic direction — some form of planning — is needed and will appear as the next phase of industrial society. There is always a bit of concluding critique and an effort to put each writer into the context of institutional thought by assaying the "nature and scope" of his particular type of institutionalism.

Two things especially interest me in these general reviews. One is the forward-looking emphasis among the institutionalists on where the system is going — the insistent reminder that today's economy is not yesterday's.

Certainly the most basic difference between heterodoxy and orthodoxy is this recognition of process and change: the repudiation of the mechanistic equilibrium syndrome that makes conventional analysis so sterile. The second is appreciation, which I think is unique, at least in degree, in Gruchy's surveys, that the *psychology* of institutionalism differs radically from that of orthodoxy. This sentiment has been with me since I was a parallel psychology and economics major at Oberlin, and while the psychological man of the behavioralists is not everyone's vision of the well-rounded human being, he is a good deal more interesting than orthodoxy's economic man. If nothing else he is capable of learning and changing. Even before I had heard of institutionalism (and I was asked whether I had acquired my skeptical and deviant views from them on a ruthless senior honors oral), I found the orthodox conception of man repugnant: amoral, hedonistic, deficient in not admitting of mutual empathy, unappreciative of the variety of individual and cultural differences, homogenizing of individuals, knowing all but understanding nothing.

Certainly no one has ever been as stupid, shallow, inhuman, and uncalculating — that is, as unable to think as a true human being — as is orthodoxy's economic man, whom Veblen so satirically labelled a "spinning globule of desire." Gruchy does a real — and I think unappreciated — service in making explicit the efforts of the early institutionalists, who were limited needless to say by the level of development of the psychological sciences that prevailed when they wrote, to create a full-bodied and real human being, who is not detached from a cultural context, as the centerpiece of their analysis.

Gruchy is not only alert to the shortcomings of Marshallian neoclassical economics. He also should be credited with the early recognition that Keynesian economics and its policy suggestions could only partially cope with the business cycles of evolving capitalism. Before many economists had even absorbed Keynes's deep teachings about economic fluctuations, Gruchy warned that they did not contain a panacea. In January 1949, he published an article in which he argued that Keynes's economics represented a major advance, compared to neoclassicism, having in particular a greater appreciation of the nature of mid-century capitalism and of the need for governmental supervision of the economy. Yet, Keynes's economics was still "fragmentary," because it did not break with the Cambridge formalistic tradition and develop a theory of process and development. Keynes might have benefited, Gruchy argues, from a reading of institutionalists.[24]

Later, in *Contemporary Economic Thought,* Gruchy says, "Keynes had little to say about the problems of a full-employment, affluent society. He was not especially concerned with the roles of the large industrial corporation or the individual consumer in an affluent society, with the problem of the hidden and unpaid social costs of continuous economic growth, or with the question of what direction an affluent society should take."[25] Keynesians have generally failed to perceive the need for some sort of long-run analysis of the economy and for democratic national economic programming.[26]

PLANNING

The heart and soul of Gruchy's writing is the concern with planning as a means of improving mass human well-being. For all his affection I do not think that planning is ever viewed as more than an instrument, a better way of helping people attain their share of the fruits of affluence, freedom from immediate and compelling material need, and greater collective control over their economic destinies. Planning is a means of breaking the concentrated power of big business and, one might also add, of big regulatory agencies unmindful of their charge to serve the public interest rather than that of their industrial bedfellows. Planning is thus not the forerunner of a "big brother" state but a liberalizing device that will enhance individual freedom. Planning is an instrumental process, a series of learning-by-doing experiments leading toward a better life. There are no unchanging abstract goals based on inflexible values, but only aims that shift over time as the economic system evolves and new problems emerge that need to be solved by collective action working through the political and programming process.

These ideas so permeate Gruchy's writings that it is both unnecessary and impossible to untangle, cite, and cope with them separately. Two key papers are the one in the *Southern Economic Journal* of October 1939 and that in the *Journal of Economic Issues* of June 1977.[27] Large portions of *Modern Economic Thought* are also important, and the whole of *Comparative Economic Systems* bears on the subject. A related paper is "Government Intervention and the Social Control of Business: The Neoinstitutionalist Position."[28]

The logic of Gruchy's case is direct and simple. The economy is no longer automatically self-adjusting, failing to generage satisfactory levels of inflation and unemployment and failing equally to achieve a suitable sharing of incomes and consumption, largely because of distortions attributable to the power of big business. Institutionalists, in perceiving and writing about these problems and their structural origins, have put forward, with some individual differences, national planning schemes. Mitchell, Clark, Tugwell, Myrdal, and Colm are among those who have suggested various versions of democratically governed planning systems. Because institutionalists are by nature forward-looking they want to know where the economic system is heading. They are particularly aware of existing structural problems and their consequences, and since they can at least broadly sense the direction of movement of the economic system as a whole, they realize that to gain some measure of control and direction over the economic process nations will of necessity resort to planning.

An underpinning idea of Gruchy and the institutional economists is that the conflict of various interests determines governmental policies towards the economy and thus helps shape patterns of economic behavior and the distribution of consumption and income. Democratic planning is a means of reconciling these competing interests and, importantly, of shifting relative power towards the public. In 1973, Gruchy wrote:

> If the national economic program were successful it would bring an end to the favorable treatment accorded to business and other private economic organizations by legislatures, regulatory bodies, and courts. . . . The institutionalists advocated a solidaristic or pluralistic approach which called for the strengthening of the labor and consumer interests so that they would be able to balance the power of the business interests. There would be created a harmony of interests that would eliminate power conflicts through compromise and adjustment. There would be a fusion of private and public power with public power, represented by the state and the courts, acting as the final arbiter in the settling of economic and social problems. Business, labor, and other interest groups would retain the right to defend what they took to be their legitimate interests, but the overriding power would be public.[29]

Why has planning not come into effect in the United States? Interestingly enough, Gruchy does not believe that the time is yet ripe. He writes, "Most institutionalists . . . do not see national planning as imminent in the United States. They believe that this course is inevitable in the long run, but it may require a more serious economic crisis than we are now witnessing to make national planning politically feasible in the United States. . . . The function of the institutionalists is educational or instructional. It is their task to explain to the American public how the logic of industrial evolution has carried the advanced industrial system to the point where its good performance requires much more national guidance."[30]

GRUCHY AND THE CONTRIBUTIONS TO THIS COLLECTION

The papers in this volume are divided into four sections. Part I begins with this paper on Gruchy's writings. The remaining two contributions in Part I touch on other aspects of Gruchy's activities as an economist. H. H.

Liebhafsky responds to a set of reviewers' remarks, made when the *Journal of Economic Issues* published multiple reviews of *Contemporary Economic Thought*. John Gambs relates the history of the founding and development of The Association for Evolutionary Economics, of which Gruchy was the initial moving force. The role of that organization, as Gruchy conceived it, was to be a vehicle for the expression of institutionalism and for mobilization of institutionalists who favored adoption of planning. Gruchy himself has recently discussed the present lack of a consistent philosophy and purpose behind that Association in his paper, "Institutional Economics: Its Influence and Prospects," which appeared in the *American Journal of Economics and Sociology* of July 1978.[31]

The other three parts in this book revolve around major themes that reflect Gruchy's lifelong interests: the evolution of institutionalist ideas, problems of managing industrial societies, and planning and development in the Third World. Leading off Part II, Wendell Gordon restates and develops the instrumental value theory of institutional economics. Philip A. Klein discusses the meaning of "holistic" economics and shows that macroeconomics, while supplementing microeconomics, still leaves unresolved such major analytical problems as economic power, the character of "economic man," and others. Royall Brandis exhibits the lasting concern of institutionalists with the philosophical basis of economics, and their absorption with problems of valuation, in his assessment of the work of Rawls and Nozick on economic justice. Anne Mayhew argues that economic anthropologists are embroiled in a debate — the "substantivist-formalist" controversy — that parallels the institutionalist-orthodox division of economics. Milton D. Lower has written a comprehensive and long-needed survey of the institutionalist theory of consumption. James R. Millar provides a Gruchy-type survey of the works of Morris A. Copeland.

In Part III Anthony Scaperlanda contrasts the rates of developmental progress in Eastern European countries and develops an explanation of differences using the Veblen-Ayres theory. Continuing the thematic concern of this section — the problems of managing advanced industrial economies — Walter C. Neale explains how a loss of consensus in Britain over the appropriate principles for income distribution undermines efforts to develop an institutional mechanism for resolving distributional issues. Thomas Havrilesky finds a link between monetary policy vacillations and distributional disputes in the United States. Robert L. Bennett argues that new microsimulation techniques are a tool institutionalists could use to operationalize and test certain hypotheses about the economy.

Part IV contains contributions dealing with problems of technology, development, and planning in the less-industrialized nations. Thomas R. de Gregori shows that the institutionalist conception of technology sheds more light on the process of technological transfer than does either the orthodox view or that of Schumacher. Edward Van Roy examines the impact of the tax policies of Asian countries on the region's distribution of foreign investment. Latin American corporatism is the subject of William Glade's essay, and James H. Street contrasts the institutional analysis of developmental problems with those of the dependency school.

THE FUTURE OF ALLAN G. GRUCHY'S
FUTURISTIC ECONOMICS

The originality and vigor of the essays in this commemorative collection are testimony to the continuity of institutional economics. No one has done more than Allan Gruchy to nurture and carry forward the legacy of institutional thought. No one has been more forward-looking in his hopes for the future of our industrial way of life and for the ultimate validation of institutional interpretations of the economic process. In a set of seminars during his retirement year Gruchy addressed faculty and students at The University of Maryland. These sessions made two things abundantly plain: most orthodox economists do not know what institutionalism is and most American economists are not willing even to engage in debate about the efficacy of planning as a policy reform capable of solving existing economic problems. That Gruchy has been successful in raising considerably the profession's and the public's understanding of institutionalism and planning, in the face of ignorance and apathy, is a major achievement.

Gruchy tells the story of being accosted by a new graduate student who remarked, "Let me shake your hand; I understand you are the last of the institutionalists."[32] I have had similar experiences and suspect most institutionalists have too. Is institutionalism waning? Are we an endangered species? I do not think so. If anything, institutionalists have probably been too quiet and too timid. A case can be made for greater activity on all fronts — publication, organization, creation of courses, training of students. But I will not go into those things here. I am not at all concerned that institutionalism will decay and vanish. There will always be institutionalists for a very simple reason: the character of orthodoxy is such that it will inevitably breed dissent and criticism, much of which will parallel, interact with, and reinforce institutional economics. The existence of grave, lasting economic problems, which orthodox measures cannot resolve, will also compel questioning and the search for alternative perspectives. Ultimately, and probably by an evolutionary process, institutionalism of some kind will surround and embed the market economics of orthodoxy. At about the same time, in all likelihood, the market economic system and the purview of private economic power will be brought under collective oversight. Gruchy will be remembered, not as the last of the institutionalists, but as one of the first.

ENDNOTES

1. Allan G. Gruchy, *Modern Economic Thought,* 1st ed. (Clifton, N. J.: Augustus M. Kelley, 1967); *Contemporary Economic Thought* (Clifton, N. J.: Augustus M. Kelley, 1972); *Comparative Economic Systems,* 2d ed. (Boston: Houghton Mifflin, 1977).

2. Allan G. Gruchy, *Supervision and Control of Virginia State Banks* (New York: Appleton-Century, 1937).

3. Allan G. Gruchy, "The Concept of National Planning in Institutional Economics," *Southern Economic Journal* 6 (October 1939): 121-144.

4. Allan G. Gruchy, "Institutionalism, Planning, and the Current Crisis," *Journal of Economic Issues* 11 (June 1977): 431-448.

5. Gruchy, *Modern Economic Thought,* p. 126.

6. Gruchy, *Contemporary Economic Thought,* p. 130.

7. The instances are so ubiquitous as to need no citation, but a few are: "in the opinion of the holistic economists," and "the holistic economists see a pattern of things quite different," (*Modern Economic Thought,* pp. 20, 585); also, "the critics of conventional economics state" and "the neoinstitutionalists do not agree" (*Contemporary Economic Thought,* pp. 15, 291).

8. Allan G. Gruchy, "Neoinstitutionalism and the Economics of Dissent," *Journal of Economic Issues* 3 (March 1969): 10.

9. Gruchy, *Modern Economic Thought,* pp. 23-24.

10. Gruchy, "Neoinstitutionalism and the Economics of Dissent," pp. 9, 11.

11. Gruchy, *Comparative Economic Systems,* 2d. ed., pp. 18-20.

12. Gruchy, "Neoinstitutionalism and the Economics of Dissent," p. 9.

13. Commons of course is discussed in Gruchy, *Modern Economic Thought,* Ayres in Gruchy, *Contemporary Economic Thought.*

14. Gruchy, *Modern Economic Thought,* pp. 25-26.

15. Ibid., p. 628.

16. Ibid., p. 573.

17. Ibid., p. 561ff; also see Gruchy, "Institutionalism, Planning, and the Current Crisis," pp. 431-32.

18. Gruchy, *Contemporary Economic Thought,* pp. 15ff; also relevant are large portions of Allan G. Gruchy, "Law, Politics, and Institutional Economics," *Journal of Economic Issues* 7 (December 1973): 623-43, esp. 640-42.

19. Technology and the corporation are discussed in Gruchy, *Modern Economic Thought,* pp. 568ff; see the chapters on Veblen and Ayres in *Modern Economic Thought* and Gruchy, *Contemporary Economic Thought.*

20. Gruchy, *Comparative Economic Systems,* p. 671.

21. Ibid.

22. Gruchy, *Contemporary Economic Thought,* p. 17.

23. Ibid., p. 18.

24. Allan G. Gruchy, "J. M. Keynes' Concept of Economic Science," *Southern Economic Journal* 15 (January 1949): 249–66.

25. Gruchy, *Contemporary Economic Thought,* p. 3.

26. Ibid., p. 8.

27. Cited above, Gruchy, "The Concept of National Planning in Institutional Economics" and Gruchy, "Institutionalism, Planning, and the Current Crisis."

28. Allan G. Gruchy, "Government Intervention and the Social Control of Business: The Neoinstitutionalist Position," *Journal of Economic Issues* 8 (June 1974): 235–249.

29. Gruchy, "Law, Politics, and Institutional Economics," p. 633.

30. Gruchy, "Institutionalism, Planning, and the Current Crisis," p. 444.

31. Allan G. Gruchy, "Institutional Economics: Its Influence and Prospects," *American Journal of Economics and Sociology* 37 (July 1978): 271–281.

32. Gruchy, "Neoinstitutionalism and the Economics of Dissent," p. 5.

2 ALLAN GRUCHY, NEOINSTITUTIONALIST

H. H. Liebhafsky

This essay consists of two parts. In the first I will discuss the concept of "neoinstitutionalism" expounded by Gruchy in his *Contemporary Economic Thought*[1] and make some comments concerning the extent to which some of the reviewers of the book displayed their understanding, or lack of it, of his usage of this term. In the second part I propose briefly to point out that Gruchy's book is not limited to an exposition of the views of the four neoinstitutionalists (Ayres, Galbraith, Myrdal, and Colm) to whom he has devoted complete individual chapters but must be understood and read to contain the views also of a fifth neoinstitutionalist. The fifth, of course, is Gruchy himself. He was too modest to make explicitly the claim I now make on his behalf.

The concluding paragraph of *Contemporary Economic Thought* reads:

> It is quite clear that there is a well-defined image to which the economist must conform if he is to be described as a neo-institutionalist. This does not mean that all economists who may be described in this manner will neatly fit the image of the typical neo-institutionalist constructed above. Not all the neo-institutionalists have well developed views with respect to the nature and scope of economics.

As usual, I am indebted to my colleagues, Wendell Gordon and Carey Thompson, for their helpful comments.

When we turn, however, to an overall survey of the work of Ayres, Galbraith, Myrdal, Colm and other neo-institutionalists there emerges a common way of comprehending economic reality that can properly be described as "neo-institutionalist." It is this common way discussed above that makes a neo-institutionalist a neo-institutionalist and that distinguishes him from the representatives of conventional orthodox economies.

Apparently some of the reviewers of Gruchy's book either did not read or did not comprehend the meaning of the paragraph quoted above. Thus, for example, Coats neatly, and presumably unconsciously, missed the point of Gruchy's book by writing:

A basic weakness stems from the inherent implausibility of Gruchy's effort to present his four exemplars [read "examples" unless a visceral reaction is desired] as representatives of a *coherent neo-institutionalist movement*.[2] [Italics mine]

A fair reading of Gruchy's concluding paragraph quoted above leads one to the conclusion that he has there made no claim concerning the existence of "a coherent movement" but instead has emphasized that what neoinstitutionalists have in common is "a way of comprehending economic reality" that is different from that of conventional orthodox economics.

Indeed, Gruchy's concluding paragraph is more than a little reminiscent of James's explanation of the meaning of what he called "Pragmatism" when he wrote:

Pragmatism represents a perfectly familiar attitude in philosophy, the empiricist attitude, but it represents it, as it seems to me, both in a more radical and in a less objectionable form than it has ever yet assumed. A pragmatist turns his back resolutely and once and for all upon a lot of inveterate habits dear to professional philosophers. He turns away from abstraction and insufficiency, from verbal solutions, from bad *a priori* reasons, from fixed principles, closed systems, and pretended absolutes and origins. He turns toward facts, toward action and toward power.

At the same time it does not stand for any special results. It is a method only.[3]

The reader need only to substitute the words "institutionalism" for "Pragmatism" and "economists" for "philosophers" in the preceding quotation to produce the meaning of Gruchy's conception of the difference between institutionalism and orthodox economics. And Coats, who decried Gruchy's conception of orthodox price theory as a "caricature," failed for reasons best known to himself to cite an example in which an orthodox economic theorist had established an empirical conclusion by means of a reliance on deductive reasoning alone. Accomplishment of this result would surely net its author Nobel prizes both in economics and in philosophy since it would contradict Kant's conclusions that because, however, the mere form of a cognition, accurately as it may accord with logic laws, is insufficient to supply us with material (objective) truth, no one, by means of logic alone, can venture to predicate anything of or decide concerning objects, unless he has obtained, independently of logic, well-grounded information about them, in order afterwards to examine, according to logical laws, into the use and connection, in a cohering whole of that information, or what is still better, merely to test it by them.[4]

Coats's comment suggests that he does not understand that the concepts of economic *theory* are purely analytical concepts, a point that becomes painfully clear when one studies price theory and realizes that no econometrician has produced an empirical counterpart of the purely analytical concepts of *demand*. All of which raises some interesting questions concerning the validity of the results of the quantitative statements of qualitative judgments that are produced in cost-benefit studies. Indeed, one may artfully ask, how many digits are significant in such studies? And do the "equilibrium conditions" in a piece of economic analysis refer to a purely analytical state of affairs or to a real-world condition?

I have intentionally used the word "institutionalist" rather than "neoinstitutionalist" in the preceding paragraphs. Gruchy is emphatic throughout his book in his insistence on the proposition that the "neoinstitutionalists" work within the institutionalist tradition established by Veblen in the early decades of this century.[5] He does *not* draw a contrast between institutionalists and neoinstitutionalists in terms of method or of philosophical orientation such as Coats has implied. Instead, his contrast is one of the neoinstitutionalist (and thus also institutionalist) and the orthodox positions. Thus, in his Preface (which his reviewers also apparently did not read or comprehend) Gruchy has written:

For those who wonder why the rift between neo-institutional and conventional economists continues after three-quarters of a century, it should be pointed out that this rift is maintained because neo-institutional and conventional economics are in essence two different ways of comprehending economic reality, the one evolutionary and the other static or cross-sectional. Behind these different ways of grasping economic reality lies a difference in intellectual outlook which, as Clarence Ayres explains in *The Industrial Economy,* is not "a mere matter of opinion," but involves instead "our basic conceptions of the nature of man and of society." The neo-institutionalists' way of comprehending economic reality leads them to adopt a cultural or social view of this reality, while the conventional economists' manner of grasping economic reality makes them prone to pattern economics after [their conception of] the physical sciences. . . . The main disagreement between the conventional and neo-institutional economists is over what should be included within the scope of economics.[6]

And, of course, what is true of the neoinstitutionalists in this regard is also true of the institutionalists who preceded them.

What then is the difference between the neoinstitutionalists and institutionalists whose state of mind they share? In the preceding quotation, Gruchy has, after all, clearly identified the state of mind of neoinstitutionalists with that of the institutionalists, saying that the rift between them and conventional economists has continued "for three-quarters of a century."

Gonce, another of the reviewers of Gruchy's book, has presented his interpretation of the difference between neoinstitutionalism and institutionalism by writing:

> Contemporary institutionalism by nature is a *new,* indeed a neo-institutional economics (vi, vii, 16, 85); its significance is that it can come to grips with the set of economic problems that orthodox economics of today cannot handle.[7] [p. viii]

But Gonce's selective portmanteau citation of pages reflects on his part also a failure to read carefully or to comprehend the concluding paragraph appearing at the end of Chapter 1 of Gruchy's book. Gruchy there wrote:

> The institutionalism of Veblen and his immediate followers was essentially the economics of a maturing industrial economy. Neo-institutionalism is the economics of an industrial economy that has not only matured but has passed into the current era of the post mass consumption society. The difference between the old institutionalism of Thorstein Veblen and the neo-institutionalism of Galbraith, Myrdal, Ayres, Colm, Lowe and Perroux is in large part the difference between the 1920's and the 1960's.[8]

The difference between the neo-institutionalists and the institutionalists, then, arises out of the difference between the kinds of problems that confront the former and those that confronted the latter.

And at the top of page viii, cited by Gonce in support of his own view, Gruchy wrote a more generalized statement of the idea contained in the preceding quotation:

> It is now well established that the problems that economists work on and the kinds of economic theories they develop reflect the times in which they live. Economists as a whole do not draw their inspiration from some remote and pristine fountainhead of scientific universalism in spite of what some orthodox members of the economics profession assert. We are clearly living in a transitional era just as did the classical economists of the eighteenth and nineteenth centuries.[9]

It may be that Gruchy erred tactically using the term "neo-institutionalism" in his book which, after all, was entitled *Contemporary Economic Thought.* He did so because he was attempting to deal with a problem that those of us who were long personally associated with Ayres as friends and colleagues know he also wrestled with. Gruchy stated the problem clearly in his book, but his reviewers ignored the existence of the problem altogether. Gruchy wrote:

> If the popular image of the institutional economist that has prevailed in recent decades in the United States had been based more on the work of Commons, Mitchell, Clark, and other post Veblenians than on Veblen's work, this image might have been quite different from what it has been in the minds of much of the economics profession. This image, based on Veblen's work *as interpreted by orthodox economists* is, as we have already seen, that of an economist who spurns inherited economics but puts nothing substantial in its place, who may be a sociologist but who can hardly be classed as an economist, who is a misguided advocate of technological determinism, and who has never gotten beyond the stage of writing descriptive monographs. In view of Veblen's major role in the development of American institutionalism it would have been very difficult for the post Veblenians to alter this popular image of the institutionalist even if they had had a special interest in doing so. [Of the five post-Veblenians discussed by Gruchy] only Mitchell may be regarded as a disciple of Veblen. Commons, Clark, Tugwell and Means were not Veblen's students. . . . [Italics mine]
>
> Since the late 1930's, and especially since the close of the Second World War, there have appeared a number of economists who have worked along institutionalist lines but who have drawn their inspiration for the reconstruction of economics from non-Veblenian, West European intellectual sources. Prominent among these latter-day heterodox economists are Gunnar Myrdal, Gerhard Colm, and Adolph Lowe. Even in the United States a new generation of heterodox economists, represented [in this book] by J. K. Galbraith and taking little or nothing from Veblen's work, has made its appearance. It is quite clear that the criticism directed against Veblen has no relevance to the work of Myrdal, Colm, Lowe and Galbraith. [Nor does it have in the case of Ayres who took from Veblen the distinction between the technological and the ceremonial but who was not Veblen's student either and whose theory of value owes far more to the work of Peirce than it does to the ideas of Veblen. As Gruchy notes, "Ayres excluded from his own economics various unacceptable parts of Veblen's work."] It is for this reason that it is appropriate to refer to these present-day heterodox economists as "neo-institutionalists" to distinguish them from the "old" institutionalists generally associated by the economics profession and others with Thorstein Veblen.[10]

What Gruchy saw as his task when he published *Contemporary Economic Thought* in 1972 was that of correcting the stereotyped caricature of institutionalism that Homan had presented to the American Economic Association in 1928 and that still permeates the minds of contemporary orthodox economists who have conveniently utilized the stereotype to avoid dealing with the problems with which heterodox economists consistently confront them. Given their explicit confessions as to what they had learned as graduate students from his *Modern Economic Thought* (1947), one may perhaps excuse those of his reviewers who missed his point (on grounds that their personal experiences of economic history and economic thought are considerably less than his).

Not only the opening and closing chapters of Gruchy's *Contemporary Economic Thought* but also his other works mark Gruchy as a contemporary institutionalist, a "neoinstitutionalist" if you will. He too shares the state of mind of the men whose works he has discussed in individual chapters in his later book. And his personal commitment to the use of a national economic budget as "a framework within which fiscal, monetary, wage, price and other economic policies can be coordinated" is clearly related to his admiration for the work of Colm and to his own intensive study of the practice of economic policy making, in the participatory democracies of Western Europe in particular. And he has stated his own point of view as much as he has described those of others when he has written:

> [It is] a shift in interest from "automaticity" to "control" that distinguishes the neo-institutionalists from orthodox economists. It is also the source of the basic difference between the model of the economy found at the core of conventional economics and the model that is central to the theorizing of the neo-institutionalists. This shift in interest from the automatic working of the competitive economy to the controlled functioning of the large-scale industrial economy results in a shift in interest from predicting the outcome of spontaneous economic behavior to controlling spontaneous economic behavior. The neo-institutionalists do not predict the course of economic behavior on the basis of what individuals are expected to do automatically in a competitive situation where the objective is to maximize gain or utility, and self-correcting forces in the market place are expected to lead to the establishment of an equilibrium. Instead the neo-institutionalists with the aid of national economic budgets set forth a planned future economic state or situation in which various macro national economic goals are to be achieved along with the micro goals of individuals and groups operating in the private enterprise sector.[11]

Gruchy has elsewhere emphasized that neoinstitutionalists substitute the concept of *process* for the concept of *equilibrium*, and it seems to me that the view expressed in the preceding quotation would have been considerably clarified and strengthened if he had added to it a short explanation to the effect that the goals set in the national economic budgets are not final, ultimate goals established on the basis of "first principles" but are to be modified and corrected on the basis of experience in the process of the implementation of those goals initially set. These initial goals, like legal rules handed down in decisions of courts, are to be considered as working hypotheses subject to correction on the basis of the experience gained in the process of their implementation. In other words, they are subject to correction on the basis of value judgments functionally or instrumentally made in keeping with the theory of value of Ayres, which Gruchy has discussed more lucidly than has many another writer.

ENDNOTES

1. Allan G. Gruchy, *Contemporary Economic Thought* (Clifton, N. J.: Augustus M. Kelley, 1972).

2. A. W. Coats, "Four Reviews of Allan G. Gruchy, *Contemporary Economic Thought,*" *Journal of Economic Issues* 8 (September 1974): 598.

3. William James, *Pragmatism* (New York: Longmans, Green & Co., 1907), p. 51.

4. Immanuel Kant, *Critique of Pure Reason,* rev. ed., J. M. D. Meiklejohn, trans. (New York: Wiley, 1900), p. 50.

5. Gruchy, *Contemporary Economic Thought,* p. 16.

6. Ibid., pp. vi–vii.

7. R. A. Gonce, "Four Reviews of Allan G. Gruchy, *Contemporary Economic Thought,*" *Journal of Economic Issues* 8 (September 1974): 607.

8. Gruchy, *Contemporary Economic Thought,* p. 8.

9. Ibid., p. viii.

10. Ibid., p. 85. The quotation within the brackets is from p. 29. In his review cited in note 7 above, Gonce commented on Gruchy's assertion that only Mitchell was a disciple of Veblen by asking "Where did Commons come from?" Paradoxically, Gonce also claimed that early portions of the book were a restatement of Gruchy's *Modern Economic Thought,* first published in 1947. Of course, readers familiar with the latter book will recall that Gruchy there emphasized the influence of Richard Ely on Commons's ideas!

11. Ibid., p. 314.

3 ALLAN GRUCHY AND THE ASSOCIATION FOR EVOLUTIONARY ECONOMICS

John Gambs

For a period of more than fifteen years, Gruchy gave much of his time, energy, and heart to the creation and guidance of an association supporting heterodoxy in economics. It is fitting that this volume will devote a chapter to that period of his life. The story begins in 1958 at an annual meeting of the American Economic Association that convened at the Wardman Park Hotel, Washington, D.C. Gruchy sent several dissenting economists (including myself) an invitation to attend a gathering at a nearby hotel, the purpose of the meeting being to inquire into the possibility of organizing a group of heterodox economists. A dozen or so showed up. We talked about the difficulty we had exchanging views, since much of what we had to say did not interest standard economists or the editors of the journals or the publishers of the textbooks. True, there had been some particularly gifted exceptions, such as Mitchell, Clark, and Tugwell, who did get published more or less regularly. But they had to be *very* good; they were the cream of the profession. On the other hand countless papers were welcomed if they did not stray from the well-worn paths of economic foolishness.

We decided that perhaps we could reduce this discrimination against us by working together more closely, meeting regularly, and publishing a modest newsletter from time to time. We ended on the note that we should carry on next year at the meeting of the American Economic Association and we requested Allan to send us minutes of this meeting and notice of the time and place of the next. And thus The Association for Evolutionary Economics (AFEE) was launched.

Unhappily, fifteen years later, Allan wrote the following of the big fat journal that now was a product of this group's endeavors:

> While I personally have felt greatly rewarded by my efforts to explain and defend the work of the American institutionalists, I do not feel the same about my efforts to bring into being an organization or association for institutional economists. In 1958, along with several other favorably disposed individuals, I started the movement that resulted in the establishment of The Association for Evolutionary Economics. Looking back over the past fifteen years since the beginning of our Association I have come to wonder whether or not there can be enough agreement among our members to make our Association a viable organization with a well-defined image. It may have been a mistake on my part to believe that institutional economists are organizable. It might have been wiser for me to have limited my efforts to elucidating and defending institutionalism.[1]

What had happened in that period? Any why did Allan part ways with the Association he had founded? I wish to tell that story, partly because in matters relating to this group I was as close to him as anybody up until two years ago, when from his point of view the association could go climb a tree.

I now return to the second meeting of AFEE. It was not yet AFEE in those days, but the Wardman Group, named after the hotel that the American Economic Association had designated as its headquarters that year. Gruchy did not attend the annual meeting — I've forgotten why. So I took over for him and appointed myself as the officer to run this organization for the next year. Well, the next year we continued our modest meetings and went on for awhile increasing our membership slightly and, what was perhaps more important, trying to define ourselves. What were we? We were not socialists or single taxers, or technocrats or Fabians or Christian socialists or Populists or Locofocos or anything of that sort. Several of us preferred to be called Veblenians — that included me. Allan was also a Veblenian but apparently wanted to go some steps further and to press for the planning of the national economy. We were both also admirers of Ayres and therefore also of Dewey.

Most of the members, I think, could not or would not identify themselves with any school, man, or movement. They were just standard economists, but slightly liberal politically and socially: they were for birth control, minimum wages, progressive taxation; against the sales tax and the trickle-down theory of prosperity. Some of them actually used Samuelson's many splendored textbook of their own free will. This diversity bothered both of us; at first Gruchy more than me, I think. But eventually both of us came to feel that this diversity should be accepted and that eventually we would seek to define our position through the appointment of a committee, of which I regret to say I was chairman. We were to compose position papers and to put them before the membership for discussion, and through this discussion we hoped to work our way towards some kind of consensus. But our efforts were balked by the democratic process. Nobody on a committee ever listens to anybody else, and each committee member thinks he is right and that when he has said his say nothing more needs to be done. Second, nobody really wants to put much effort into committee work; having given his opinion, each committee member wants to go home. Third, when travel is required to meet together, somebody far away sacrifices time and travel money; our organization was too poor to reimburse anybody for anything. At one point, despite obstacles, I thought we had a good report and I presented it to our governing body only to be met with complete dissent on a very important point by the most senior member of the committee. I could not say to him, "But you stinker, you agreed to this only last week." So I gave up, for that time at any rate, feeling that perhaps later an opportunity might arise to make the point more palatable to our dissenter.

Despite our fuzziness about ourselves the organization grew and prospered. Ayres arranged with The University of Texas to help finance a journal. At first I was almost deliriously happy about this, but Gruchy, I noticed, was a little doubtful. I think he could see that we were not the kind of organization that should have a full-fledged journal almost the size of the *American Economic Review* but rather that we should stay small. We also finally agreed upon a name that expressed our attitude — at least those of us who had founded the organization — better than the Wardman Group. I later wished that we had kept the original, because AFEE meant very little to many people. Well, for weal or woe we were now provided with a registered name, and this helped us a great deal because we could now promise people that their subscriptions or gifts would be tax free. What we now needed was a constitution. The moving spirits of AFEE hurried to get the document approved so that we might enjoy the benefits dependent upon our having a complete educational organization with constitution and officers.

Several small things bothered me about the constitution — despite its excellence — but what bothered me most was its statement of purpose. The purpose of AFEE as it appeared in the document was to bring together people with an "interdisciplinary approach to economics" or, to be more precise, the only significant difference between AFEE and any other general economic association that might conceivably be dreamed up was to be interdisciplinary. But almost every economist is interdisciplinary nowadays and the word does not shock people as it did when Robbins was a little boy. Actually, even the purest and most nearly exact sciences are interdisciplinary. Without physics and chemistry modern astronomy would have to disappear; biology is sustained by the same sciences. Besides being interdisciplinary, then, what was our program to be like? Speaking for myself I guess I'm a born-again Veblenian; that is, I've learned little since Veblen's death. Gruchy is a more complicated fellow and has become interested in planning, and he reserves much of his admiration for Colm and others who have gone ahead in the field of planning. I am by no means against planning, but it seems to me that other things must come first. Thus I throw my efforts into making the world of economics appear to be ridiculous to all who study it. What we need to do is what Galbraith has recommended in his general theory of reform. He says, "The emancipation of belief is the most formidable of the tasks of reform and the one on which all else depends." Laughter emancipates belief.

Several minor things kept popping up to irritate Gruchy and me. A glowing tribute appeared in our journal to honor an economist who had just been awarded a Nobel Prize. How come? Where did the authority come from to praise a bunch of Scandinavians for selecting an economist who did not represent us? We had no objections to the economist or to the Scandinavians, but only to the making of AFEE policy without authorization. This was the beginning of what might be called a squabble — or more than a squabble. Both Gruchy and I were on the editorial board, and I felt that we should have been consulted before such a strong policy statement was made. It seems to me a matter of terribly important policy for the journal of an organization to give accolades to people who are unsympathetic with its goals.

The question was who was running the journal? Indeed, who *was* really running the Association? The second tiff revolved around the origin of the curious policy that governed the reviewing of Gruchy's book, *Contemporary Economic Thought.*[2] This book should have been considered something of a guiding light to AFEE. The reviewing of it was delayed, and even the American Economic Association printed a review before AFEE. Moreover, the book was reviewed by four people, a custom the Association had adopted because it allegedly promoted eclecticism; some thought the organization should not be accused of taking sides. But taking sides was exactly what I thought, and what Gruchy thought, the organization was all about.

To return to the reviews of Gruchy's book, it seemed almost as if the least friendly or qualified reviewers had been selected. Gruchy was annoyed. Some thought he should have been able to take a bad review in stride. But the truth was that a book that was supposed to represent the heart and soul of our organization was treated cavalierly.

In 1973 Fusfeld, Gruchy, and I agreed upon the draft of an amendment to the constitution that would clearly state the purpose of AFEE, namely, to promote dissident non-Marxian economics. The board of directors turned it down. To Gruchy and me this was the crowning insult and we both resigned about that time. We had not really coordinated this act but had experienced a common reaction: we did not want to be members of an organization that we had never made. AFEE may continue to survive, and Allan and I have many good friends who remain members; we urge them to remain members; we urge them to remain as long as they feel they are doing something worthwhile. May they improve it and make of it the kind of organization that Allan wanted it to be.

ENDNOTES

1.   Allan G. Gruchy, "Remarks upon Receipt of the Veblen-Commons Award," *Journal of Economic Issues* 8 (June 1974): 207.

2.   "Four Reviews of Allan G. Gruchy: *Contemporary Economic Thought. The Contributions of Neo-Institutional Economics,*" *Journal of Economic Issues* 8 (September 1974): 597–615.

II INSTITUTIONALISM TODAY AND TOMORROW
The Evolution of Ideas

4 NEOINSTITUTIONALISM AND THE ECONOMICS OF DISSENT

Wendell Gordon

The title of this essay was also the title of Gruchy's presidential address to The Association for Evolutionary Economics, December 1968. It was a fine statement then and it remains a fine statement. Gruchy was arguing that economics should take a long view rather than a short view.[1] "The difference between the conventional view of economics as a narrow study of economic decision making and the neoinstitutionalist view of economics as a broad study of the evolving goal-directed economic system is also the difference between a short-run view and a long-run view of the economic system."

Gruchy further said: "Economics is a science not of efficiency but of values." But when the neoinstitutionalists say this: "They are not raising any normative issues in the form of what 'ought' to be. What they do say is that economics, viewed not as a technical but as a social science, deals with the material aspects of values or wants." "The ultimate purpose of economics is to provide an interpretation of the way in which the industrial system operates with respect to the satisfaction of personal and collective wants or goals." "These dissenting economists, as scientists, do not propose to tell the people what goals they should seek to achieve. However, they do propose to explain to the people how their wants or goals come into being. . . . "

Such is the value theory of institutional economics and that is what this essay is about. What matters is to understand life, society, and the economy as process rather than as an exercise in static equilibrium, neoclassical, steady-state growth, optimizing and/or maximizing. Most economists probably presume that they are dealing with change and process — and saying something useful — when they attempt to answer questions of policy, having to do with change, with price theory and national income theory and neoclassical growth theory tools. They have been so indoctrinated with these methodologies that the incongruity of calculating and using the assortment of constant parameters, elasticities, propensities, exponents, and miscellaneous other parameters escapes them. They miss the implication for error of using analytical tools that presume underlying relationships do not change, when they must know that changing structure is an essential part of the process. Or perhaps they are not unappreciative of this problem, explicitly recognize it, and, then, somewhere along the way, forget the implications.[2]

But the orthodox economist using his price theory, national income theory, and neoclassical growth theory tools has another problem also. He is likely to claim that he does not make value judgments. He takes values as given, he says, and then he attempts logically to explain how the economy works and what the effects of various policies will be. But what are the values that are taken as given in order to manipulate this quasi-logical exercise? Chiefly they are that income distribution is given and that the profit motive or the desire for material gain is given and overriding and that the "name of the game" is to maximize such gain either at the individual or social level. That it cannot handle the implications of income redistribution is a weakness of the approach. And that, in effect, motivation is assumed given and unchanging in the form of uniquely quantifiable profit is an even more "powerful" weakness.

THE VALUE THEORY OF
INSTITUTIONAL ECONOMICS

The frame of reference of institutional theory is different. It concerns itself with the process of change in a context where changing structure is allowed for. And it also attempts to explain the processes by which motives and values adapt and, at the same time, guide the process.

A "value" is a judgment made by an individual (or, in a sense, also by an institution or by technology) as to what is desirable, useful, effective, or esteemed.[3] The conception that something has value involves the identification by one of these custodians of value (the individual, institutions, or technology) that that something has desirability or is worthy of esteem. And "value theory" is the study of the process by which judgments about values are made and values are identified.

But it should be added that, of these three custodians of value, it is the individual who matters, at least if individuals are the actors and they think so. But this does not mean that the values of individuals are unique, or permanent, or instinctive, or definitive, or clairvoyant, or quantifiable — quite the contrary. Values are changeable results of changing circumstances (evolving in the process of self-correcting value judgments), and they reflect attitudes, not omniscience of eternal verities.

The forces influencing the ever changing ideas of individuals about values are here alleged to be:

1. the individual's biological heredity,
2. the dynamic process of technological accumulation,
3. the inhibitions of institutionalized behavior norms (which are pretty much what they are as a response to technology), and
4. the natural setting (which includes resources and Zimmermann's neutral stuff).[4]

The biology of the individual — his heredity, which is a result of the processes of mutation and natural selection — beyond doubt influences the individual's conception as to what is desirable or estimable in the world around him. A being that did not drink water would have a different opinion as to the value of water than would a being that did.

But what of the individual in relation to technology and institutions? Dewey wrote:

> Man has beliefs which scientific inquiry vouchsafes, beliefs about the actual structure and processes of things [one may say: beliefs about the efficacy for certain purposes of particular techniques]; and he also has beliefs about the values which should regulate his conduct. The question of how these two ways of believing may most effectively and fruitfully interact with one another is the most general and significant of all the problems which life presents to us.[5]

Technology is the dynamic force that is, over time, overwhelmingly influential in determining the nature of change, the behavior norms of institutions, and the values of individuals. The institutions of the period since the Industrial Revolution — corporations, banks, and labor unions — came to have very different behavior norms from those of the dominant institutions of the Middle Ages (the guilds, the feudal manors, chivalry, and slavery) precisely because the effective use of the steam engine and the open hearth required institutions different from those called forth by the three-field system and handicraft manufacturing.

Technology plays its influential role both because it embodies the capability for changing the physical face of the world and because the effecting of such change forces institutions to adapt and change their norms or values. So, institutions acquire behavior norms or values in response to the exigencies of technology, to permit the effective use of the technology. But a behavior pattern in existence as an aspect of the norms or values then held by an institution tends to be continued until some positive new influence comes along to coerce a change. Consequently, at any given time, the behavior norms (or values in being) of institutions are characteristics that came into being at an earlier time and may be said to be, in all likelihood, more appropriate to the conditions of that earlier time than to the changed conditions of the present. But to say that behavior norms are thus antiquated does not preclude the possibility that they may represent values that individuals may wish to continue.

The institutions of society may be said to have norms or values in this sense, as Ayres has pointed out.[6] And Ayres does use the term *values* to describe the phenomenon.

At all events, at any given time an institution may be said to have certain eternally antiquated values or behavior norms. Bankers are more likely to consider would-be borrowers to be creditworthy if they come from what the bankers consider to be good families, rather than from "red-lined" districts. Labor union members want their leaders to sound a bit uncouth and either to wear dirty shirts or silk shirts, nothing in between. And such currently held values may contribute little to the efficacy of either bank or labor union activities at the given time.

So also, individuals brought up in the setting of certain institutions (the family and church and their ethics, certain clubs and fraternities [or hippie cells], corporations and their profit seeking, politics and its lack of ethics) form their values in large measure in conformity with the exigencies of these institutions, as constrained by the individual's biology, as permitted by the natural setting, and as guided by technology.

As to the natural setting and the role of resources, it may be said that the importance of one resource by comparison with another or by comparison with neutral stuff (petroleum in comparison with clay) is going to be largely influenced by the state of technology. But also the whereabouts of the location of the new industry and even its feasibility is going to be heavily dependent on resource availability. A type of clay, if it is bauxite, may cease to be neutral and become a valuable resource for making aluminum when technology so decrees. And the location of bauxite deposits determines where bauxite mining will occur and influences the pattern of aluminum production in general.

The value theory of institutional economics, which may also be called instrumental value theory (and is, in the general tradition of Peirce, James, and Dewey), views value determination as a process involving continuously testing technique (used in an effort to implement values) against the consequences of the use of the technique. It involves evaluating the technology against the results obtained when one uses that particular technology in an effort to implement a value. But at the same time that the quality, or the value, or the effectiveness of the technique is being tested, the value itself is subject to reappraisal in the light of the consequences of the effort to implement it and in relation to all the other "held values" and their changing implications. Values themselves are reappraised against the consequences of trying to give effect to the values, and against their relation to all the rest of the individual's frame of reference, involving in particular the institutions and their stylized behavior norms mediating the process. And, meanwhile, the quality and changing nature of the dynamically accumulating technology dominates the whole process and the physical look of the world.[7] This is the ends-means-ends continuum, which has no beginning and no end. This is no teleological process. There is no paradise at the end of the road or to be had right after some revolution that is just around the corner, if we could just carry it off. Rather, this is a process that is ever ongoing, and in the course of the process the individual is continually reappraising. One is changing opinion as to which technologies work best and is discovering new technologies as a by-product of the internal dynamic of the technology-accumulation process. One is rejecting some technologies and assimilating others. One is then looking at the results of those efforts. And the innovation and use of the better and more desirable technologies is a process that occasions changes in the structure of institutions and in their behavior norms, which those institutions are imposing on individuals. And those institutionalized behavior norms are the values of institutions and in their turn are affecting the values of individuals. And we have gone full circle and a half.

Truth and values evolve and are relative to time, and place, and institutions, and technology (and heredity and natural setting). Human nature and its scheme of values are being created and recreated every day. As Ayres says in the *Industrial Economy*:[8] "The present nature of man — what human beings as we know them are — is a function of life in society . . . . "

The test of behavior and/or technique is whether it gives results that the individual considers relatively satisfactory, whether it is effectively instrumental. The value theory then is that values are created and identified (instrumentally determined) in a process involving self-correcting value judgments. One does things differently next time if things did not work out in a relatively satisfactory manner the ways one did them before. "The proof of the pudding is in the eating." And the values, as to the desirable or the estimable, which the individual holds at any particular time, are also determined in this process of self-correcting value judgments in the intermix with technology and institutions, biology and nature.

An important facet to instrumental value theory is the ongoing nature of the process. The values of individuals change as individual attitudes change in a context of biological evolution, changing institutional norms, evolving technology, all constrained by the natural setting and our evaluations of valuable resources and neutral stuff. No definitive judgment can be made now as to what is best for all time. No blueprint for the Garden of Eden or for a communist Utopia can be drawn up now, with the thought that this is the ideal social order toward which we should all work and that once we have arrived at this "promised land" all will be for the best in this best of all possible worlds — permanently. This is not the name of the game. And the game would be a big bore if it were.

It should be noted that value theory, stated in this form, is (if the approach is correct) common to all cultures; that is to say, it involves a principle that can be applied to all cultures. Certainly, different cultures may value particular, different goods or circumstances differently, but that is not the crux of the matter. There is here a common principle, even though it may result in different evaluations of particular commodities or attitudes in different cultures at a given time. The value theory is general, though the concepts as to what is valuable are not the same. For example, two cultures may have different views as to the appropriateness of collecting interest on debts. And yet the value theory should be capable of explaining how those conceptions were arrived at in each.

CATALOG OF CURRENTLY HELD VALUES

To say that different institutions or different cultures may value things differently does not mean that it is bootless at a given time and place to attempt to catalog the currently commonly held values. And certain values may be quite generally held and for long periods of time, maybe even forever. An attempt at a catalog of currently held values or wants in "Western Culture" at the present time should be worthwhile even though it is both tentative and, even where confirmed at the moment, subject to change.

Gruchy offered such a tentative list in his presidential address. The items were "such wants as economic abundance, economic freedom, economic security, economic justice, and economic quality."[9]

I attempt a similar listing, alleging, tentatively rather than dogmatically, its applicability to "Western Culture" in the 1970s. The first value is the possession of decent, minimum, material level of living for all, accompanied by the right on the part of the individual, not too obstreperously, to pursue an improved level of living. (This concept can have meaning as a right only if there is productive capability to meet it and an agency with the corresponding duty to make the right operational. The world does have the necessary productive capability to provide everyone with a decent minimum, and it is feasible to organize arrangements that can make the decent minimum available to all.) The second value is the conception that people have the right to expect other people to be pleasant and cooperative and have the obligation to behave so themselves. The third value is the conception that the individual has a right to a degree of freedom of action such as will permit the individual to be proud of his or her own behavior. The fourth value is the right to such security as is reasonably attainable, security of several kinds: against unemployment, considerate care during illness, old age, and childhood. And there is also the matter of security against the ravages of war.

A good deal could and perhaps should be said at this point in explanation of such a list and its role. But I should rather merely concede that the list is highly tentative and claim that some such listing may exist, even had better exist, if society is to be halfway coherent and stable. And in this setting I should like to speculate on one implication of such a list. This is the aggregability question. The ability to aggregate the ingredients in welfare is necessary if a unique welfare maximum is to be identified.

AGGREGABILITY

Something more needs to be said about the implications of working with an assortment of nonhomogeneous values such as these. In general, they cannot be aggregated. They cannot be subsumed, with the aid of some common denominator, into a quantifiable or consistent total, either cardinal or ordinal.

It is possible to straitjacket the problem or to simplify the assumptions to a degree that permits identifying a unique maximum. If the best practice techniques for producing commodities can be identified, if a production possibility frontier can be derived that is concave with respect to the origin and stays still, if a pattern of nonintersecting community indifference curves that are convex with respect to the origin — if such conditions and more exist, a unique welfare maximum may be identifiable at the point of tangency of the production possibility curve with the furthest outlying community indifference curve that it can reach.

But these conditions are unrealistic to the point of being contrary to fact in many ways. To illustrate the difficulty, assuming one among many possible steps in the direction of the real world seems appropriate. One possible such step is to check out the implications of a redistribution of income on the realistic assumption that there exists no "hard" criterion for saying that one degree of inequality in the distribution of income is better than another except as a self-correcting value judgment sort of process in the context of institutional value theory.

The accompanying graph (Figure 4-1) illustrates the situation. Assuming initially an income distribution corresponding to community indifference curves in the AA' and BB' pattern and production possibilities corresponding to the curve CPC', welfare is maximized at P. Since the slope of the tangent through P represents exchange ratios between luxuries and necessities that are satisfactory to both consumers and producers, it may be argued that (in lieu of money) either homogeneous luxuries or homogeneous necessities may be used as a yardstick for measuring national income. If luxuries are used, national income is OG; if necessities are used, national income is OG'. Up to this point there is no problem in terms of inconsistent results. OG is prima facie equal in value, if not in linear distance, to OG', and a unique welfare maximum has been found at P.

But there might exist a different income distribution resulting in a different demand pattern corresponding, one may allege, to the community indifference curves in the DD' and EE' pattern.

With demand patterns changed by income redistribution, but with production capabilities remaining unchanged, the new possible welfare maximum is at P', at the tangency with the farthest outlying community indifference curve in the DD'/EE' pattern that the production possibility curve can reach. And national income measured in necessities is OF' and measured in luxuries is OF. Measured in luxuries as the numeraire income has risen, measured in necessities it has fallen. And there is no way, in the context of the standard assumptions of pure competition/laissez-faire, to prove whether P or P' is "better."

Such is one of many possible examples of the difficulty of aggregating nonhomogeneous items (such as luxuries and necessities) in a context where some other significant element in the picture — in this case income distribution — is allowed to change. Somewhat the same graphic proce-

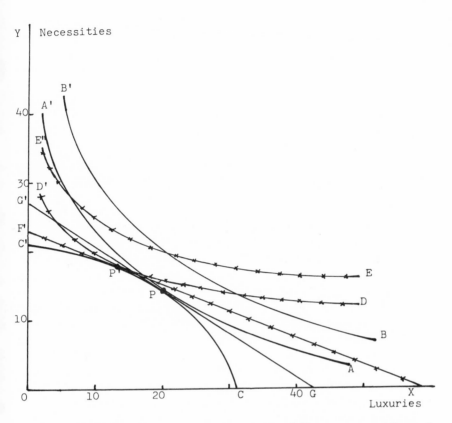

Figure 4-1   Indifference curves, production possibility curves, and the welfare optimum or maximum

dures can indicate the inherent possible inconsistencies in estimates of total income or welfare when an expansion in production capability occurs, when a choice is being made among possible production techniques, and when an effort is made to establish whether one growth rate is more rapid than another.

That aggregation, in an effort to identify a unique total (and check whether it is a possible maximum), cannot be performed in a theoretically satisfactory manner is a point that needs to be emphasized in economics because a large percentage of the profession is spending an awful lot of time playing with econometric models based on a presumption that some such aggregation is meaningful. The concepts of economic abundance, freedom, justice, economic quality, and security are separately meaningful and "move-toward-able." But the concept of a maximum combination of such ingredients is without precise theoretical meaning.

As one backs down from the general equilibrium level to the level of microeconomic price theory, this means that concepts such as the equating of marginal products across industries and the equating of cost ratios and utility ratios at the margin are not definitive guides to the desirability of certain price and cost relations in the general welfare context. This argument does not deny that it is presumptively good judgment for a businessman to try to cut costs and for a buyer to try to buy for less. (Prices and costs and profits are important.) But it does mean that these considerations have their relevance in a setting involving a genuine ceteris paribus assumption and without a precise tie-in with the concept of a general welfare maximum.[10]

There are other circumstances that emphasize the theoretical impossibility of conceptualizing a unique welfare maximum in a halfway realistic world. There is ambiguity as to what is the "best" income distribution. There is ambiguity as to what is the "best" total population and rate of population growth. There is the ambiguity that results from the fact that, as per capita productive capabilities rise, our appreciation of the relative values of things will change. There is the ambiguity that results from the fact that efficiency cannot be identified (that is to say the best-practice-technique cannot be identified) by knowledge about the comparative capabilities of techniques alone. The identification of relative efficiency of techniques is contingent on demand patterns, and demand patterns are contingent on income distribution and tastes and changing tastes. So the identification of the "best" income distribution is itself a value judgment and possibly an ever-changing value judgment.

In the context of the institutional theory of value, society is indeed ever changing its conception as to what is desirable. We need to appreciate the nature of this process and that it means that there is no eternally "best" that can be revealed to us either by logical positivism or by natural law or by our instincts or by some clairvoyant idealist.

CONCLUSION

Economics does not integrate into a neat package starting with values assumable and given from outside the economic process. Circumstances economists should take into account influence values; "the whole" does not make sense otherwise. Thus, decisions as to desirable public policy cannot reliably be made on the basis of the assumption that equating marginal utility ratios on the demand side with marginal cost ratios on the supply side assures an optimum result and a welfare maximum. There is every presumption that such equating, even if pure competition existed (which it obviously does not), would not provide a presumptively reliable test of policy desirability, even if the allegedly relevant data could be compiled in reliable form. In this context it is an almost trivial postscript to say that the relevant data (say, for constructing a demand curve) are not to be had. Meanwhile econometricians misspecify models and use unreliable or irrelevant data in pseudosophisticated procedures to grind out results that would generally not be theoretically defensible even if the models were specified correctly, the data reliable, and the statistical method appropriate.

It is proper for an individual to have values and to change them, and it is appropriate for one to try to convince one's fellows of the merits of the values one holds at the moment. It is appropriate for society as a whole to hold values in the manner of a consensus and to change them, perhaps under the influence of most anyone's arguments. It is important to try to understand the influences guiding these changes.

The implication of these concepts, which envisage values as changing with changing circumstances, may perhaps not be what one might expect at first glance. The implication is probably not that there is a tendency toward a decline in ethical standards because there are no eternal verities to guide us in our quest for certainty.[11] Actually the implication for the quality of individual ethics may well be quite the contrary and quite wholesome. The individual is "on his own" and society is "on its own." They can make something of themselves that they can be proud of if they will. But people have to do it for themselves, and they have to do it again and again every day. People can only do it for themselves as a cooperative venture — not in a "dog eat dog" or essentially competitive manner. This way of thinking may well be conducive to the creation of improved ethics and improved relations among people. (Adam Smith's glorification of selfishness via the invisible hand concept has not been the value concept society has needed. [Note: this is a self-correcting value judgment made by the author at a given time and place]). The institutional way of looking at things also implies that values inhere in the means used to accomplish human purposes as well as in the ends that may be envisaged as following from any given conduct.

A quotation from Ayres seems appropriate: "This naturalistic, instrumental, technological theory of value is not 'mere' theory. As I have already said and will continue to repeat, it is not a theory of how value judgments ought to be made. It is an account of how we do, now and always, actually evaluate the things we value."[12]

Yet it is also a theory that permits us, even enjoins us, to have an opinion as to how things ought to be, even if there is nothing eternally definitive about the quality of "oughtness." This is normative not positive economics. We do have values, and economists (as economists) should take an interest in understanding where they come from and how economics can contribute to their implementation.

And we have gone full circle back to Gruchy's statement: "These dissenting economists, as scientists, do not propose to tell the people what goals they should seek to achieve. However, they do propose to explain to the people how their wants or goals come into being. . . ."[13]

ENDNOTES

1. Allan G. Gruchy, "Neoinstitutionalism and the Economics of Dissent," *Journal of Economic Issues* 3 (March 1969): 3–17.
2. Robert Solow, *Growth Theory* (New York: Oxford University Press, 1970), p. 7.
3. The individual has to be identified as central. Technology and institutions have to be considered secondary. See John Dewey, *Individualism Old and New* (New York: Putnam's, 1929). Also it may be mentioned that the author is not unaware of the distinctions that have been made between "value in use" and "value in exchange" and of alternative value concepts such as the labor theory of value.
4. W. N. Peach and J. A. Constantin, *Zimmermann's World Resources and Industries,* 3d ed. (New York: Harper & Row, 1972), p. 9.
5. John Dewey, *The Quest for Certainty* (New York: Minton, Balch, 1929), p. 18.
6. C. E. Ayres, *The Industrial Economy* (Boston: Houghton Mifflin, 1952), pp. 300 et seq.
7. To say that technical knowledge accumulates dynamically is to say that a new bit of knowledge follows more or less automatically from the preceding as the human mind considers and reconsiders the implications of each new development. So, in large degree, the process of accumulating technical knowledge is self-sustaining and in only limited degree is induced by considerations such as the profit motive.
8. Ayres, *Industrial Economy*, p. 11.
9. Gruchy, "Neoinstitutionalism," p. 11.
10. The individual decisions at the microeconomic level, made in the ceteris paribus context, are subject to correction by a society influenced by its values and using the decision-making processes available to it, including especially the democratic political process or whatever other (political and otherwise) decision-making processes a given society may have foisted on itself.
11. Dewey, *The Quest for Certainty,* passim.
12. C. E. Ayres, *Toward a Reasonable Society* (Austin: University of Texas Press, 1961), p. 34.
13. Gruchy, "Neoinstitutionalism," p. 4.

5 A RECONSIDERATION OF HOLISTIC ECONOMICS

Philip A. Klein

There is general agreement that Veblen, Commons, and Mitchell were the intellectual progenitors of a distinctive movement in the history of economic thought in the United States. While it had some clear antecedents in various European groups, e.g., the German historical school and some of the socialist groups (notably the Utopian socialists), the American version was sufficiently distinctive to warrant giving it a new name and putting it in a class more or less of its own. The name most often applied is institutionalism. But this is a poor choice for a variety of reasons. As Ayres once wrote,

> As a designation of a way of thinking in economics the term "institutionalism" is singularly unfortunate, since it points only at that from which an escape is being sought. Properly speaking, it is the classical tradition that is "institutionalism," since it is a way of thinking which expresses a certain set of institutions. As a designation of the way of thinking which recognizes the decisive part played by technology in economic life the term "instrumentalism" is far more satisfactory.[1]

Despite Ayres' preference for instrumentalism that term never caught on, and in retrospect one can understand why. Ayres meant it to refer to the fundamental dichotomy around which he built his own thinking concerning the nature of the economy: the constant interaction between what he called technology and institutions.

45

This distinction is similar to the Veblenian distinction between the output of the machine process which he termed industrial, and the motivation of business enterprises, whieh he termed pecuniary.[2] Ayres himself sometimes spoke of a dichotomy between the scientific and the ceremonial. Dewey emphasized this basic distinction as well, and Dewey's instrumental process is roughly coterminous with Ayres's technological process.

The point to note is that all institutionalists have in common a view about how the political economy operates and how it is related to the rest of the life process. Institutionalism, instrumentalism, evolutionary economics, and heterodoxy are all efforts to capture the essence of the perspective in a single memorable word or phrase. One of the more perceptive, if neglected, such attempts was Gruchy's concept of "holistic economics." Although the term is not often used today, it not only speaks to what is most distinctive in institutionalism, but suggests other implications.[3]

HOLISTIC ECONOMICS DEFINED

In his 1948 volume, *Modern Economic Thought,* Gruchy took pains in the first few pages to suggest that American economic heterodoxy encompassed not only the work of Veblen (to whose views the term institutionalist was originally applied) but also Commons, who used the term "collective economics," Clark, who preferred "social economics," and Tugwell, who coined the term "experimental economics." Mitchell's work was known as "quantitative economics," a term that is surely inadequate to encompass his overall perspective. Feeling the need for a term covering all these, Gruchy suggested "holistic economics." The word holistic comes from the Greek *holos* meaning whole and was originally used by the South African, Jan Christiaan Smuts, in 1926 in a book entitled *Holism and Evolution.*[4] Writes Gruchy, "Smuts used the term to describe the kind of scientific thinking which grew out of the researches of Charles Darwin (1859) in biological evolution, of Antoine Henri Becquerel (1895) in radioactivity, and of Albert Einstein (1915) in the theory of relativity. This type of scientific thought is evolutionary or dynamic rather than mechanistic or static in its emphasis.[5]

Gruchy employed Smuts's term because no single word had emerged in the post-Veblenian period that adequately described the viewpoint of these heterodox economists. Gruchy offers the following holistic definition of economics:

> Economics is the study of the structure and functioning of the evolving field of human relations which is concerned with the provision of material goods and services for the satisfaction of human wants.[6]

Added Gruchy, "The term 'holistic' has been selected because it called attention to what is most characteristic in the new economics: Its interest in studying the economic system as an evolving, unified whole or synthesis, in the light of which the system's parts take on their full meaning."[7] There is another thread to Gruchy's view, namely that orthodox theory developed in the period when capitalist industrial society (in England as well as in the United States) was characterized by many small-scale enterprises. From such a background Hutchison's notion that orthodox theory could be "extended" or "modified" to encompass the reality of modern industrialism more fully by what Hutchison called "deductive manipulation" made more sense than it could to Veblen and his followers, who saw the economy and its functioning as well as its ultimate role in society in quite a different light than did the orthodox economists.[8]

HOLISTIC ECONOMICS
AND MACROECONOMICS

One reason why the term holistic economics failed to catch on may be because many equated holism with macroeconomics. But an institutionalist would conclude rather easily that whatever macroeconomics is, it is not coterminous with holism. Consider the confusion that exists to this day about the difference between microeconomics and macroeconomics. Numerous definitions tell us that the former considers "the trees" whereas the latter is concerned with "the forest."[9] One recent macroeconomics text begins:

> There is not one branch of economics, microeconomics, which uses supply and demand analysis, and another branch of economics, macroeconomics, which uses some other apparatus. Both microeconomics and macroeconomics are concerned with the interaction of transactors on *markets,* and as a result, each is amenable to analysis with the same tools.[10]

This view may be contrasted with the following:

> Microeconomics analyzes the behavior of the individual consumer, firm, or industry, using price theory as its tool, whereas macroeconomics studies the vast aggregates at play in the economy, using national income analysis and theory about the behavior of our markets — goods, money, labor, and bonds.[11]

There is little point in extensive discussion here of the appropriateness of these definitions. Whatever is involved in macroeconomic analysis it clearly does not address the central concern of institutionalism. One tends to forget how recently the term macroeconomics was introduced. The Keynesian revolution of 1936 focused on the macroeconomy, but Samuelson does not even introduce the term until the fourth edition of his text (1958); through the third edition (1955) the term does not appear.

Keynes's focus was distinctive, but his concerns were not the same as those of American institutionalists. Some similarities have been suggested by Peterson.[12] But there is one significant difference between Keynes's Weltanschauung, or even the broadest possible perspective one can attach to post-Keynesian macroeconomics, and the perspective of institutionalism. Macroeconomics and holistic economics do not regard the economy as "whole" in the same way. The key new concept in Keynes's *The General Theory* was the concept of effective demand. Effective demand refers only to the *quantity* of aggregate demand relative to the quantity required to give full employment. Indeed, Keynes's whole concern was with quantities of aggregate activity, and this concern is distinct from the institutionalist's focus on the essential thrust of economic direction and activity. Keynes's "propensity to consume," for example, never involves consideration of consumer sovereignty, demand manipulation via advertising, or the deployment of market power. Institutionalism has never ignored the impact of concentrated economic power on the economy. One seeks awareness of this issue in vain in Keynesian macroeconomics.

The impact of Keynes's macroeconomics was transcendingly important but also very different from the institutionalist impact. Peterson is not wrong in stressing some common concerns, but his view is incomplete. Keynes's celebrated comment that digging holes and filling them up might sometimes be effective economic policy presents a trivial example of a broader lack. Keynesian macroeconomics may avoid fallacies of composition, but it is not concerned with *where* the economy is going or with how its emergent operation impinges on its participants. To be at an underemployment equilibrium, a full-employment equilibrium, or an overfull-employment equilibrium does not tell what it is the employed are producing, how output-mix decisions were made, or what the implications are of these results for resource use, technology, and energy. These are the concerns of holistic economics. I once commented,

> The disproportionate attention given to theoretical apparatus which concentrated on simplistic allocation while the economy itself wrestled with valuation increasingly is being recognized. Perusal of any basic text will underscore this discrepancy between the complexity of our apparatus to deal with 'markets' and the paucity of our apparatus to deal with value (in static terms) or progress (in dynamic terms).[13]

Even when one looks at the economy as an aggregated structure as in the Keynesian framework one is still regarding the economy as an allocative rather than a valuative mechanism.

The output of Keynes's macroeconomy is *measured* but not evaluated. Keynes himself says: "The outstanding faults of the economic society in which we live are its failure to provide for full employment and its arbitrary and inequitable distribution of income."[14] Despite the presence of the normative word "inequitable," he makes it clear that his concern with income distribution is largely of the Malthusian or Hobsonian variety, that is, with the macroimpact of differential marginal propensities to consume on savings, interest, investment, and hence on income and output. He argues further that the implications of his theory are in certain respects quite conservative and that it makes no overwhelming case for state socialism.

Keynes concludes,

> Our criticism of the accepted classical theory of economics has consisted not so much in finding logical flaws in its analysis as in pointing out that its tacit assumptions are seldom or never satisfied, with the result that it cannot solve the economic problems of the actual world. But if our central controls succeed in establishing an aggregate volume of output corresponding to full employment as nearly as is practicable, the classical theory comes into its own again from this point onwards.[15]

The classical theory may come into its own again for Keynes, but it surely does not for the institutionalist. The results emerging from the macroeconomy for Keynes need only be measured against the yardstick of what full-employment output might be, whereas the institutionalist would wish to know a great deal more about the implications of that full-employment output. In short, in an economy with a deflationary gap Keynes's concern is filling the gap, with converting C + I to whatever level of C + I + G is required to achieve full-employment income. He spends no time on what it is that income consists of, how the decisions concerning the nature of the income are reached, or on judging the quality of emergent economic life.[16]

HOLISM AND THE INSTITUTIONALIST PERSPECTIVE

Keynes's model is frequently characterized as only quasi-dynamic or comparative statics. Dynamism in Keynes is surely not the same thing as progress in Ayres or holism to Gruchy. The term holism says precisely where the locus of attention should be: the whole economy as an *evolving, choosing, culturally conditioned entity.*

Macroeconomics was in part an effort to free economic analysis from fallacies of composition. One person on tiptoe can see over a crowd; everyone cannot. If each person tries to increase his saving, the result will be to lower income, and savings in the aggregate will go down not up. Macroeconomics became necessary because the aggregate performance of the economy was not adequately comprehended by summing the performance of individual households and firms.

Examples of the fallacy of composition accentuate the relationships between the total results emerging from market processes and the myriad parts of the market process (e.g., households and firms). But holism encompasses the ultimate thrust of a political economy, and here one cannot take market operations as "given." The political economy is larger than the market both quantitatively and qualitatively. Prices in the public sector are set by means of a process reflecting more than the customary motivations of households and firms in markets. The entire culturally conditioned process, moreover, by which valuation is made by the participants in an economy far transcends market allocation. The allocative operations of an economy are evaluated and debated via political contests. Elections to governmental bodies select public officials pledged to certain attitudes toward taxation, public expenditures, key wages and prices, public responsibility for minimal standards of economic welfare, and so forth. It is clear, therefore, that the economy is a great deal more than the macrosum of all the households and firms as they express themselves in markets. Thus, in the end, the distinction between microeconomics and macroeconomics, while useful for a number of limited purposes, obscures the crucial distinction between the viewpoint of orthodox economics and the institutionalist emphasis on the whole economy.

POWER AND THE FALLACY OF COMPOSITION

Nothing makes the dangers of mere microsummation, as in macroeconomics, clearer than factoring power into the economic equation. Inclusion of power makes abundantly clear that structuring economic analysis with a primary aim only of avoiding fallacies of composition may well be useful, but holistic economic analysis must be understood to go farther, as a few examples may clarify.

Macroeconomics regards the economy as consisting of the same sovereign consumers motivated by the same rational pursuit of "utility" as does microeconomics. The same (presumably competitive) firms are considered to operate in macroeconomics and are motivated by rational pursuit of maximum profits. The role of the government is primarily that of participant of last resort, standing ready to fill deflationary gaps and to tax away inflationary gaps. There might be a minor refereeing role for the govern-ment—as when union and management need assistance in settling collective bargaining disputes or when business firms become rambunctious from excessive zeal in pursuing profits and the antitrust laws are utilized. Macro-economics considers where consumers get their notions of "satisfaction" and the implications of what firms may do to affect these notions. Advertis-ing is conventionally assumed, of course, but misinformation, rechan-nelling of consumer objectives, and similar intrusions into consumer moti-vation are not customarily treated. Similarly, the impact of firms on the resource base, and on the environment, is not easily included in orthodox macroeconomics, nor are the consequences of concentrated power as it intrudes via huge business firms into the information channels of the government, the political process, and the social structure of a society.

The role of the government in macroeconomics is radically different than its role in holistic economics. We have already seen that the role of govern-ment in conventional macromodels is largely quantitative. Those who de-velop a "positive" macroeconomics consider the macropolicy alternatives and discuss the best means for accomplishing this quantitative manipu-lation. Institutionalists, in contrast, will relate firm-household-government interaction to the political process and all this to the cultural and institu-tional seedbed from which the community's whole value structure emerges. This value structure is partly expressed in the market, partly outside the market. It manifests what a society, given its attitudes, its resources, and its technology, chooses to produce and what the consequences of this choosing will be. The deployment of power permeates the whole process and is criti-cal in the determination of the character of both the private and the public parts of the economy. The inequities, the distortions, the expansions and contractions in various sectors, the growth, the patterns of distribution and development are all affected by the power structure. Indeed, it is not too much to say that it is the allocation of power far more than resource alloca-tion that conditions and shapes the development of the economy and its ongoing operations. This is the fundamental allocation that mainstream economics, micro or macro, prefers to ignore.

The process by which economic valuation emerges is a process that ante-dates any market activity, in the sense that the participants in market alloca-tion arrive in the market with a set of then-current attitudes and a perspec-tive shaped by their culture. It has been affected by prior manipulation, and continues to be manipulated in the market by a wide variety of groups, all of whom have vested interests in particular market results they wish to encourage. They bring to bear on these results as much power as they may possess. Beyond the market, the process of valuation is sociopolitical and finds expression in the legislators chosen, the constraints that the election process brings into operation on the legislators, the pressures that lobbyists and others bring to bear on legislative activity, the realities that shape both spending and taxing programs, the contemporary standards of minimal permissible poverty and maximum permissible wealth, and a whole host of related factors. Out of all this comes — in a continuous and changing stream — the values which the economy projects as well as partially shapes.

The view of the economy just presented is what institutional economists have always meant by the "whole economy" and hence "holism" points to a crucial aspect of institutional thought. The role of government is crucial in a qualitative sense and is fundamentally affected by concentrated economic power in private hands. That the importance of this qualitative participation by government probably far transcends any mere quantitative functions of government seems abundantly clear. That the role of government is far greater than mere refereeing of household and firm behavior, even in a market-oriented enterprise economy such as that of the United States, should be equally clear. Governmental activity is shaped by and shapes the economy and so plays a pivotal role in the ongoing valuation process.

Some years ago Galbraith suggested that the power interplay in the contemporary concentrated economy may produce less disastrous results than many might fear because organized power blocs could offset each other's power. Thus big business and big labor may have customarily held each other somewhat in check — their market objectives of maximizing profits or wages are not fully achievable. Galbraith included big agriculture and big government in this perspective and concluded that the American market economy might work somewhat better — presumably somewhat more as the competitive model assumed it might — than it would have had each of these conflicting power blocs not existed to "countervail" the power of the others. Galbraith made it clear that the rise of government to bigness was at least partially a response to the prior rise to power of the other groups. A major weakness in the Galbraithian view is that there is nothing to prevent any of the countervailers from agreeing to cooperative endeavors to exploit the unorganized and widely dispersed consuming public. There was, in short, no automatic guarantee that countervailing power would protect the "public interest." Since Galbraith developed the notion in 1952 he has developed a more thorough analysis of the American economy and would no doubt wish to elaborate this notion.[17] The rise of consumerism to at least the status of a quasi-power might ameliorate some of the ganging up on the public, but not all.

HOLISTIC ECONOMICS AND THREE TRAPS IN ORTHODOX THEORY

The requirement of holism is nothing less than explicit recognition of the need to focus attention on the way in which community values develop and on the implications of these emergent values for how the economy functions. We have suggested, therefore, that the term holistic economics may bring to economic analysis the framework institutionalists would regard as essential. It may assist economists in revising their perspective toward their discipline from the economics of allocation to the economics of valuation.[18] *valuation* In trying to isolate economic analysis from broader considerations conventional economics employs at least three devices, which may be regarded as traps that ensnare and limit its perspective.

Often it is necessary in economics or any other field to concentrate on certain aspects because it is impossible to consider everything at one time, and it is equally impossible to master every relevant field. Economics has carried this process furthest and often to a self-defeating extreme. Nowhere is this clearer than in the *assumption of Economic Man.* An early formulation was that of Mill:

> Economics is not concerned with ". . . the whole conduct of man in society. It is concerned with him solely as a being who desires to possess wealth, and who is incapable of judging the comparative efficacy of means for obtaining that end. It predicts only such of the phenomena of the social state as to take place in consequence of the pursuit of wealth."[19]

Robbins has commented that the construct "assumes a world of economic men concerned only with money-making and self-interest" and is, therefore, apt to appear "foolish and exasperating . . . to any competent economist." But Robbins insists it "is worth further examination" because it can serve as "a certain expository device of pure analysis."[20]

Robbins argues in this fashion because, as he continues, economics is concerned with "relative valuations" and "we do not regard it as part of our problem to explain why these particular valuations exist. We take them as data."[21] Institutionalists would argue that the determinants of "relative valuation" *cannot* be taken as data and hence ignored. These valuations are part of the whole economy — hence the appropriateness of the term holism. The economy itself is intimately involved in making these valuations, although it is not the sole instrument of their determination. To take an obvious example, consumers may value a particular product highly because business firms in pursuit of profits, power, or whatever, have persuaded them to value that product more than they would on the basis of their own independently determined motivations. The relative valuations that emerge are, therefore, vastly different than they otherwise would have been. Are all agents equal Economic Men or is not the firm given greater voice than the consumer? The public sector, moreover, cannot be comprehended at all within the customary confines of the Economic Man construct, nor can most of the dynamic and environmental concerns of the day.

So in effect, the essential argument of holistic economics is not that one must try to consider all aspects or problems simultaneously, when clearly this is impossible, but rather that the economy itself is involved in the conditioning of economic decisions. As such, it is both shaped by and a determinant of what the economy does. Economists as economists cannot, therefore, escape consideration of the implications of economic decisions, and this involves them in the valuation process.

Closely related to the Economic Man trap is the ceteris paribus trap. The Economic Man trap shunts critical aspects of the economy and its functioning out of the way by declaring them to be "noneconomic." The ceteris paribus trap, however, recognizes that the factors it deals with are a legitimate aspect of economic problems, but it determines that economists can, "for expository purposes," declare such factors off limits. A noteworthy orthodox debate revolved about whether Marshallian demand curves were based on the assumptions that Marshall held constant tastes and preferences, *money* incomes, and the price of all other products, or whether what he held constant were tastes and preferences, *real* incomes, and all other prices.[22] The debate in effect considered the implications of altering the income assumption, but the tastes and preferences assumption — really critical if one is concerned with how valuation takes place in an economy — was never relaxed.[23] The problem is of significance to economists precisely because the economy and its participants are very much involved in the process of shaping tastes and preferences. The process involves not only allocation through the market but public sector attitudes as well.

If the assumption of constant tastes and preferences is very closely related to the previous discussion of Economic Man, the ceteris paribus trap can be further clarified by referring to the other assumption mentioned — that of given income. Whether the income referred to is money income or real income is not half so crucial as the assumption that purchasing power — whether monetary or real — is assumed to be given before the economist commences his analysis. The result is that *how* income distribution is determined (a process that most assuredly occurs in the economy), *how* the wealth distribution that frequently determines the income distribution came about, *how* economic power and economic opportunity came to be what they are in an economy — all are ignored by banishing them from consideration via the ceteris paribus assumption. What the implications might be of limiting or distorting the full economic potential of given resources by accepting uncritically and unquestioningly whatever distribution of wealth, power, or opportunity a given economy happens to incorporate cannot even be described, let alone evaluated by so structuring economic analysis. But these questions are most definitely economic questions; never is this really disputed. We merely agree via ceteris paribus that we shall never investigate them or their implications.

The notion of *externalities* is not new. A recent definition says they "arise when the voluntary economic activities of agents — in production, consumption, or exchange — affect the interests of other economic agents in a way *not* setting up legally recognized rights of compensation or redress."[24] The author says this definition is "too broad," and so we must restrict the definition to impacts directly on technological opportunities or preferences. Here, "direct externalities, beneficial or harmful, lead the Invisible Hand astray."[25] The externalities problem, so viewed — as "sources of gain or loss that do not get translated into market signals" — is very restricted. The author suggests that the way in which externalities may be handled is to make adjustments via taxes and subsidies, by "unitization" (putting the "harmer" and the "harmee" in a water pollution situation into the same "unit" for analysis), or by reassignment of property rights. That viewing externalities in this way constitutes a trap from a holistic perspective can be seen fairly readily.

In all the examples cited the object of adjustment is to bring into balance "private marginal costs" and "social marginal costs." But what are "social marginal costs"? How are they derived? What allowance for time is made, so that we know whether or not, as in a question of resource conservation, any effort has been made to include future generations in the calculation of costs or benefits? The term "social marginal cost" is used to suggest that the economy has derived values, as institutionalists use the term, but without in fact recognizing that determining values is a primary function of the economy itself. In short, the most significant task of the economy is assumed away so that economic decisions can be trivialized into mere "market mechanics."[26] The result, in my judgment, is to lead economists into assuming they have coped with "the economic problem" when in fact they have distorted it by equating a valuational problem with an allocational problem. Valuation subsumes allocation, but it is scarcely coterminous with it.

In short, the "externalities trap" like the other two considered enables conventional analysis to assume it is dealing successfully with the economic problem when, in fact, the most fundamental aspect of that problem — namely how the economy develops its values — has simply been ignored or assumed away. But because the economy itself plays a critical role in shaping values and in changing values the problem cannot be shunted off to some other "noneconomic" aspect of social investigation.

CONCLUSION

Followers of the Veblen-Ayres tradition in economics have earned the right to be known as something more than "mere dissenters." While there is variation among them in the details of their views, the fundamental perspective from which this group regards the role and operation of the economy has a considerable consistency. The movement was originally called institutionalism, and more recently has come to employ Veblen's own term, calling itself evolutionary economics. I have suggested here that the term Gruchy used in the 1940s — holism, or holistic economics — has a good deal of merit because it emphasizes the globalism that is an essential aspect of the Veblenian perspective. It stresses what is advanced rather than what is rejected in conventional economics.

Holism is not coterminous with macroeconomics, because the latter was designed to rescue mainstream economics only from the fallacy of composition in broadening the perspective of microeconomics, particularly competitive theory. This was a useful move, but it stressed quantitative rather than qualitative changes. Macroeconomics represents a broadening of the economics-is-allocation perspective — no doubt a critically important broadening — but it does not represent recognition of the economics-is-valuation perspective fundamental to holism. The dynamic equivalent of this static framework is recognition that the economy is concerned with progress rather than growth alone.

Economic power affects both the interrelationships of households and firms as they interact in markets and the interrelationships as well of all the participants in the political and cultural process that shapes economic values. The nature of the public sector; the role and responsibility of various levels of government; the sensitivity to and awareness of the environment, the future, and the world outside the home economy in making economic decisions for the present; the importance attached to leisure; the notions of acceptability in participation in the society in general and the economy and its opportunities and possibilities in particular — all these questions and more are part and parcel of the economy as a valuating mechanism.

Various efforts to constrain economic questions to a more convenient framework have only succeeded in obscuring the nature of political economy. The assumptions of Economic Man, ceteris paribus, and a few, simple externalities advance precision at the cost of avoiding difficult questions. Holistic economics has the distinct advantage of serving to point up this necessary perspective, and there is considerable evidence that a number of economists are in fact realizing that it is the political economy — the ongoing process of valuation — that must command our attention.

ENDNOTES

1. C. E. Ayres, *The Theory of Economic Progress* (Chapel Hill: University of North Carolina Press, 1944), pp. 155-156n.
2. See, for example, T. Veblen, *The Theory of Business Enterprise* (New York: Charles Scribners, 1904), Chs. 2 and 3.
3. One recent use of the term, which however appeared too late for consideration here, is in C. K. Wilbur with R. S. Harrison, "The Methodological Basis of Institutional Economics: Pattern Model, Storytelling, and Holism," *Journal of Economic Issues* 12 (March 1978): 61-89.
4. J. C. Smuts, *Holism and Evolution* (New York: Macmillan, 1926).
5. Gruchy, *Modern Economic Thought: The American Contribution* (New York: Prentice-Hall, 1947), p. 4.
6. Ibid., p. 550.
7. Ibid., p. vii.
8. T. W. Hutchison, *The Significance and Basic Postulates of Economic Theory* (London: Macmillan, 1938), pp. 73-76. See Gruchy, ibid., pp. 549-50.
9. See, for example, the definitions in Milton Spencer's Dictionary of Economic Terms and Concepts at the end of his *Contemporary Economics,* 2d ed. (New York: Worth Publishers, 1974).
10. Robert L. Crouch, *Macroeconomics* (New York: Harcourt Brace Jovanovich, 1972), p. 3.
11. John H. Makin, *Macroeconomics* (Hinsdale, Ill.: Dryden Press, 1975), p. 6.
12. "Although the language is different, the disequilibrium economics of Keynes is much like the evolutionary economics of Veblen. Both see economics as a process, as a movement through time." W. Peterson, "Institutionalism, Keynes, and the Real World," *Journal of Economic Issues* 11 (June 1977): 216.
13. Philip A. Klein, "Economics: Allocation or Valuation?" in *Journal of Economic Issues* 8 (December 1974): 804.
14. J. M. Keynes, *The General Theory of Employment, Interest, and Money* (New York: Harcourt, Brace, 1936), p. 372.
15. Ibid., p. 378.
16. Gruchy has viewed Keynes in essentially the same way. See *Contemporary Economic Thought* (Clifton, N.J.: Kelley, 1972), pp. 2-5.
17. Galbraith is never one to understate his case. He wrote of countervailing power, "The contention I am making here is a formidable one. It comes to this: Competition, which at least

since the time of Adam Smith, has been viewed as the autonomous regulator of economic activity and as the only available regulator apart from the state, has, in fact, been superseded." *American Capitalism: The Concept of Countervailing Power* (Boston: Houghton Mifflin, 1952; Sentry edition, 1962), p. 112.

18.   P. A. Klein, "Economics: Allocation or Valuation?" *Journal of Economic Issues* 8 (December 1974): 785-811.

19.   J. S. Mill, *Essays on Some Unsettled Questions of Political Economy,* 1874, pp. 137-40. Quoted in Eric Roll, *A History of Economic Thought* (New York: Prentice-Hall, 1942), pp. 397-98.

20.   Lionel Robbins, *An Essay on the Nature and Significance of Economic Science* (London: Macmillan, 1946), p. 94.

21.   Ibid., pp. 84-95.

22.   Milton Friedman, "The Marshallian Demand Curve," reprinted in W. Breit and H. M. Hochman, eds., *Readings in Microeconomics* (New York: Holt, Rinehart and Winston, 1968), pp. 104-14. M. J. Bailey, "The Marshallian Demand Curve," reprinted in Breit and Hichman, *Readings,* pp. 115-22.

23.   As an exercise in seeing whether or not it could in fact be relaxed in the confines of an otherwise untouched mainstream paradigm, I tried to relax the assumption myself some years ago. I thought the result showed rather conclusively that the assumption could be relaxed, but not surprisingly no one has ever been much interested. Relaxing ceteris paribus assumptions is not an effort that garners much support, let alone enthusiasm, among mainstream economic theorists. (See P. A. Klein, "Demand Theory and the Economist's Propensity to Assume," *Journal of Economic Issues* 7 (June 1973): 209-39.

24.   J. Hirschleifer, *Price Theory and Applications* (Englewood Cliffs, N.J.: Prentice-Hall, 1976), p. 449.

25.   Ibid.

26.   P. A. Klein, "American Institutionalism: Premature Death, Permanent Resurrection," *Journal of Economic Issues* (June 1978): 251-76.

6 JUST ECONOMIC INSTITUTIONS
Two Philosophical Views
Royall Brandis

> The economist as a social scientist is concerned not with efficiency alone, but with efficiency in relation to the wants of the individuals and groups operating within the evolving economic system. These individuals and groups are interested in such wants as economic abundance, economic freedom, economic security, economic justice, and economic quality. — Allan G. Gruchy

Two of the several ways in which the question of justice in economic arrangements can be attacked have recently found detailed exposition in books by philosophers: John Rawls, *A Theory of Justice*,[1] and Robert Nozick, *Anarchy, State, and Utopia*.[2] Consideration of the approaches taken by these two authors, as well as the very different conclusions arrived at, may lead us to a better understanding of the difficulty of reaching agreement as to what are (and what are not) just economic institutions. We should say, by way of introduction, that neither the tools of analysis used nor the institutions scrutinized by these authors are exclusively economic. But economic analysis and economic institutions bulk large in both expositions, and the focus of our attention will be restricted to those areas, more

The author would like to acknowledge the help of two colleagues: Professor Emeritus of the Philosophy of Education Harry S. Broudy and Professor of Philosophy B. J. Diggs. Neither, of course, is to be held responsible for what follows.

narrowly to the economic institutions of property and inheritance. This restriction is not as serious as might at first appear, for the character and developmental path of an economic system are shaped by the design of its institutions regarding property, property rights, and the rights to bequeath and inherit.

It is a curious anomaly that institutional economists have been often concerned with righting or, at least, exposing perceived economic injustices while generally avoiding the question of what, precisely, is economic justice.[3] In Gruchy's classic "review of the troops," he finds little to be said on the subject of justice in discussing the work of men like Veblen, Commons, Mitchell, Clark, Tugwell, and Means.[4]

The accuracy of this treatment by Gruchy is confirmed and, perhaps, explained by an examination of Commons's definitive *Institutional Economics*.[5] Commons rejected Locke and the idea of a Social Contract in favor of Hume's principle of scarcity and the conflict of interests. He is quite clear on this:

> Institutional economics goes back to Hume. Taking our cue from Hume and the modern rise of such a term as "business ethics," ethics deal with the rules of conduct arising from conflict of interests and enforced by the *moral* sanctions of collective opinion. Economics deals with the same rules of conduct enforced by the collective sanctions of economic *gain* or *loss*. Jurisprudence deals with the same rules enforced by the organized sanctions of *physical force*. Institutional economics is continually dealing with the relative merits of these types of sanctions.[6] [Italics in original]

In fact, of course, Commons concentrated his own efforts on the latter two legs of the tripod—economics and jurisprudence. With Locke's Social Contract ideas studied only in philosophy and with utilitarianism the ruling creed of orthodox economics, the Humean view never really penetrated. Indeed, when Ayres came to write *The Theory of Economic Progress,*[7] he lumped Hume and Smith together; they "summed up the moral nature of man in 'sympathy.' "[8] Commons had treated two philosophers as opposed. "Hume derived both self-interest and justice from Scarcity, but Smith . . . derived them from Abundance."[9] While it is true that each man was dealing with slightly different aspects of the philosophers, it is also true that neither Ayres nor Commons was led in his seminal works to make a frontal attack on the question: What constitutes economic justice?

BASIC VIEWS

We might try to derive the appropriate criteria for judging the justice of economic institutions in the following way: Imagine a situation in which self-interested, fully rational human beings meet under certain conditions to decide upon a social contract that will specify the principles of justice to which their economic (and other social) institutions must conform. Imagine further that all are in a special sense equal in this gathering. They know inequality exists, but each is ignorant of the nature of his own position — favorable or unfavorable. Thus, one cannot be influenced to advocate principles that would serve to favor himself at the expense of others. Each does possess a "sense of justice" (Rawls, p. 19).[10] Economic institutions in the real world that conformed to the principles of justice agreed to in this hypothetical "original position" could then be said to be just economic institutions. Those that did not conform would be unjust institutions. This, in essentials, is Rawls's approach.

A second possible approach is to imagine man in a (Lockean) state of nature in which each person is completely isolated from every other person. Now let all come to be in (at least, sometimes) contact with each other. Each will wish to enforce his rights and to defend himself. He will wish to do so efficiently and effectively. His wish will create a demand for enforcement-defensive services. "Protective associations" (Nozick, p. 13) will arise as entrepreneurs respond to market demand by offering to sell protective services.[11] From this beginning, we can trace in a hypothetical manner the developmental history of those institutions that would grow out of individual needs and desires freely expressed in a kind of market place as well as the supply response to those demands. These institutions would be, by virtue of their origins, just institutions. Any other institutions, in particular any that affect the distribution of income and wealth — whose (hypothetical) history cannot be traced in this fashion — are unjust institutions.[12] This is, essentially, Nozick's approach.

For Rawls, then, the criteria for judging the justice of institutions are to be found outside those institutions. For Nozick, these criteria, although derived from original individual rights, are internal to the institutions. For Rawls, the result of the operation of a given institution on those persons affected by it and on society generally is an important basis for judgment of the justice of the institution. For Nozick, the result is not relevant to the judgment; it is the process by which the result was obtained that serves as our guide in judging the justice of the arrangement. Another way to see the difference in basic views between Rawls and Nozick is to note that Rawls has no need for history, while historical principles are fundamental to Nozick's view. Rawls begins with a synthetic situation, "the original position," in which the principles of justice are worked out. These principles are then applied in judging the justice of modern institutions and in proposing just institutions to replace those existing ones now found wanting. Nozick, on the other hand, wants to know the history, real or hypothetical, of an institution. It is on the basis of that history from origin to the present that the institution is to be judged.

DISTRIBUTIVE JUSTICE

Now one might suppose that, if "justice" meant — even approximately — the same thing to both Rawls and Nozick, then the two should come out at about the same point when the principles each derives are applied. But, in fact, this is far from the case, and the differences are particularly marked in the area of distributive justice in economic matters. How does it come about that, starting from what might be thought to be opposite ends of the same track, Rawls and Nozick do not meet at a common conclusion, but rather arrive at near opposites?

Rawls, for example, finds his principles of justice lead to government's guaranteeing "a social minimum either by family allowances and special payments for sickness and unemployment, or more systematically by such devices as a graded income supplement (a so-called negative income tax)" (Rawls, p. 275). Further, the government "imposes a number of inheritance and gift taxes, and sets restrictions on the rights of bequest. The purpose . . . is not to raise revenue . . . but gradually and continually to correct the distribution of wealth" (Rawls, p. 277).

Nozick, on the other hand, argues for what he calls an "entitlement theory of justice in distribution" (Nozick, p. 153). If wealth has been acquired justly or, when acquired unjustly, if rectification of the injustice has been accomplished, then justice in distribution requires obedience to the maxim:

> From each according to what he chooses to do, to each according to what he makes for himself (perhaps with the contracted aid of others) and what others choose to do for him and choose to give him of what they've been given previously (under this maxim) and haven't yet expended or transferred. [Nozick, p. 160]

This maxim is consistent with Nozick's more general conclusion that only a minimal state can be justified. In contrast to the positive injunction to redistribute placed upon government by Rawls, Nozick's maxim only hints of any distributive role for the state in his reference to the (possible) "contracted" cooperation of others in production. Presumably, the authority of the state must stand ready to enforce contracts. Clearly, however, the state must also be prepared to defend legitimate holdings by the use of its power. But both of these functions are envisaged in Nozick's minimal state. Indeed, it was the demand for the performance of these two functions that led to the origin of "protective associations" in the (hypothetical) history of the origin of the state.

Perhaps we should note one possible way of viewing the two philosophers' approaches to distributive justice. Rawls seems already convinced that the results of any existing (or conceivable?) economic system will, left to its own devices, yield an unjust distribution of income and wealth. Hence, justice without government intervention in the distributive process is impossible. And, presumably, Rawls would place the burden of proof on those who would argue for the justice of existing arrangements. Nozick appears to take the opposite stance. For Nozick, the burden of proof lies on he who would argue that state intervention in the distribution process can yield justice despite the restriction that would thus be placed on the individual's liberty to dispose of his property as he wished.

RAWLS ON JUSTICE BETWEEN GENERATIONS

No aspect of economic life causes so much difficulty for both Rawls and Nozick as that which involves the passage of time. This should not surprise economists who have long known that some of our thorniest theoretical problems lie in the areas of capital and interest, saving and investment, and economic growth generally. For Rawls and Nozick, the problems arise (explicitly for Rawls, implicitly for Nozick) when they consider the institutions of (private) property and inheritance and their relation to the state.

Rawls runs into difficulty over the question of justice between generations because of the unidirectional nature of time. Rawls's theory, on a strict interpretation, allows no inequalities in a just society except those that benefit the least advantaged. Now, if the first generation saves, its consumption must, perforce, be reduced below what it might otherwise have been. This saving, assuming (as Rawls does throughout) that saving is always converted into productive capital, serves to raise production and consumption for future generations. But this has a perverse effect in terms of Rawls's theory: The creation of this inequality between generations has been at the expense of the least advantaged, namely, the first generation. Furthermore, if the saving process continues, each succeeding generation would enjoy greater production (and consumption) at the expense of all the earlier, less-advantaged generations.

Put differently, if we take the view (as Rawls does for other reasons) that all those in the "original position" are contemporaries although they do not know which generation they are, then they might well agree not to save anything for their posterity. If previous generations have saved, the present generation cannot do anything about it; it cannot compensate its ancestors. Thus, again, regression would lead each generation to the no-saving conclusion. Now, Rawls's concern that this not be a result of his theory does not appear to lie in a Calvinistic urge to promote the sanctity of thrift. Rather, it lies in the very practical belief that one cannot hope to establish a just society without achieving some minimum level of productivity and standard of living. Thus, economic growth (up to a point) is necessary to achieve a just society, and saving is necessary to economic growth. So, saving is moved outside the main lines of Rawls's theory:

> It is a natural fact that generations are spread out in time and actual exchanges between them take place only in one direction. We can do something for posterity but it can do nothing for us. This situation is unalterable, and so the question of justice does not arise.

> It is now clear why the difference principle does not apply to the savings problem. There is no way for later generations to improve the situation of the least fortunate first generation. [Rawls, p. 291]

Rawls's solution to the problem is to modify the otherwise strict requirements of the "original position." The modification is that "the parties are regarded as representing family lines, say with ties of sentiment between successive generations" (Rawls, p. 292). This is a particular, not a general, fact and thus violates the rules that Rawls had previously set up about the parties' ignorance of particulars in the "original position." However that may be, Rawls has now solved to his satisfaction the problem of justice between generations. For now that those in the original position are tied by the bonds of family sentiment to future generations, they can be expected (indeed, they have a duty) to save and accumulate capital in order to improve the well-being of future generations.

The rate at which this saving will occur will be determined by "balancing how much at each stage they would be willing to save for their immediate descendants against what they would feel entitled to claim of their immediate predecessors" (Rawls, p. 289). This Rawls calls the "just savings principle." It is still the least advantaged who hold our attention. The rate of accumulation of capital in a particular generation must be approved by them, and the accumulation must be designed to improve the lot of the least favored (although not these exclusively) of future generations.

While the rate of capital accumulation will be specified as described above by the "just savings principle," the economic growth that is thus made possible is not continuous but, rather, has a clearly demarcated and, presumably, abrupt end. For economists concerned with growth theory or economic development problems, Rawls's specification for the end of the process is, at the least, a challenging one:

> The last stage at which saving is called for is not one of great abundance. . . . Further wealth might not be superfluous for some purposes; and indeed average income may not, in absolute terms, be very high. Justice does not require that early generations save so that later ones are simply more wealthy. Saving is demanded as a condition of bringing about the full realization of just institutions and the fair value of liberty. . . . To achieve this state of things great wealth is not necessary. In fact, beyond some point it is more likely to be a positive hindrance, a meaningless distraction at best if not a temptation to indulgence and emptiness. [Rawls, p. 290]

Thus, there is a dual inequality between generations. For the first, and possibly for the other early generations, there is a positive reduction in consumption to provide capital for later generations. For the last generations there is no mandate to save, but only an injunction to replace the existing capital as it wears out so that the appropriate level of income is produced continuously. One can make adjustments in these matters depending upon his assumptions about population — whether rising, falling, or stable — but they would lead us ultimately to the same conclusions.

IS INHERITANCE NECESSARY?

For Rawls, saving and inheritance are linked; indeed, he appears to believe that saving depends on inheritance. If capital is to be accumulated and the capital stock maintained, he believes inheritance is necessary. Strictly speaking, this is not the case. If each individual saved during his working years solely for the purchase of a life annuity upon retirement, there would be no inheritance of wealth because there would be no wealth at death to bequeath. Yet, there would be a stock of savings and a corresponding stock of real capital in existence at all times; only the names of the claimants to that stock of savings would change as individuals entered the labor force and began the purchase of their postretirement life annuities; meanwhile, annuitants would be dying.

While the above possibility moderates the need for savings to be transmitted through inheritance, it does not necessarily eliminate it. For there is no assurance that the total stock of capital resulting from this process will be sufficient to raise per capita income high enough to allow a just society to flourish. On the other hand, the transmission of property ownership through inheritance opens the way for a particular family over time to acquire so much income-yielding wealth as to be, in Rawls's view, unjust. Consequently, Rawls (p. 277) proposes inheritance and gift taxes and "restrictions on the rights of bequest" (Rawls, p. 277). He is very clear on this point: "The purpose of these levies and regulations is not to raise revenue (release resources to government) but gradually and continually to correct the distribution of wealth and to prevent concentrations of power detrimental to the fair value of political liberty and fair equality of opportunity" (Rawls, p. 277).

Rawls's dilemma is also clear: He wants to allow bequest in order to stimulate saving and capital accumulation. Yet, he fears the result of inheritance on the just society. But it is hard to conceive of a policy that discourages inheritance that may not also discourage saving. Rawls adds to his problem by suggesting a proportional expenditure tax as superior to either a proportional or progressive income tax (Rawls, p. 278). This further encouragement to saving would, presumably, require even higher inheritance taxes and even stricter restrictions on bequest. Indeed, it does appear that Rawls's view comes down to this: Everyone has a right to bequeath; no one has a right to inherit.

There is one other possibility that should be noted. It is possible that some individuals will retain their goal of what they desire for their heirs and simply save whatever additional amount is necessary to achieve this goal *after* taxes. Since there is no reason to expect each individual to react in the same way to the existence of an inheritance tax system, Rawls really has no solution to this problem. The best he can offer is a suggestion of Meade's to make inheritance taxes progressive but have the progressivity based upon the preinheritance wealth of the beneficiary. The ability of such a tax to redistribute wealth without discouraging saving is — to say the least — questionable, so Rawls has not really solved his problem. (Meade has no similar problem because he would be happy to have the foregone private saving replaced by government saving.)

NOZICK ON INHERITANCE

It is more difficult to criticize Nozick's views on saving, inheritance, and capital accumulation, because he really never comes to grips with the difficulties involved. In the first place, the "minimal state" that arises through the process of the market is, according to Nozick, "the most extensive state that can be justified, any state more extensive violates people's rights" (Nozick, p. 149). Consequently, his concern is to develop a theory of distributive justice (which he calls "the entitlement theory" leading to a minimum of governmental action affecting the distribution of income and wealth. The theory consists of three "principles": (1) "the principle of justice in acquisition." (2) "the principle of justice in transfer," and (3) "the principle of rectification" (Nozick, pp. 150–152).

If it were not for this third principle, Nozick's view would be clear. The only question to be asked about a person's wealth ("holdings," to use Nozick's somewhat broader term) would be whether he received it freely from its previous owner either in exchange or by gift or bequest. The principle of rectification, however, is to provide for those cases in which the wealth-holder or a predecessor has violated one of the first two principles (of acquisition or transfer) in obtaining a holding. This would seem to open the door to much the same questions of distributive justice with which Rawls is concerned. Nozick is quick to make clear, however, that the *results* of the distributive process are not to be accepted as evidence of past injustice: only the *process* of aquisition and transfer are at issue in any specific case. Furthermore, such cases are not thought to be numerous or hard to identify. According to Nozick, "Deviation from the first two principles of justice [in acquisition and transfer] will involve other persons' direct and aggressive intervention to violate rights, and since moral constraints will not exclude defensive or retributive action in such cases, the entitlement theorist's problem rarely will be pressing"[13] (Nozick, p. 173).

To the economist, aware of all the subtle, hidden forms that market power may take and the manifold ways in which it may be exercised (not even to speak of overt fraud or deception), Nozick's view of the economic system is not an easy one to comprehend. Whether a more realistic view of the world in which we live would alter Nozick's satisfaction with the entitlement theory we, of course, do not know. But the theory itself is not a watertight one, as we shall argue.

Nozick's entitlement theory fails to recognize that one must not only be entitled to give, but the receiver must also be entitled to receive. Thus, the victim of a highwayman is entitled to turn over his holdings to the robber, but the robber is not entitled to receive them (as Nozick, of course, recognizes). Is an inheritor entitled to his inheritance? Does entitlement to a holding during one's life extend to determining the disposition of one's property after death? Is that not just a matter of law (e.g., trusts running only to those living at time of death or only to the third generation)? Nozick will have a difficult time showing that the heir even has a right to "defensive or retributive action" if one puts forth the argument that entitlement to holdings ceases with death and cannot be transmitted to others after death. In truth, Nozick's view of inheritance violates his radical individualism, for it is only by a social agreement that the living undertake to carry out the wishes of the dead.[14]

Nozick argues that, "were people's reasons for transferring some of their holdings to others always irrational or arbitrary, we would find this disturbing . . . . We feel more comfortable upholding the justice of an entitlement system if most of the transfers under it are done for reasons" (Nozick, p. 159). But he continues immediately, "This does not mean necessarily that all deserve what holdings they receive" (Nozick, p. 159). Well, then, how do we determine which are deserved? Does Nozick mean that one could be "entitled" to a holding but not "deserve" it? Then, Nozick adds, "Gifts to loved ones, bequests to children . . . are nonarbitrary components of the fabric [of individual transactions and transfers]" (Nozick, p. 159). What is the basis for this last statement as justification for entitlement to inheritance? Does it differ from the highwayman because bequest is "freely given"? What does it mean to say that someone dead makes a gift freely? What is the deceased giving up? Nozick's answers to these questions are not easy to find.

CONCLUSION

One way to understand the wide difference between Rawls and Nozick is to see each, despite his professional background in philosophy, as representative of two fundamental — and fundamentally different — intellectual traditions. Rawls is, at bottom, a Darwinian; Nozick, on the contrary, is a Newtonian. Of course, this influence is mostly implicit in their work, but it surfaces at one point with Rawls when, after referring specifically to the theory of evolution, he says, "The capacity for a sense of justice and the moral feelings is an adaptation of mankind to its place in nature" (Rawls, p. 503). The instant case, incidentally, would seem to go beyond Darwin in that a sense of justice in its members might well enhance the chances of survival of a particular group, but it might not enhance, or even might reduce, the chance of survival of a particular individual exhibiting that sense.

With Nozick as with Rawls, this scientific influence is mostly implicit in his work, but something approaching explicit treatment is found in his discussion of the "moral boundary" that surrounds each individual (Nozick, p. 57ff.). For example, "A line (or hyperplane) circumscribes an area in moral space around an individual" (Nozick, p. 57). The individual, then, is an encapsulated congeries of rights reacting to other individuals when their force impinges upon him and, in turn, exerting force upon them. It is not difficult to see behind this picture a universe of Newtonian atoms that, even when engaged in the closest interaction, still retain their individual identities — inviolable, independent, and influential.

Rawls's view of man in society is an organic one. We shape, and are shaped by, the social institutions that comprise our social environment. Especially, man's identity as human is based upon his linkage with his fellows. This is evidenced in many ways in Rawls's exposition, but nowhere more clearly than in his approach to the problem of distributive justice. The question for Rawls is: What would be the characteristics of an institution that justly distributed among *all* the social product resulting from the direct productive activity of *some?* For, in the Rawlsian view, production is a social activity carried on by a part of the society for the benefit of the whole society. And all are entitled to a share. Justice might require allocation of somewhat larger portions to those who contribute directly to the output, but, conceivably, it might not. Production is a cooperative activity; it could not be carried on without the organizational arrangements made possible by society. Thus, the product belongs to the society; no individual has a superior claim.

Nozick's view of man is atomistic. As such it leads him to the obverse of Rawl's approach to distributive justice. Production is an individual activity even when carried on as a group endeavor (via "the contracted aid of others"). The act of producing carries with it an individual entitlement to the product or to the appropriate contracted share of the product — in the case of group production. Society's claim to a portion of the product extends only to the competitive price of the individually demanded protective services of the minimal state. If the state takes more, either for its own purposes or to redistribute to others, it does so unjustly.[15] In general, an organic view of society is, to Nozick, belief in an illusion. It is an illusion analogous to the belief that a gas as an organic whole exerts pressure on the walls of its container when, in fact, it is the random impact of individual molecules that yields the resulting pressure.

Both Rawls and Nozick fall victim, each in his own way, to a fallacy that is all too familiar to economists. The fallacy arises in the search for a link between production and distribution. In economics it might be called the mono-factor theory of production. Since without factor of production A (A = land, or labor, or capital, and so on), production would not occur; therefore, factor A is responsible for *all* production and is entitled to all of it. With Rawls, factor A is society;[16] with Nozick, factor A is the individual. Their very different theories of distributive justice flow from these very different beginnings. Alas, in truth, production is the result of a combination of many factors — those of the economists' classifications as well as, in a different classificatory scheme, both society and the individual.

Neither the social contract view of Rawls nor the radical individualism of Nozick can provide us with a wholly satisfactory theory of justice with which to assess the institutions of economic life. The evolutionary outcome which yielded self-interested human beings with family ties, coupled with the necessity for capital accumulation if the economy is to provide more than brute existence, may well prevent our devising appropriate economic institutions that also fully satisfy our desire for justice. Even if the dilemma is a true one, the search for just institutions will continue.

Of particular interest to institutional economists should be the fact that Rawls makes a clear distinction between the principles of justice for institutions and those that apply as between individuals. And his work is an exposition of a theory of justice for institutions. Rawls's definition of an institution is very close to that of Commons:

> By an institution I shall understand a public system of rules which defines offices and positions with their rights and duties, powers and immunities, and the like. These rules specify certain forms of action as permissible, others as forbidden; and they provide for certain penalties and defenses, and so on, when violations occur. [Rawls, p. 55]

and,

> The principles of justice for institutions must not be confused with the principles which apply to individuals and their actions in particular circumstances. These two kinds of principles apply to different subjects and must be discussed separately. [Rawls, pp. 54–55]

This may be compared with Commons's statement:

> If we endeavor to find a universal principle, common to all behavior known as institutional, we may define an institution as Collective Action in Control of Individual Action.[17]

On the other hand, institutionalists are not likely to find much common ground with Nozick. Commons argued for the importance of a distinction between justification of ownership and ownership itself. While couched in the context of the relation of law to these matters, his statement (had it not been made forty years earlier) might be taken as direct rejection of Nozick's entitlement theory of distributive justice. Thus Commons:

> All that the present owner, therefore, can get out of his contemplation of the past is some kind of justification, argument, or pleading for his present claim to rights of ownership. . . . [Institutional] economics asks, What *is* that right to do as one pleases now and hereafter? . . . What *ought* to be the right or its value in view of conflicting rights of others, and of the social consequences of exercising that right?[18]

The Rawls and Nozick works represent in the 1970s a renewal of an ancient controversy in social philosophy. At the same time, by the amount of attention paid to economic institutions they remind us again of the very fundamental nature of the questions asked by institutional economists. Their study might well be the basis for consideration anew of the principles of justice for economic institutions.

ENDNOTES

1. John Rawls, *A Theory of Justice* (Cambridge, Mass.: Harvard University Press, 1971).
2. Robert Nozick, *Anarchy, State, and Utopia* (New York: Basic Books, 1974).
3. Professor Broudy, in critically reviewing an early draft of this paper, commented that the concept of justice may well be a primitive notion not susceptible of rigorous definition. Consequently, he suggested it may be more helpful to think about remedying injustice than to think about achieving justice.
4. Allan G. Gruchy, *Modern Economic Thought* (New York: Prentice-Hall, 1947).
5. John R. Commons, *Institutional Economics* (New York: Macmillan, 1934; reprint ed., Madison: University of Wisconsin Press, 1959 and 1961).
6. Ibid., p. 71.
7. C. E. Ayres, *The Theory of Economic Progress* (Chapel Hill, N.C.: University of North Carolina Press, 1944; 2d ed., New York, Schocken Books, 1962).
8. Ibid., p. 72.
9. Commons, *Institutional Economics*, p. 161.
10. The Rawls and Nozick works will, hereafter, be referred to in this manner.
11. Nozick never faces up to the question of how one could, even hypothetically, have a market *before* one has the most basic institutions of human society. One might hazard the guess from the general tenor of the work that Nozick adopts Smith's view of man as possessing an innate "propensity to trade, barter, and exchange."
12. Once an institution, e.g., private holdings of property that obey the entitlement principle, infra, is found to be just in this way, its operation in the real world is, of course, anything but hypothetical. It becomes a measure by which we can determine the justice of holdings in that real world.
13. But see Nozick, p. 231, for statements that would appear to modify this view in certain extreme cases.
14. I am indebted to Professor Diggs for this characterization of Nozick's position.
15. I neglect here the Principle of Rectification, which allows redistribution if required to correct a past injustice. It should be remembered that evidence of inequality in distribution is *not* evidence of a past injustice requiring rectification.
16. This is not meant in the sense of government's being entitled to the whole product, but rather in the sense that, production being a cooperative process, it could not occur except within society; therefore, all have a right to participate in the decision as to how the output of the process is to be divided.
17. Commons, *Institutional Economics*, p. 69.
18. Ibid., pp. 408–409.

7 ATOMISTIC AND CULTURAL ANALYSES IN ECONOMIC ANTHROPOLOGY
An Old Argument Repeated

Anne Mayhew

Most economists and certainly all institutionalists are aware of the long debate within economics about the usefulness of standard economic theory, but some may be unaware that a similar debate has been taking place in economic anthropology. The dispute has become known as the "Formalist-Substantivist Debate."[1] It not only involves a controversy over the usefulness of standard economic theory but also a dispute over the way in which some anthropologists understand and try to use that theory.

Gruchy has described the conflict between economic orthodoxy and institutionalism as one between "atomistic" and "logical" analysis, on the one hand, and "evolutionary" and "cultural" analysis on the other.[2] Precisely the same terms could be used to describe the conflict between the substantivists and the formalists.

The formalists have, like standard economists, stressed the importance of individual decision making and have advocated using the tools of standard economic theory in studies of primitive and peasant economies. The substantivists have, like good institutionalists (as several of them are), replied that to focus on the individual is less informative than to analyze cultural patterns, and they have argued that standard economic theory is of little use in understanding primitive and peasant economies. It would strike most economists upon reading the formalist-substantivist arguments that

72

the old arguments between institutionalist and standard economists had merely been reworded by anthropologists. Institutionalists may be surprised at this turn of events in economic anthropology, anthropology long having served as a source of examples for institutionalists from Veblen to Polanyi and Ayres.

THE DEBATE IN OUTLINE

Anthropologists have long recognized the subfield of economic anthropology, and earlier in this century there were specific discussions of the applicability of economic theory to anthropological analysis.[3] The modern formalist-substantivist debate did not, however, develop until the early 1960s. In 1962 and continuing for several years thereafter a number of articles appeared in the *American Anthropologist* and elsewhere arguing vociferously that primitive and peasant peoples employ the same kinds of "economic strategies" employed by people of Western, industrialized societies. It was argued that standard economic theory is, therefore, universally applicable and should be used more often by anthropologists.[4]

The exponents of the formalist position were responding to the writings of Polanyi, Arensberg, Pearson, and their associates in *Trade and Market in the Early Empires*[5] and quite specifically to an article by George Dalton (a disciple of Polanyi) that appeared in 1961.[6] Dalton restated a theme first argued by Polanyi in *The Great Transformation*[7] and then elaborated in *Trade and Market in the Early Empires:* self-regulating markets of the kind that characterize modern industrial capitalistic economies are recent phenomena in human history, and the standard economic theory developed to analyze events in self-regulating markets is not applicable to much economic activity that was not or is not now organized through self-regulating markets.

Dalton's restatement of Polanyi's argument caused a furor among anthropologists. Published several years earlier it might have passed without much comment, but it appeared at a time when a number of anthropologists were becoming disenchanted with the conventional anthropological analysis of human behavior.

A DILEMMA IN ANTHROPOLOGY

In the twentieth century "culture" has been the central concept of anthropology. This concept has been used to organize information on the diverse technologies, kinship patterns, patterns of thought, and social structures of different peoples. Not only have anthropologists spoken of a culture as encompassing these patterns, they have also used the concept of culture to *explain* human diversity[8] (which is the central problem of anthropology, just as value and price have been the central problems of economics). Because historical studies of nonliterate people are impossible, anthropologists have not ordinarily tried to describe how mankind's diverse ways developed but have explained these diverse ways as consequences of differing ongoing systems. Each society is said to have its own culture — a unique set of functionally integrated rules, tools, and thought patterns — and each individual is then viewed as a product of his culture. As powerful as this concept of culture has been for anthropology — and indeed for much of twentieth century social science — it does present a problem. If man is viewed as a product of his culture, he may then be perceived as little more than a puppet, a blind follower of rules.

Much to the distress of a number of the present generation of anthropologists, individuals and individual action tended to disappear in anthropologists' accounts. The idea that man is a "product of his culture" led, they argue, to picturing man as an unthinking obeyer of rules. But anthropologists — particularly those working in areas of the world where rapid social change is taking place — are acutely aware that man is a sentient, reasoning creature who makes decisions. They find it difficult to integrate this view of man with the view that he is a product of his culture, doing what he does because of the dictates of rules that he did not make but simply inherited.

Man, many anthropologists now stress, is not a passive actor following a set of rules and fitting into a niche of society. Instead, man is a thoughtful being who considers his position and makes decisions. The actual behavior of a person may or may not correspond in any particular situation to the rules that the individuals involved say are supposed to apply. According to this dissenting view, older ethnographies have tended to be catalogs of ideal behavior rather than accounts of actual behavior. The rules of various societies, as they have been recorded by anthropologists, are only one of a number of factors considered by individuals in deciding upon actual behavior, not *the* determinants of behavior.

Within the "cultural paradigm," individual actions — for all their importance — are difficult to explain because man is seen as an obeyer of rules. If everyone is an obeyer of rules, how can one then account for new rules, for emerging patterns of behavior, for social and economic change? A "disobeyer of rules" — an innovator, a calculating and experimental person — is needed in the model. It is after all an individual, the modern anthropologist is likely to point out, who seeks work outside the village and thereby opens the village to change; it is an individual who takes or does not take the development officer's advice to experiment with a new cropping pattern; and so on.

THE APPEAL OF ECONOMIC THEORY

Many anthropologists have understood standard economic theory to be a universal and highly successful theory of human choosing. As one anthropologist, Strickon, says, "Economics, supposedly the least humanistic of the social sciences, is also the only one which explicitly has a position for the individual in its larger systemic theories. . . ."[9] Stating the formalist position concisely, he argued that — although one view of human behavior is that "individual actions are passive, and predetermined, responses to the imponderable workings of 'the system' " — nevertheless " 'the system' as we know it consists of statements which represent abstractions generated from the observation of human behavior, and the latter is inseparable from decision-making."[10]

It follows that a theory of decision making would be useful, and many anthropologists leaped to the assumption that economic theory was such a theory. In this view they have had the support of some sociologists, Homans, for example,[11] and of some economists, Robbins, for example.[12]

THE SUBSTANTIVE RESPONSE

Dalton and other substantivists responded to the emerging formalist position in an innocently wrong manner. They perceived the issue as economists concerned with misuse of economic theory and were not mindful of the anthropologists' search for a theory of individual behavior.[13] What Dalton and the others feared was that in attempting to use the concepts of standard economic analysis anthropologists would be tempted to assume — or at least to imply to others — the existence of a market system where none existed. They responded under the misapprehension that they were engaged in battle with would-be neoclassical welfare economists, not with anthropologists seeking a theory of individual action.

THE RESULTING CONFUSION

In the rather limited number of cases in which anthropologists have actually set out to use economic theory, they have frequently made rather serious errors in doing so, errors that result from inadequate understanding of economic theory and of the uses to which it may be put. Ortiz, for example, in writing about the Paez Indians of Colombia, argues that part-subsistence farmers are rational in their decision making and that their allocation of time and other resources can best be analyzed through the use of "decision-making models" rather than in terms of what is "traditional."[14] In describing the behavior of the Paez she argues that output is largely determined by household needs. Perhaps because she fears this may appear "irrational" or "traditional," she states her proposition in terms borrowed from economics: "Farmers do not attempt to *maximize indefinitely their marginal revenue* by increasing production. Quantity produced, therefore, should be restricted to the needs of the producing unit"[15] (Italics mine). She appears quite unaware that to "maximize indefinitely their marginal revenue" would be a most irrational kind of behavior for any firm or farm.

Schneider, one of the leading proponents of the formalist approach, has written a book designed to introduce anthropologists to basic economic concepts and terminology and it is full or errors. A typical example follows. The reader who doubts that it is typical is referred to the book for myriad similar examples. Schneider suggests that the concept of "elasticity" will be useful to anthropologists:

> Elasticity refers to the fact that the response of demand and supply to price changes varies from reflecting them perfectly to not reflecting them at all. We can think of this as a relationship between units of price and quantity such that where there is maximum elasticity the maximum quantity is offered for a small change in price. For example, if the units of price were 100-ton gold bars and the quantity available was one pound of peanuts, a single bar of gold, when offered, would suck up the whole supply of peanuts. . . . Zero elasticity is the situation in which a change of price produces no change whatever in the quantity supplied. That is, the price unit is so small that a change can't equal the smallest unit of quantity. Thus, a one-cent change in the price offered for a diamond would have no effect on the supply of diamonds. . . . The importance of the concept of elasticity in general is that it warns us to not always expect an intimate equilibrium between supply and demand.[16]

This long quotation gives a taste of the confusion that can arise. The reader is assured that the deleted passages are just as wrong and as silly as those quoted.

Formalists have borrowed words from the language of economics and frequently misused them because they assume that by doing so they can prove "rationality" and can prove that decision making is important in primitive societies. Schneider, in his account of the Wahi Wanyaturu of East Africa, asserts that the Wanyaturu are profit-seeking, rational decision makers. He tries to prove this by arguing that "equilibrium prices" are established through the workings of the "laws of supply and demand."[17] He defines the "demand" for millet as that amount required by an adult for survival. "Supply" is that amount produced by each household in excess of the amount required by members of the household. Thus both demand and supply (at least over the period of a year) are fixed. Without realizing it, Schneider has described a situation where both the demand and the supply curves are vertical, making it impossible for supply and demand to determine price.[18]

The passages cited from Ortiz and Schneider may be ludicrous to economists, but the problem of the misuse of economic theory is a very real one and often occurs in more subtle form. Pospisil asserts that the economy of the Kapauku of Papua "resembles a simplified version of capitalism" and argues that sales of commodities "are usually heavily influenced by the law of supply and demand."[19] But his statement that "particular relationships between the trading partners" and "customary prices" play a role in determining prices and his statement that "the native 'businessmen' do most of their selling and buying on special occasions of a ceremonial nature"[20] cast doubt on whether he is actually describing a market system as economists understand it. More importantly, totally missing from his account is any mention of additional supplies being called forth by higher prices or of changes in the quantities demanded. In short, he is not describing an equilibrating feedback system and his use of "supply," "demand," and other terms from economics does not persuade the reader that his shell- and pig-mad Kapauku are maximizing capitalists.

Formalists such as Ortiz, Schneider, and Pospisil say they use terms of economic theory because these terms help them to analyze the systems they are studying. They also appear to believe that they are *proving* individual rationality by doing so, but a rather odd test of rationality has been adopted. One way to prove that people are not passive followers of rules is to collect and present evidence of leadership, of change, and of manipulation of others and of control over situations. This has in fact been done, and it is because it has been done that many anthropologists have rejected the older approach of describing societies as integrated sets of rules. Nevertheless, there seems to be a desire among the formalists to go further in *proving* rationality. This is the reason that using economic theory to describe and analyze is so important to Schneider, Pospisil, and other formalists. If they can find some sort of "supply and demand," this is taken as proof of, or at least as very strong evidence of, rationality. The following syllogism appears to have been adopted:

1. All people choose and are rational.
2. Microeconomic theory is *the* theory of rational choice.
3. Therefore, microeconomic theory must be useful for describing and analyzing all social systems.

The syllogism has never been spelled out in the literature but when it is, it appears to be foolish. Nevertheless, something like it must have been accepted by the formalists since they apparently equate rationality with choosing behavior as described by standard economic theory.

When the substantivists say the formalists do not present persuasive evidence of prices determined by supply and demand, formalists have understood them to say that the Wanyaturu and Kapauku and other primitive and peasant peoples are irrational or nonrational followers of rules. Of course, this has not been the substantivist argument — no substantivist has denied the proposition that all people are manipulators. What the substantivists have disagreed with is the implicit assumption that standard microtheory is the only theory of rational choice and must therefore explain all rational choices.

Adding to the confusion has been the fact that much of the debate has been carried on at a highly abstract level. If this has meant that many formalists have not had to apply the frequently treacherous concepts of standard economic theory, it has also meant that there has been no real meeting of minds between substantivists and formalists on the question of the role of the individual. Because the substantivists have denied the usefulness of the orthodox concepts, formalists have assumed that they were endorsing the view that man is a passive follower of cultural rules.

Examination of substantivist work on primitive and peasant economies shows that this is not so. In Van Roy's work on the Thai peasant economy, there is no standard economic theory (metaphorical use aside), but there is considerable emphasis on individual decision making.[21] Van Roy stresses the fact that Thai hill dwellers are constantly "jockeying for improved standing." The peasant is "rarely certain of his position" and "must continue to treat the [patron-client] relationship carefully, continually appraising its cost-benefit ratio from his point of view and continually working to move the ratio in his favor."[22] This is clearly not an endorsement of a view of man as a passive follower of rules. Nor is man treated as a blind obeyer of rules in other descriptive works of substantivists (e.g., Neale, Dalton, Polanyi, and Adams).[23] Formalists have, however, rarely treated the actual descriptive work of substantivists as important to the debate in anthropology. What alone has been important is the stand on the value and relevance of economic theory.

CONCLUSION

Although the formalist-substantivist debate has been a confused one, there is for anthropologists (and other social scientists) a real issue. It is easy for economists to dismiss the efforts of anthropologists, whose attempts to use economic theory are misplaced and frequently foolish, but they should not overlook the fact that it is difficult to incorporate thoughtful humans into cultural models. Unfortunately, because so much of the debate has been over the usefulness of standard economic theory, this difficulty has been obscured.

As mentioned at the beginning of this paper, it is possible to use the same terms Gruchy has used to describe the conflict between orthodoxy and heterodoxy in economics to describe the debate in economic anthropology. It is in a sense a debate over the merits of "atomistic" analysis as opposed to "cultural" analysis. Nevertheless, there are somewhat different issues involved in the two debates.

Among economists the issue has been how much to emphasize the cultural rules — the institutions. In emphasizing the need for "evolutionary" and "cultural" analyses, institutionalists have not been arguing that the individual could be ignored. Certainly in the work of Veblen and Ayres the tinkering individual is important in the process of technological change; in Commons's analysis the contentious, suing individual initiates the process of legal change.

Among anthropologists the issue is how to put more emphasis upon the individual. They are not abandoning the anthropological study of cultural norms and patterns — rather they seek to understand how these have evolved and how they change. It is for this reason they have turned to standard economic theory and, in so doing, have adopted a theory they neither understand nor can put to good use.

If anthropologists had been aware of the long methodological struggle in economics between its standard and its institutional branches, they might have understood that skepticism about the usefulness of conventional economic theory does not entail a view of man as a cultural puppet, and that there are better ways to study people who are making decisions within a context of cultural norms and rules.

ENDNOTES

1. Probably the best single source from which to learn more about the dispute is George Dalton, "Theoretical Issues in Economic Anthropology," *Current Anthropology* 10 (February 1969): 63–101 and the "Comments" on Dalton's article in the same issue. Dalton provides a very complete bibliography.

2. Allan G. Gruchy, *Modern Economic Thought: The American Contribution* (New York: Prentice-Hall, 1947), ch. 1.

3. Bronislaw Malinowski is usually given credit for founding the field. He published in the *Economic Journal* as early as 1921: "The Primitive Economics of the Trobriand

Islanders," *The Economic Journal* 31 (March 1921): 1–16. His *Argonauts of the Western Pacific* (London: Routledge, 1922) and *Coral Gardens and Their Magic* (New York: American Book Company, 1935) are both classics in the field. D. M. Goodfellow in his *Principles of Economic Sociology* (London: Routledge, 1939) and Raymond Firth in his *Primitive Polynesian Economy* (London: Routledge and Kegan Paul, 1939), as well as in his other works, discussed the application of economic theory to the study of primitive economies. The most famous earlier exchange on the topic was the Knight-Herskovits exchange: (Frank H. Knight, "Anthropology and Economics," *Journal of Political Economy* 49 (April 1941): 247–68 and Melville J. Herskovits, "Anthropology and Economics: A Rejoinder," *Journal of Political Economy* 49 (April 1941): 269–78.

4. Among the most important of these articles were Robbins Burling, "Maximization Theories and the Study of Economic Anthropology," *American Anthropologist* 64 (September 1962): 802–21; Edward E. LeClair, "Economic Theory and Economic Anthropology," *American Anthropologist* 64 (December 1962): 1179–1203; Scott Cook, "The Obsolete 'Anti-Market' Mentality: A Critique of the Substantive Approach to Economic Anthropology," *American Anthropologist* 68 (April 1966): 323–45. Also, see the articles collected in E. E. LeClair, Jr. and Harold K. Schneider, eds., *Economic Anthropology: Reading in Theory and Analysis* (New York: Holt, Rinehart and Winston, 1968).

5. Karl Polanyi, Conrad Arensberg, and Harry Pearson, eds., *Trade and Market in the Early Empires* (Glencoe: Free Press, 1957).

6. George Dalton, "Economic Theory and Primitive Society," *American Anthropologist* 63 (February 1961): 1–25. Although I am here arguing that it was this article that set off the debate, it should be noted that there was an earlier skirmish over the question of whether or not one could legitimately speak of an "economic surplus." This was a reaction to Harry Pearson, "The Economy Has No Surplus: Critique of a Theory of Development," in K. Polanyi, C. M. Arensberg, and H. W. Pearson, eds., *Trade and Market*. Marvin Harris responded to Pearson's chapter in an article titled "The Economy Has No Surplus?" *American Anthropologist* 61 (February 1959): 185–99. Dalton then responded to Harris and was thus drawn into the fray: "A Note of Clarification on Economic Surplus," *American Anthropologist* 62 (June 1960): 483–90.

7. Karl Polanyi, *The Great Transformation* (New York: Rinehart, 1944).

8. For an excellent discussion of the evolution of the concept of culture, see George W. Stocking, Jr., "Franz Boas and the Culture Concept in Historical Perspective," in his book *Race, Culture, and Evolution* (New York: Free Press, 1948).

9. Arnold Strickon, "Comment," *Current Anthropology* 10 (February 1969): 93.

10. Idem.

11. George C. Homans, *Social Behavior: Its Elementary Forms* (New York: Harcourt, Brace, and World, 1961). This work and others are discussed in Anthony Heath, *Rational Choice and Social Exchange: A Critique of Exchange Theory* (Cambridge: Cambridge University Press, 1976), which is a critical review of the uses to which both sociologists and anthropologists have put economic theory.

12. Lionel Robbins, *An Essay on the Nature and Significance of Economic Science,* 2d ed. (London: Macmillan, 1935).

13. See Dalton's article in *Current Anthropology* ("Theoretical Issues") for the best example of this type of substantive response.

14. Sutti Ortiz, "The Structure of Decision-Making among Indians of Colombia," in Raymond Firth, ed., *Themes in Economic Anthropology* (London: Tavistock, 1967), pp. 191–228.

15. Ibid., pp. 203–204.

16.   Harold K. Schneider, *Economic Man* (New York: Free Press, 1974), pp. 83–84.

17.   Harold K. Schneider, *The Wahi Wanyaturu: Economics in an African Society* (New York: Viking Fund Publications in Anthropology, No. 48), ch. 5.

18.   I am indebted to William C. Schaniel, University of Tennessee, for pointing out this peculiarity.

19.   Leopold Pospisil, *The Kapauku Papuans of West New Guinea* (New York: Holt, Rinehart and Winston, 1964), p. 18.

20.   Ibid., pp. 20–29.

21.   Edward Van Roy, "An Interpretation of North Thai Peasant Economy," *The Journal of Asian Studies* 26 (May 1967): 421–32.

22.   Ibid., p. 432.

23.   For examples see Walter C. Neale, "Land Is To Rule," in Robert Eric Frykenberg, ed., *Land Control and Social Structure in Indian History* (Madison: University of Wisconsin Press, 1969), pp. 3–15; George Dalton, "History, Politics, and Economic Development in Liberia," *Journal of Economic History* 25 (December 1965): 569–91; Karl Polanyi, *Dahomey and the Slave Trade* (Seattle: University of Washington Press, 1966); and John Adams and Nancy Hancock, "Land and Economy in Traditional Vietnam," *Journal of Southeast Asian Studies* 1 (September 1970): 90–98.

8 THE EVOLUTION OF THE INSTITUTIONALIST THEORY OF CONSUMPTION

Milton D. Lower

The theory of consumption, within the institutionalist conception of the economy, is inseparable from the general theory of cultural and economic evolution. The earliest coherent treatment of consumer behavior within this holistic and evolutionary perspective was that of Veblen in his first book, *The Theory of the Leisure Class.*[1]

Veblen's novel insights in this work, regarding such modes of institutionalized behavior as "vicarious leisure," "conspicuous consumption," and "pecuniary emulation," stirred wide public interest at the turn of the century; and they remain the hallmark of his thought in the popular apprehension. In this and other works, moreover, Veblen drew a sharp distinction between these institutional (or ceremonial) varieties of consumption, which utilize resources as invidious symbols, and consumption that is in a generic sense "instrumental." This "consumption dichotomy" (a cultural artifact more or less detached from Veblen's broader scheme of thought) has found a secure place in the corpus of knowledge of each of the social sciences, including mainstream economics.[2]

INSTITUTIONALISM AS EVOLUTIONARY THEORY

Less widely appreciated and less deeply assimilated were the evolutionary concepts and methods that enabled Veblen to arrive at these and other novel formulations. It was these concepts and methods, however, that provided the foundation for a distinct "school" of institutional economic thought. Within this theoretical tradition, the Veblenian concept of two mutually exclusive but interactive aspects of human culture and behavior, the instrumental or technological and the institutional or ceremonial behavior functions, has been developed into a powerful tool of evolutionary economic analysis.[3]

The consumption dichotomy familiar to students in social science survey courses is one expression of this principle of analysis. But the aim of such an analysis, as applied to consumption or other economic activities, is grossly misunderstood if the Veblenian dichotomy is construed as a taxonomy or system of classification, however insightful. Rather, the instrumental and ceremonial varieties of consumption are of interest, in common with and in relation to other economic behavior, for the distinct functional bearing of each through time on the direction and development of the economic life process. We shall return to this point later.

As evolutionary economics, the institutionalist approach has been nourished from Veblen onward by developments in the life sciences, in philosophy, in anthropology, sociology, psychology — and by other economic approaches concerned in some measure with holistic cultural change. Conversely, wherever the evolutionary perspective has been taken, or the economy has been analyzed as part of culture, there has been a high rate of combination, recombination, and independent invention of "institutionalist" concepts and methods.[4]

Since Veblen, consequently, there have been many "institutionalisms," some of them owing little or nothing to Veblen directly, some adopting and some eschewing the name "institutional economics." The search for likeness among these heterodox economic approaches has itself constituted an important contribution to the development of an evolutionary paradigm in economics, whatever it be called. To this effort, no one has contributed more than the economist we honor with this volume, Allan Gruchy.[5]

It has frequently been remarked, nonetheless, that it is easier to say what institutional economics is not than to say what it is. The social sciences generally take economic and other institutions as variable in time and space. The observation that institutions are variable is, however, consistent with many different views of economic systems, and it does not necessarily lead to a thoroughgoing evolutionary perspective. Macroeconomic theory, for example, allows certain aggregates to vary in accordance with causes that are related to institutional change. Fields, such as labor economics and economic development, are eclectic mixtures of orthodox and institutionalist analyses.

Yet for all who entertain a serious theoretical purpose as institutionalists, or evolutionary economists, there exists a common and substantial dissent. Orthodox economics as a *system* of theory explores the behavior of ideal-typical "economic men," acting under the very particular political and economic institutions of an exchange-integrated economy that came to flower in the late eighteenth and early nineteenth centuries.[6] Hence the ease of saying what institutional economics *is not*: it is not this.

CRITIQUE OF THE ORTHODOX THEORY OF CONSUMER BEHAVIOR

Critique has been a vital aspect of the development of institutionalist thought, and remains an important element in the holistic method. This method strives to relate the parts to the whole of an evolving cultural situation, focusing analysis upon a general or a specific economic problem. Such a procedure requires, inter alia, a critique of the partial, "economistic" analysis of the situation, as given by orthodoxy, for two reasons.

First, within contemporary market economics, some of the behavioral tendencies represented as "laws" by orthodox theory are in fact institutionalized modes of behavior.[7] The scope, the relevance, even the basic conceptual categories (supply, demand, markets, resources, value, GNP) of orthodox models require reevaluation in cultural and evolutionary terms. Secondly, orthodox theory and its history are part of the changing institutional situation to be analyzed in evolutionary terms.[8] The mainstream has not only interpreted but has considerably influenced the course of economic evolution through its impact upon the prevailing economic ideologies and policies.[9]

There is no branch of orthodox theory to which these considerations apply more forcefully than to the neoclassical theory of consumer behavior. With respect to this body of doctrines, systematic dissent and critique have been defining characteristics of institutionalist thought. The problems posed for the institutionalist theory of consumption have largely been defined by the failure of mainstream theory and method to address the most basic scientific and policy questions regarding the manner in which consumption has been instituted in the changing industrial economy.

THE CLASSICAL PRECONCEPTIONS

Since Adam Smith, consumption has been both a normative and a positive terminus for mainstream economic thought. When Smith made it so, he merely gave expression to the liberal "natural rights" wisdom of his age. Within his "obvious and simple system of natural liberty," it was self-evident that consumption was the "end" of all economic activity and that the "wants" of sovereign individual consumers should decide the composition of production.[10] This preconception was of a piece with Smith's plea for laissez-faire; and, in the context of the late eighteenth century, laissez-faire was arguably consonant with the unexceptionable purpose of relieving undifferentiated "want." For the majority in want, moreover, consumption as an *end* was equally society's *means* to maintain and improve the human resources upon which the increasing wealth of the nation depended. The growth of production was Smith's interest, and it was perhaps true at the time that nothing of comparable importance was overlooked by taking the underlying distribution and content of consumption as "given." The problem was that Smith's preconception acquired the force of a dogma.[11]

The later classical economists became tangentially aware that "who consumes what, how much, and why" is a matter of potentially great bearing on economic well-being, including production itself. Ricardo contrived his entire economic theory to show that, in the overall context of "diminishing returns in agriculture," the distribution of product among the classes of society determined the growth of production.[12] Given his "iron law of wages," according to which population growth would hold wages to the subsistence level, this became a question of whether the diminishing surplus would go to the capitalists, who would invest it, or to the landlords, who would squander it in sumptuary uses. Ricardo, as is well known, concluded that the resort to marginal land would increase the share of the landlords across the board, thereby halting economic progress in an eventual "stationary state."[13]

But Ricardo did not allow his conclusion to divert him toward an *institutional* inquiry on these questions of distribution and consumption. The problem inhered, he believed, in the niggardliness of Nature, the scarcity of the "original and indestructible powers of the soil." The landlords' rent, he said, "is the effect of circumstances over which they have no control, excepting indeed, as they are the law makers and lay restrictions on the importation of corn."[14] Once free trade, laissez-faire, and the sanctity of property were secured, then nothing further could be done to improve upon that dismal state into which Nature has delivered us. Thus were the institutions of society enshrined as laws of nature and limits to policy in the classical tradition.[15]

The classical legacy to the later orthodox theory of consumption comprised, finally, the unexamined assumptions with which the classicals had started: wants are phenomena of individual human nature. And in Ricardo's words: "Give men but the means of purchasing, and their wants are insatiable. . . ."[16] The classicals also bequeathed the assumption of the "paramount importance of production" to meet these given wants, using the given scarce resources, under laissez-faire.[17]

But even as these doctrines were received into the neoclassical theory of consumer behavior, in the late nineteenth century technological development had brought production to levels of want-abatement beyond Ricardo's imagination. And the substantive content of "wants" had attained a degree of pecuniary and industrial complexity that demanded an institutional analysis of the sort that Veblen would shortly provide.

THE NEOCLASSICAL THEORY

The neoclassical theory was nevertheless erected squarely on the classical preconceptions and took no account of the related "macroeconomic" dilemmas of distribution and growth that the classical analysis had left unresolved. The broadly utilitarian assumptions of the classicals were drawn out and refined by the concept of "marginal utility" and the mathematical means of its representation, which were developed more or less simultaneously by "marginalists" in several countries.[18]

The key idea was the "diminishing marginal utility" of goods, which paralleled the classical "law of diminishing returns" in production. According to this idea, while wants in general are insatiable, each separate want of the individual is limited, so that successive units of any want-satisfying thing yield diminishing increments of "utility." Thus, the individual, who will seek to maximize the total utility obtainable from his given income, compares the marginal utility of each contemplated quantity of a good against its market price. He then chooses to purchase that quantity of each good which will yield a ratio of marginal utility to price just equal to that for every other good he buys. This theory of "consumer equilibrium" in terms of utility maximization was formalized as the "demand" side of a complete model of equilibrium price determination by Marshall in the 1890s.[19]

With the completion of this neoclassical "microeconomics," the last vestiges of classical political economy (which at least had taken cognizance of questions of growth and change) were exorcised from mainstream economic theory.[20] The theory of consumption became a mathematical elaboration of the assumption that individuals maximize utility in satisfying their given wants, with given incomes. The theory of production became an elaboration of the assumption that individuals maximize profit or minimize disutility in transforming given scarce resources. The individual schedules of demand and supply so determined were presumed to add up to the market demand and supply for each good and service, and supply and demand then determined the price and quantity of every component of the national product. Beyond supply and demand the economist could not inquire.

It has been widely suggested in the history of economic thought that neoclassical economics gained ready acceptance just because it circumvented the classical problems and issues. Ricardo's labor theory of value, which he had used to explain the existence of the "surplus" that was available for capitalist investment or landlord dissipation, had been preempted and carried to its logical and systematic conclusion by Marx. The utility theory of value offered an alternative, wholly static way of looking at the economy. The economy became an automatic mechanism that allocated the limited production that could be wrung from Nature to the uses desired by the individuals — no longer the classes — who produced it.[21] By hewing to the assumption that society is an aggregation of individuals, that is, by ignoring how people come to own what they own, it even became possible to demonstrate the fundamental justice of the existing distribution of income. According to the marginal productivity theory of income distribution, each individual received an income, under perfect competition, that was equal to the marginal product of the land, labor, or capital he furnished to the productive process.[22]

As Robinson has said: "This is an ideology to end ideologies, for it has abolished the moral problem."[23] So far as the theory of consumption is concerned, Smith's broad assertion that consumption is (ought to be) the "end" of economic activity had become a rigorous defense of the status quo in regard to the distribution and content of consumption. Unfortunately, this came at a time when the *instrumental* grounds for Smith's undifferentiated consumers' sovereignty, if not yet his grounds for the paramount importance of production, had all but disappeared.

THE RETREAT FROM UTILITY

In one respect, however, the doctrine of diminishing marginal utility proved troublesome, if the desired result was, indeed, that the theory should allow no scope for judgment upon the given distribution of income and consumption. The notion of diminishing marginal utility seems to imply the further notion that Galbraith calls the "diminishing urgency of wants."[24] And if there is diminishing urgency of wants, it follows that the wants of the poor are more urgent and therefore more deserving of productive effort to meet them than the wants of the rich. Or, in traditional utilitarian terms, the maximum total utility from a given output — the "greatest good of the greatest number" — would seem to be achieved by equality in the distribution of consumption.[25] This result, however, would wholly vitiate the normative basis for consumers' sovereignty, absent redistributive policies, and with it the justification for maximizing production and growth in response to the dictates of the free market. As Galbraith has commented, "it was remarkable indeed that the situation was retrieved. This was done — and brilliantly. The diminishing urgency of wants was not admitted."[26]

The entire subsequent development of the neoclassical theory of consumer behavior may fairly be viewed as a series of retreats from the implication of a diminishing urgency of wants. First, while continuing to employ the concept of diminishing marginal utility, neoclassical theorists denied the possibility of interpersonal or intertemporal comparisons of utility. The consumption of bread may decline for every individual as income rises, but this yields no utilitarian imperative to subsidize bread to the poor. Let the rich man eat cake, and the marginal utility society derives from the last penny he spends may be as high as that obtained when the poor man buys his penny's worth of crust. Let the poor eat cake, and the collective utility may still be higher if the rich add circuses at the margin. We cannot compare the individual enjoyments, however clearly a pattern of diminishing urgency of wants may emerge from the observed facts.[27]

The pattern can emerge, moreover, only with the passage of time, which allows for changes in income and tastes. Thus, we cannot even infer from the "bread — cake — circuses" sequence for a given individual that there is diminishing urgency of wants. We can only say that yesterday the rich man had a taste for bread, today a taste for cake, and tomorrow he may have a taste for circuses. Each day — indeed, each moment — he is a different individual with a different utility function.[28]

While the situation was thus formally retrieved, not all practitioners of the science felt comfortable denying the apparent fact of diminishing urgency of wants by resort to such evasive and essentially "picky" arguments. Somehow the suggestive parallel of diminishing marginal utility with the realm of fact had to be broken altogether. This was done by disavowing the notion of cardinal or measurable utility, by abstracting from equivalent ordinal utilities the colorless idea of "indifference," and then ceasing to speak of utility at all.[29] Most recently, the theory of consumer equilibrium has taken the posture that the prices consumers pay for goods simply "reveal their preferences," and this insight is coupled with a plea of ignorance as to the unit of inner satisfaction so measured. This agnosticism stops short, however, of suggesting that whatever remains concealed behind preferences is less worthy of society's concern than was old-fashioned utility.[30]

ORTHODOX THEORY IN THE SCIENTIFIC BALANCE

The fundamental flaw of the received theory runs deeper than an expedient "moral agnoticism" can cure.[31] The purge of metaphysical utility — certainly desirable as far as it goes — is very nearly beside the point. It remedies neither the "positive" nor the "normative" defects of the orthodox theory of consumer behavior. The problem is not any *particular* conception of subjective value but the *fact* of it: the fact that the evaluative "springs of actions" are placed beyond inquiry, whether by the self-evident truth of "natural rights," the given curves of "marginal utility" or "indifference," or by the retreat to "revealed preference" and values nihilism.[32]

Whether cast in terms of utility, indifference, or revealed preference, the theory remains hostage to its restrictive, contrary-to-fact assumptions about the range of behavior it purports to explain.[33] It is scientifically, therefore, neither a theory of consumption nor a theory of behavior. It cannot explain consumption because it assumes away the cultural determinants of the quantity and quality of consumption; and it cannot explain behavior, since it has posited in its place the ideal type of the economic man. Strictly speaking, the theory *explains* nothing. It is an empathetic exploration of the rational processes of a maximizing consumer, choosing in the market, with given ordered wants and perfect knowledge of the alternative means and costs of satisfying them, under an income constraint. The theory asks us to think of how that would feel.[34]

Under the theory, the consumer will have "sufficient reason" to purchase that particular (equilibrium) bundle of goods and services which he apprehends will maximize his utility, leave him indifferent to further substitutions, or express (reveal to economists) his preferences. However, nothing in the theory pertains to the actual purchase or experience of goods and services, or to the demonstrable causes or consequences of such behavior.[35] In fact, the theory and method have what economists call an "opportunity cost." By virtue of the same contrary-to-fact institutional assumptions that permit the theory to cast its light upon the sufficient reasons of hypothetical consumers, there is excluded, within the terms of the theory, any formulation or testing of the "efficient causes or effects" of actual wants, consumer behavior, or substantive patterns of consumption. As Veblen summarized this orthodox dilemma nearly seventy years ago: "The acceptance by the economists of these or other institutional elements as given and immutable limits their inquiry at the point where the modern scientific interest sets in."[36]

ORTHODOX THEORY IN THE POLICY BALANCE

But it is not only the scientific interest that is shut off; it is the policy interest as well. By relegating all questions of value and choice to the subjective limbo of the individual "mind," orthodox economics justified consumers' sovereignty and laissez-faire. By placing all questions of "who consumes what, how much, and why" theoretically off-limits, neoclassicism put its stamp of approval on the given distribution and content of consumption, and affirmed the paramount importance of production for given market ends. The consequence, however, was an increasing irrelevance to the problems and issues surrounding the role of consumption in the evolving corporate economy.

Contemporary macroeconomics was born in the Great Depression, in response to the inability of traditional theory and its policy of laissez-faire to deal with the problem of effective demand. At the bottom of the theoretical difficulty, of course, was Say's Law of markets, which held that there could be no such thing as inadequate aggregate demand because the act of production (supply) creates the income (demand) to clear the market. And of course the income will be spent, by sovereign consumers or profit-seeking investors.

The Keynesian refutation of this law, anticipated by some early classicals and by "underconsumption" theorists, relied, inter alia, upon a forbidden inquiry into at least some of the determinants of consumption.[37] Keynes's remedy for inadequate demand went on to suggest both a theoretical and a practical role for government expenditure (public consumption). The Keynesian arguments for these heresies, it seems safe to say, would have found no more acceptance than those of earlier heretics but for one circumstance: Keynes reconciled the facts of "general glut" and massive unemployment, as well as the ideal of effective demand at full employment, with the concept of equilibrium. Not only might the macroeconomy be in equilibrium at any given level of activity, but at each such level the existing theories of microeconomic equilibrium still fully explained producer and consumer behavior. Such departures from laissez-faire as would be required to restore full employment need have none but a quantitative effect on the basic allocative mechanism.[38]

Since Keynes, the orthodox mainstream has accepted a theoretical, or functional, distinction between private and public consumption, as well as the notion of a "consumption function," which is in part institutionally determined, as central to the explanation of the *level* of aggregate demand and employment.[39] Unfortunately, this "neo-classical synthesis" does not appear to have contained enough "institutionalism," for now we are in the middle of what Joan Robinson calls the "second crisis of economic theory," which "arises from a theory that cannot account for the *content* of employment [and demand].[40]

Let us turn then to the institutionalist theory, where the evolving content of consumption and its economic consequences have been at the center of theoretical concern since Veblen.

THE INSTITUTIONALIST THEORY OF CONSUMPTION

The year before Veblen published *The Theory of the Leisure Class*, he wrote an article entitled "Why is Economics Not an Evolutionary Science?" In this article he scored the various schools of economic theory then existing — in the yet incomplete transition from classical to neoclassical orthodoxy — for their common metaphysics of "normality" and "controlling principles." The outcome of their common method "at its best, is a body of logically consistent propositions concerning the normal relations of things — a system of economic taxonomy."[41] But if we grow restless under this taxonomy and this metaphysics, "What are we going to do about it?"[42]

> There is the economic life process still in great measure awaiting theoretical formulation. . . . For the purpose of economic science the process of cumulative change that is to be accounted for is the sequence of change in the methods of doing things — the methods of dealing with the material means of life.[43]

From the most general to the most particular level of his analysis of the "economic life process," Veblen made use of the concept of a technological-ceremonial dichotomy. Earlier it was noted that this dichotomy involves a *functional* distinction between two aspects of human culture and behavior. As Ayres noted, the dichotomy "undertakes to distinguish two aspects of what is still a single, continuous activity, both aspects of which are present at all times. Indeed, they bound and define each other as do the obverse and reverse of a coin."[44]

Technology is tool-using behavior. It encompasses the skilled use of tools, materials, working principles, and matter-of-fact ways of doing things in any culture. Because of the objective character of the tools and materials and the operational character of the working principles and methods, moreover, there is an inherent tendency for such cultural elements to proliferate, through the "tool-combination process." This inherent dynamism of the technological process occurs both within culture and across cultural frontiers, and the evolution of technology (including what we now call science) has demonstrably been continuous and progressive throughout culture history.[45]

Within any particular culture and within any particular span of time, however, the pace and direction of such tool-combination (the "logic" of technology) is dependent upon institutional order. In any field of operations in which tool-using behavior goes on, it will be found interwoven with institutionalized, ceremonial behavior, which is past-binding in origin and effect. Such behavior is governed and sanctioned by the existing system of social stratification, mores, ideology or tribal belief, emotional conditioning, and ritual.[46] The institutional criterion of meaning, belief, worth, and conduct is not matter-of-fact workability, but a "ceremonially adequate" reenactment of or conformance to the details of this system of habitual usages. The institutional order is thus inherently change-resistant.

The cumulative sequence of interaction between these two aspects of culture, or behavior functions, is cultural evolution — general or specific. The outcome, viewed in terms of the livelihood of a people, is economic development (or underdevelopment). In evolutionary perspective, the central fact about an economy is the "state of the arts" achieved, which tells us more than anything else about the people's livelihood. Thus, in retrospect we recognize "hunting and gathering" societies; "yak" or "yam" cultures; "peasant agrarian societies"; "handicraft," "manufacturing," or "industrial" economies. Less definitively, we speak of contemporary "postindustrial" or even "post–mass consumption" society.[47]

Economic systems, past and present, are also meaningfully analyzed according to "the manner in which the economy is instituted in society," which is conditioned by and interactive with the evolving state of the arts. Comparative analysis of the main substantive patterns of economic systems — reciprocity, redistribution, and exchange — is particularly essential to analysis of the contemporary mixed economy, which combines elements of all three types of institutional mechanisms.[48]

VEBLENIAN FOUNDATIONS: THEORY OF THE LEISURE CLASS

One problem-area in this changing economic whole is the manner in which consumption is instituted — who consumes what, how much, and why —

and the functions and dysfunctions of this pattern for the further evolution of the system. In *The Theory of the Leisure Class*, Veblen laid the foundations for the institutionalist theory of this process. The scope of the study embraced the evolution of work, leisure, and consumption in culture generally, and the basic concepts were framed at this level of generalization. But the near focus was upon the manner in which this process of cumulative change had worked out in contemporary industrial society, especially the growth and adaptation of "leisure-class" symbolic usages under the pecuniary institutions of market economy.[49]

Veblen's detailed accounting of the evolution of consumption in the pecuniary-industrial economy cannot be summarized with justice here. In lieu of the genetic sequence — the cumulative technological expansion of potential and the "unbroken line of use and wont" from the lower barbarian culture to industrial capitalism — the bare analytical terms must be presented. Basic to the analysis was the fact that consumer behavior has in every phase of culture been instituted with and correlative to the system of work and livelihood on the one hand, and the system of exploit, status, and "ceremonial adequacy" on the other. Hence the "consumption dichotomy." The object of inquiry was to distinguish those aspects of consumer behavior deriving from each of these systematic sources and to analyze their cumulative economic consequences.

Veblen stated the criterion for distinguishing instrumental from ceremonial consumption, in general evolutionary terms: "The test to which all expenditure must be brought in an attempt to decide that point is the question whether it serves directly to enhance human life on the whole — whether it furthers the life process taken impersonally."[50] Consumption (and production) that "meets the test of impersonal usefulness — usefulness as seen from the point of view of the generically human" — is in and of the technological process of work and livelihood.[51] By contrast, ceremonial uses of goods and human effort are "incurred on the ground of an invidious pecuniary comparison" to serve the "relative or competitive advantage of one individual in comparison with another."[52] Such self-canceling expenditures are an exercise in futility and must be considered, impersonally, as "waste."[53]

In *The Theory of the Leisure Class*, Veblen's interest was focused on the development and institutional role of such conspicuous waste, and he made little effort to expand upon his concept of instrumental consumption. He tended to emphasize a rather basic and limited form of instrumental consumption, however, corresponding to what Strassman has called "energy-conserving" consumption. The latter is characterized by "its direct promotion of the functioning of men as biological organisms and as trained participants in the complex of material production. Food, clothing, shelter, household tools, transportation equipment, medicines, and training all had, and continue to have, this role."[54] It was left to later institutionalists to develop and refine the analysis of instrumental consumption, in other contexts.[55]

Ceremonial consumption, in Veblen's analysis, expresses and reinforces the canons of status, worth, and honor of the leisure-class institution, as it survives in industrial society. This institution reached its full development in higher barbarian cultures, such as feudal Europe, where the invidious distinction between the honorific and the industrial employments was rigorously instituted as a system of classes, a leisure class and a working class. The distinction itself is much older, resting ultimately upon the distinction between exploit (warfare and the hunt) and drudgery (woman's work) in the earliest predatory phases of culture; and it survives in industrial society in the distinction between pecuniary (money-making) and industrial (goods-making) employments. The term "leisure" in this context does not of course connote idleness, but "non-productive consumption of time" and "exemption from useful employment."[56]

The motive underlying all of these social distinctions is emulation—the desire for esteem, by and in comparison with one's fellows. In workmanship, this motive leads to invidious distinctions according to efficiency and the serviceability of the output. In the predatory culture, invidious distinctions among warriors and hunters, which are in some respects distinctions in point of workmanlike efficiency, evolve—through long habituation to the life of exploit, prowess, and seizure—into a sharp honorific distinction between exploit and drudgery. The evidence of invidious worth becomes the trophy, or booty from the raid, and especially the ownership of women seized from the enemy. The ownership of women by men reinforces the dishonor of the industrial employments performed by women, and eventually gives rise to the settled institution of property in goods. The leisure class proper emerges with this institution, and within the leisure class at least, emulation is thereafter centered on the possession of wealth. When the chief badge of honor becomes the accumulation of wealth, the chief economic motive, other than the acquisition and use of the common instrumentalities of the culture, becomes "pecuniary emulation."[57]

As regards this invidious distinction in terms of wealth and money power, possession is not sufficient. "The wealth or power must be put in evidence, for esteem is awarded only on evidence."[58] This is the role of conspicuous waste in the pecuniary economy, and in Veblen's analysis it has taken as many forms and tended to bulk as large as the development of production technology has made possible. In the preindustrial evolution of the leisure class, the typical form of emulative waste was "conspicuous leisure" — the expenditure of human effort in nonproductive activity. Such expenditure included not only the honorific abstention from work of the lord or head of household, but the "vicarious leisure" first of wives and female chattels, and subsequently of as many able-bodied men as he could afford to divert from production to his personal service.

In the later industrial phase, conspicuous leisure continues unabated, but it is supplanted in relative importance by the "conspicuous consumption" of produced goods. Again, such conspicuous display of wealth is carried out both by the wealth-holder and vicariously by the supernumeraries of his household. Finally, Veblen noted, in the contemporary state of the arts, the opportunity for the play of the motive of pecuniary emulation had reached quite far down into the class structure. While among the middle and lower classes there was reduced scope for achieving honor by means of conspicuous waste, the upper-class canons of decency in taste were imitated in such degree as to maintain "reputability" through the "pecuniary standard of living" appropriate to one's circumstances.[59]

Veblen's analysis in *The Theory of the Leisure Class* remains the most basic and important contribution to the institutionalist theory of consumption. It stands to this day as a coherent and consistent challenge and rebuke to the orthodox theory of consumer behavior, having never been seriously challenged as to the accuracy or power of the explanation it offers. By his critique of the theory and actual practice of "consumers' sovereignty," Veblen opened inquiry on the nature and consequences of the instituted motives, distribution, content, and level of consumption — and hence of production — in the industrial economy. In posing the central issue of "waste," which he pursued in his later work through every aspect of the corporate system of production, Veblen defined the terms of the "second crisis of economic theory" seventy years before Joan Robinson named it, and thirty years before the "first crisis."[60]

RESPONSE TO THE FIRST CRISIS OF ECONOMIC THEORY

The most important subsequent developments in the institutionalist theory and its bearing on consumption awaited the coming of these crises that *The Theory of the Leisure Class* presaged. So far as the critique and reconstruction of the "microeconomic" theory of consumer behavior was concerned, there was not much to be added to what Veblen had said in his early work. Until the entire orthodox theoretical structure fell into doubt in the Great

Depression, institutionalists restated Veblen's theory of consumption, and the mainstream economists continued to formalize theirs in ever more abstract and irrelevant terms.

Institutionalists were not theoretically "specialized" to respond to the particular range of macroeconomic questions posed by the "first crisis of economic theory" and answered more or less successfully by the Keynesian equilibrium analysis. The point is not that the institutionalist approach was ill-equipped to handle the theory of business fluctuations, since Veblen, and more particularly Mitchell, had been leading contributors to that field. The point is, rather, that in their theories and in the response of such economists as Mitchell and Clark to the "first crisis," they insisted upon answering the questions of the "second crisis." That is, their assessment of the problem of effective demand was not simply quantitative. As Gruchy notes, contrasting the institutionalists of the period with Keynes: "It was their position that *both* the volume and the direction of investment and employment were unsatisfactory from the point of view of the general welfare in the depressed 1930s."[61]

In consequence of their long-term analysis of the problem of private waste and misdirection of resources, both in consumption and in production, the institutionalists of the depression era took a broader policy approach than that encompassed in the Keynesian framework. They pointed to the drastic institutional changes wrought by the corporate revolution and the increasing concentration of economic power, and they challenged the Keynesian (and neoclassical) assumption that the private enterprise economy receives adequate guidance from the market in allocating resources in the public interest. "And," they asked, "who really decides what consumers will purchase, and what will be the content of the affluence made possible by full employment and a high and sustained economic growth rate?"[62] The policy they urged, in an outpouring of theoretical and empirical studies and from the numerous positions they occupied in the early New Deal, was movement toward "indicative national planning" of the contemporary Western Europe type.[63]

World War II ended both the Great Depression and the great debate between Keynesianism and neoclassical orthodoxy over the efficacy of government spending to maintain aggregate demand. It also began an era of rapid technological change and economic growth that was planned only in respect to the expanding sector known as the "military-industrial complex."[64] This unprecedented growth had within a decade or so after the war created a "mass consumption" society in the United States, the likes of which the world had never known. Mainstream economists, now under the "neoclassical synthesis," settled down to the theory and policy of the classical special case of Keynesian equilibrium — the full employment case — where the best of the macroeconomic and microeconomic worlds are met in equilibrium. Other economists, of a "neoinstitutionalist" bent, were more inclined to examine the developing problems and dilemmas of the "affluent society."[65]

GALBRAITH'S RESPONSE TO THE SECOND CRISIS

Galbraith, in *The Affluent Society* and other works, contributed several important dimensions to the institutionalist theory of consumption.[66] His critique of the "central tradition" in economics is very much in the Veblenian tradition, but it is framed for an era in which the classical assumption of the paramount importance of production to relieve "want," as will as the doctrine of original wants that served this assumption, requires scrutiny.[67]

Reviewing the history of economic ideas and their impact on the "conventional wisdom," Galbraith arrives at a "modern paradox" of the affluent society. "Why is it that as production has increased in modern times concern for production seems also to have increased?"[68] The beginning of an explanation, he says, is that the ancient preoccupations of economic life — with equality, security and productivity — have now narrowed down to a preoccupation with productivity and production. In the postwar period, "production has become the solvent of the tensions once associated with inequality, and it has become the indispensable remedy for the discomforts, anxieties and privations associated with economic insecurity."[69]

And yet, Galbraith notes, our concern for production is "traditional and irrational" in many respects, and our efforts to increase it are "stylized." Thus, we confine our theoretical and operative concern for increasing production to measures for improving bad resource allocation and promoting thrift and diligence, which were most relevant a century ago. Meanwhile, we "content ourselves with whatever we are getting" by way of research and development in new technology and in the volume of capital formation "despite the clear indication that these are the dimensions along which large increases in output are to be expected."[70] So that our preoccupation with production would seem to be a "preoccupation with a problem of rather low urgency," or a concern with production "only so far as the problem solves itself."[71]

What makes all of this intelligible, says Galbraith, is the "elaborate myth with which we surround the demand for goods." This "has enabled us to become persuaded of the dire importance of the goods we have without our being in the slightest degree concerned about those we do not have. For we have wants at the margin only so far as they are synthesized. We do not manufacture wants for goods that we do not produce."[72]

Thus, the first major contribution of Galbraith to the institutionalist theory of consumption is the concept of the "dependence effect," or the "dependence of wants on the process by which they are satisfied."[73] In Veblen's analysis, a large proportion of wants arise from "pecuniary emulation," whereby goods are consumed for their symbolic or status value. The items of "conspicuous consumption" of the few continuously filter down into the "pecuniary standard of living" of the many, creating wants in a manner totally inconsistent with the orthodox assumption that wants are original with the individual. Galbraith includes such emulation in the dependence effect as a "passive" element, but adds that when producers actively create wants through advertising and salesmanship, wants also come to depend on the *production* that satisfies them.[74] This is the ultimate flaw in the orthodox attempt to deny the "diminishing urgency of wants." For when wants are "contrived by the process of production by which they are satisfied . . . this means that the whole case for the urgency of production, based on the urgency of wants, falls to the ground."[75]

Galbraith's second major contribution is the concept of "social balance" which he defines as "a satisfactory relationship between the supply of privately produced goods and services and those of the state."[76] The traditional theory of consumer behavior as a theory of market equilibrium deals with this question solely by omission. Orthodox macroeconomics, as has been noted, deals with public expenditure as a quantitative term in aggregate demand, and has nothing to say on the content of such expenditure. But on the view that private wants are subject to the dependence effect, there is an inherent bias toward social "imbalance." Explicit concern with social balance becomes indispensable for intelligent allocation between the public and private sectors.[77]

DIRECTIONS IN THE POST-MASS CONSUMPTION SOCIETY

As this suggests, in the post–mass consumption society, there is no escaping the need to make social choices about some considerable part of the annual allocation of resources. But then there never has been, if indeed wants are created by the social processes of emulation and producer want-creation. It has been, rather, a question of *which* social agencies or processes made choices for nonsovereign consumers and to whose benefit. If social choices are made democratically and openly, they are not less "free," and perhaps more so, than many choices made in the contemporary market.

The broader concern to which Galbraith's work is addressed — encompassing his concern about corporate want-creation and social imbalance — is one shared rather widely in contemporary society, from many different perspectives. This concern is the "quality of life" we consume. More precisely, as Gruchy says, there is a widespread malaise about "problems such as the rise of the affluent society in which the heavy social costs of aimless economic growth are frequently ignored and in which the quality of life falls as affluence rises."[78]

Among the "heavy social costs" is environmental pollution. A part of Robinson's "second crisis of economic theory" is that the divergence between private and social costs, presented by traditional economics as "an exception to the benevolent rule of laissez-faire," is clearly the rule. "Where is the pricing system that offers the consumer a fair choice between air to breathe and motor cars to drive about in?"[79] Where, too, we may ask, is the sovereignty of the consumer who unknowingly chooses to put the children to bed in sleepwear treated with cancer-producing "Tris," because our post–mass consumption synthetics are so flammable?

Increasingly, economists find themselves confronting whole ranges of problems that are addressed as "exceptions," if at all, in orthodox theory. Increasingly, problems allocated to one compartment of theory spill over into another. Thus, production "externalities" show up as major consumer issues, and "given wants" show up as outputs of the productive process. Increasingly, GNP is considered "gross" by some, while looting becomes the normal response to a blackout in the post–mass consumption society. "Experience of inflation has destroyed the conventions governing the acceptance of existing distribution."[80]

There is no remedy but a holistic theory and policy that

accepts all cultural variables bearing on the problems;
considers the interactions of the whole and the parts;
recognizes that the "quality of life" may advance with limited growth of
     physical output and the elimination of "waste"; and
offers a plan for the macroeconomy, in conjunction with a reasonable
     incomes policy.

While institutionalists do not offer a finished plan for all of this, their theory alone has addressed the main issues as they have arisen, and that theory will be part of the solution.

ENDNOTES

1.   Thorstein Veblen, *The Theory of the Leisure Class* (1899; New York: Random House, Modern Library, 1934).

2.   Stuart Chase, "Foreword" to ibid.

3.   A leading contributor to this line of development was Clarence E. Ayres, *The Theory of Economic Progress,* 2d ed. (New York: Schocken Books, 1962). See also Allan G. Gruchy, *Contemporary Economic Thought: The Contribution of Neo-Institutional Economics* (Clifton, N. J.: Augustus M. Kelley, 1972), pp. 89–132.

4.   See David Kaplan, "The Formal-Substantive Controversy in Economic Anthropology: Reflections on Its Wider Implications," *Southern Journal of Anthropology* 24 (Autumn 1968): 228–51. See also James H. Street, "The Latin American Structuralists and the Institutionalists: Convergence in Development Theory," *Journal of Economic Issues* 1 (June 1967): 44–62.

5.   Allan G. Gruchy, *Modern Economic Thought: The American Contribution* (New York: Prentice-Hall, 1947); and Gruchy, *Contemporary Economic Thought.*

6.   Karl Polanyi, *The Great Transformation,* Part 2 (Boston: Beacon Press, 1957), pp. 33–219.

7.   "Now the money economy, seen from the new viewpoint, is in fact one of the most potent institutions in our whole culture." Wesley C. Mitchell, "The Prospects of Economics," in *The Backward Art of Spending Money and Other Essays* (New York: Augustus M. Kelley, 1950), p. 371.

8.   Thorstein Veblen, "The Preconceptions of Economic Science (I, II, and III)," in *The Place of Science in Modern Civilization and Other Essays* (1919; New York: Russell and Russell, 1961), pp. 82–149.

9.   Gunnar Myrdal, in making a plea for an "institutional" alternative in development theory, notes that "the very theories and concepts utilized in (conventional) analysis guide it away from those 'non-economic' factors." Thus, "what is needed is a different framework of theories that is more realistic. . . . In this situation even the negative accomplishment of demonstrating the inadequacy of our inherited economic theories and concepts is worthwhile.'" Gunnar Myrdal, *Asian Drama: An Inquiry into the Poverty of Nations,* 3 vols. (New York: Twentieth Century Fund, 1968), 1:27.

10.   See Thorstein Veblen, "The Evolution of the Scientific Point of View," in *The Place of Science,* p. 53n.

11.   Veblen has an extremely interesting discussion of this Smithian preconception as deriving from his "normalising the chief causal factor engaged in the process (which) affects also his arguments from cause to effect." Of particular interest "is the fact that his successors carried this normalization farther. . . ." Veblen, "The Preconceptions of Economic Science," in The Place of Science, pp. 128–30.

12.   David Ricardo, *On the Principles of Political Economy and Taxation,* vol. I of *The Works and Correspondence of David Ricardo,* Piero Sraffa and M. H. Dobb, eds., (Cambridge: Cambridge University Press, 1951), p. 5.

13.   Ibid.

14.   David Ricardo, quoted in Wesley C. Mitchell, "Postulates and preconceptions of Ricardian Economics," in *The Backward Art of Spending Money,* p. 215.

15.   See Polanyi, *The Great Transformation,* pp. 111–129. This chapter is one of the most interesting and original interpretations of classical "naturalism" in the literature.

16.   Ricardo, quoted in Mitchell, "Postulates and Preconceptions," p. 219.

17.   John K. Galbraith, *The Affluent Society,* 3d ed., rev. (Boston: Houghton Mifflin, 1976), ch. 9. The title of this chapter is "The Paramount Position of Production."

18. Ibid., p. 120.

19. H. H. Liebhafsky, *The Nature of Price Theory* (Homewood, Ill.: Dorsey Press, 1963), chs. 4 and 8.

20. Criticism of the neoclassical school, perhaps especially Marshall, must always be tempered with the observation that they were not yet wholly the captives of their own formal system. Thus, in their discursive writing, their parentheses, their footnotes, and their public pronouncements, they exhibited numerous departures from the model they passed on to the incoming generations. See Joan Robinson, *Economic Philosophy* (Garden City, N. Y.: Anchor Books, 1962), pp. 48–74.

21. See, for example, Eric Roll, *A History of Economic Thought*, 2d ed. (New York: Prentice-Hall, 1942), pp. 165–72, 187–95, and 347–411.

22. Liebhafsky, *The Nature of Price Theory*, ch. 12. Joan Robinson comments that in the marginal productivity theory, "the apparent rationality of the system of distribution of the product between the factors of production conceals the arbitrary nature of the distribution of the factors between the chaps." Robinson, *Economic Philosophy,* p. 61.

23. Robinson, *Economic Philosophy,* p. 54.

24. Galbraith, *The Affluent Society,* p. 120.

25. This was the essence of the original argument for the income tax. See Liebhafsky, *The Nature of Price Theory*, pp. 43 and 54–55.

26. Galbraith, *The Affluent Society,* p. 121.

27. Empirical work, from "Engel's Law" in 1857, had indicated such a pattern. See W. Paul Strassman, "Optimum Consumption Patterns in High-Income Nations," *Canadian Journal of Economics and Political Science* (August 1962): 364.

28. While this argument bars the diminishing urgency of wants, it proves too much. Institutionalists have always pointed to the "timelessness" of orthodox analysis as a fatal flaw for the possibility of deriving any scientific (operational) conclusions for it. See also note 30, infra.

29. Perhaps the classic exposition of this transition from marginal utility to indifference was the 1939 study of J. R. Hicks, *Value and Capital*, 2d ed. (Oxford: Clarendon Press, 1946). The achievements of this "scientific revolution" are stated with outstanding clarity by Hicks: "Thus we can translate the marginal utility theory into terms of indifference curves; but, having done that, we have accomplished something more remarkable than a mere translation. For, in the process of translation, *we have left behind some of the original data;* and *yet we have arrived at the desired result all the same"* (p. 17). Italics added.

30. Joan Robinson suggests, moreover, that whatever lies concealed behind revealed preferences will, unfortunately, just have to stay there, since "it is just not true that market behavior can reveal preferences. . . . The objection is logical, not only practical." The problem is that a preference perforce exists at a moment in time, but "we can observe the reaction of an individual to two different sets of prices only at two different times. How can we tell what part of the difference in his purchase is due to the difference in prices and what part to the change in his preferences that has taken place meanwhile?. . . We have got one equation for two unknowns." Robinson, *Economic Philosophy*, pp. 50–51.

31. See C. E. Ayres, *Toward a Reasonable Society* (Austin: University of Texas Press, 1962), ch. 3, pp. 39–54. Also Ayres, *The Theory*, pp. 205–30.

32. See Wesley C. Mitchell, "Economics, 1904–1929," in *The Backward Art*, p. 407.

33. That "invalid assumptions do make an invalid theory regardless of successful hypothesis testing" is a view that has proved useful in science, if less so in astrology. This view seems to be gaining in popularity again, following the long debate over "Milton Friedman's peculiar assertion" to the contrary. W. Paul Strassman, "Technology: Trait, Category, or Virtue Itself?" *Journal of Economic Issues* 8 (January 1974): 678–79.

34.   On the neoclassical theory of consumer behavior as an "ideal type" — hence a "personification" — and an exercise in "fellow-feeling," see John R. Commons, *Institutional Economics*, vol. 2 (Madison: University of Wisconsin Press, 1959) pp. 727ff.

35.   The consumer in equilibrium is timelessly poised on the edge of rational action. For this indefinite moment which is covered by the theory, he will forever be spared the frustrations of knowing that he was sold a "lemon," or the sorrow of having drunk up the grocery money. No unanticipated consequences will ever in this theoretical moment better instruct his rationality or, on the other hand, leave him feeling better or worse in comparison to his neighbor than he intended by his purchases.

36.   Thorstein Veblen, "The Limitations of Marginal Utility," in *The Place of Science,* p. 240.

37.   John M. Keynes, *The General Theory of Employment, Interest and Money* (1936; London: Macmillan, 1957), chs. 2, 3, 8–10, and 23. Veblen can be considered an "underconsumptionist" in the sense that he clearly rejected Say's Law and found considerable merit in the case put by underconsumption theorists from Malthus to Hobson, the "British institutionalist." Veblen specifically agreed with Hobson that underconsumption arose from the maldistribution of income, but found Hobson's redistributive remedies "manifestly chimerical" in a business-dominated society. The tendency to depression could not be checked by any form of increased consumption or "waste," Veblen argued, so long as the technological capacities of industry were subject to the pecuniary aims of business. See Thorstein Veblen, *The Theory of Business Enterprise* (1904; New York: Charles Scribner's Sons, 1936), ch. 7, esp. pp. 250–58.

38.   For an institutionalist critique of macroeconomic equilibrium theory and its orthodox underpinnings, see Wendell Gordon, "Simple Underconsumption," *Southwestern Social Science Quarterly* 31 (March 1951): 243–57; and "Orthodox Economics and Institutionalized Behavior," in Carey C. Thompson, ed., *Institutional Adjustment: A Challenge to a Changing Economy* (Austin: University of Texas Press, 1967).

39.   Some doubt may legitimately remain even at this late date, however, as to the explanatory power of the various hypotheses of the consumption function (absolute, relative, permanent income) that have been erected on the microeconomic underpinning. An excellent review of this literature not long ago had to face such doubts, in presenting empirical evidence from the field of home economics. The burden of this evidence is that an appreciable proportion of families have no clear "goals or plans . . . for allocation of income or acquisition of assets, and where they do, the goals "may lead to very different forms of economic behavior." Similar "substantial evidence" suggests that "a large proportion of consumer purchases are unplanned," such that "these findings raise questions as to whether purchases are made in a rational manner." See Robert Ferber, "Consumer Economics: A Survey," *Journal of Economic Literature* 11 (1973): 13.

40.   Joan Robinson, "The Second Crisis of Economic Theory," in *The Second Crisis of Economic Theory,* ed. Rendigs Fels (Morristown, N. J.: General Learning Press, 1972), p. 6.

41.   Thorstein Veblen, "Why is Economics Not an Evolutionary Science?" in *The Place of Science,* p. 67.

42.   Ibid., p. 70.

43.   Ibid., pp. 70–71. The first sentence in this quotation from Veblen was selected by Ayres for the frontispiece of his *Theory of Economic Progress.*

44.   Ayres, *The Theory,* p. 101.

45.   Ibid., ch. 6.

46.   Ibid., p. viii.

47.   Gruchy, *Contemporary Economic Thought,* p. 12.

48. Karl Polanyi, "The Economy as Instituted Process," in Karl Polanyi, Conrad M. Arensberg, and Harry W. Pearson, eds., *Trade and Market in the Early Empires: Economics in History and Theory* (Glencoe, Ill.: Free Press, 1957), pp. 243–70.

49. David Hamilton provides a useful descriptive analysis of more recent "symbolic" consumption in his *The Consumer in Our Economy* (Boston: Houghton Mifflin, 1962), pp. 65–76.

50. Veblen, *The Theory of the Leisure Class*, p. 99.

51. Ibid., p. 98.

52. Ibid., p. 98–99.

53. Ibid., p. 99.

54. Strassman, "Optimum Consumption Patterns," p. 365.

55. See ibid., pp. 369–72, for an interesting development of the concept of "awareness-yielding" consumption, which would appear to be predominantly instrumental. Also, Hamilton, *The Consumer*, pp. 76ff., has a good discussion of "technological determinants of wants." For the most part, the analysis of instrumental consumption has been carried out in the context of the general theory of instrumental valuation. See Ayres, *The Theory*, ch. 10; and *Toward a Reasonable Society*.

56. Veblen, *The Theory of the Leisure Class*, p. 43.

57. Ibid., p. 32. A note on Veblen's theoretical use of "motive" is perhaps in order. Unlike the orthodox conception of finished motives fixed in the individual consciousness, Veblen's is a concept of evolving cultural propensities. Subsequent scholarship has suffered the misfortune that he chose to call the more stabilized ones of these "instincts." Motive, — including Veblen's propensities, — is, however, a question of "sufficient reason" to act, and we have Veblen's insistence that the cultural sciences can only provisionally and proximately make use of this teleological aspect of the human situation for purposes of analyzing an evolving sequence of cause and effect. Both of the motives mentioned in the text are thus evolved cultural products that will evolve further. See Veblen, "The Limitations of Marginal Utility," pp. 239ff.

58. Veblen, *The Theory of the Leisure Class*, p. 36.

59. Ibid., chs. 5 and 6.

60. Robinson, "The Second Crisis . . . ." Veblen saw the tendency to depression as the normal state of the pecuniary economy "under the consummate régime of the machine, so long as competition is unchecked and no *deus ex machina* interposes." The two remedies for the situation, under prevailing institutions, were (1) elimination of competition and (2) massive wasteful expenditure. Veblen expected both expedients to be used increasingly, with military expenditures playing a large part in maintaining a suitable level of waste. This theme was introduced in 1904 in Veblen, *The Theory of Business Enterprise*, pp. 254ff., and was carried through all of Veblen's later work.

61. Gruchy, *Contemporary Economic Thought*, p. 3.

62. Ibid., p. 6.

63. Ibid., p. 7.

64. Robinson, "The Second Crisis," pp. 6–7.

65. Gruchy, *Contemporary Economic Thought*, pp. 8–18.

66. Galbraith, *The Affluent Society*. See also the chapter on Galbraith in Gruchy, *Contemporary Economic Thought*, ch. 4.

67. Galbraith, *The Affluent Society*, chs. 9 and 10.

68. Ibid., p. 99.

69. Ibid.

70.   Ibid., p. 114.

71.   Ibid.

72.   Ibid., p. 114–15.

73.   Ibid., p. 131.

74.   The impression must not be left that Veblen was somehow unaware of the role of advertising in consumer behavior, especially emulative behavior. He reserved some of his sharpest barbs for the practices of advertising and salesmanship. Such "sellers' costs" were often the largest part of the price of advertised goods and were "net waste" for the economy. "Meritricious publicity," creating "good will" or other "intangible assets," was one of the principal means by which a firm could secure a "vested interest," a "marketable right to get something for nothing." But Veblen apparently thought that the net effect was to "induce credulous persons now and again to change their mind about what things they will buy," rather than to increase total consumption. Thorstein Veblen, *The Vested Interests and the Common Man* (1919; New York: Viking Press, 1946), pp. 100–101. See also Thorstein Veblen, *Absentee Ownership and Business Enterprise in Recent Times* (1923; New York: Viking Press, 1954), pp. 284–325.

75.   Galbraith, *The Affluent Society,* p. 126.

76.   Ibid., p. 193.

77.   Ibid., p. 198.

78.   Gruchy, *Contemporary Economic Thought,* p. 8.

79.   Robinson, "The Second Crisis," p. 7.

80.   Ibid., p. 9.

9 INSTITUTIONALISM FROM A NATURAL SCIENCE POINT OF VIEW
An Intellectual Profile of Morris A. Copeland

James R. Millar

Throughout his long career as an economist, Copeland has proudly proclaimed his commitment to institutionalism.[1] For this reason, and especially as a result of criticism of the theory and practice of orthodox economics that has flowed from his unswerving adherence to the natural science point of view, Copeland has never been fully accepted into the mainstream fold.[2] Ironically, neither is Copeland fully recognized today as an institutionalist. Over the almost sixty years that he has practiced economics, the interpretation placed upon the term "institutionalist" has changed greatly, and this movement in American economic thought is less heterogeneous than in the 1920s and 1930s. To the uninitiated, and this includes most who practice economics, institutionalism means the thought of Ayres — when it is not simply confused with atheoretical, colorless descriptions of institutions or industries. But even many who style themselves institutionalists do not recognize Copeland as a member of the tribe.

Gruchy's classic study of Veblen, Commons, Mitchell, and Clark describes the rootstock of the institutionalist movement.[3] Just what has subse-

The author would like to thank Chandler Morse, Malcolm Liggett, and John Adams for helpful suggestions on earlier drafts of this paper.

quently happened to the various offshoots of this early period of luxurient growth has, however, yet to be traced. Gruchy's recent analysis of what he calls "neo-institutionalist" economists includes only one direct offshoot: Ayres.[4] The other contemporary branches remain to be charted. It seems fitting, therefore, to honor Gruchy's professional accomplishments by supplementing his lifelong study of institutionalism with an essay on the economic philosophy of Copeland. I hope to honor Copeland at the same time by explaining his methodological stance and describing several of his main achievements as an academic economist.[5]

Gruchy labeled Mitchell's brand of institutionalism "quantitative," and it would not be unreasonable to use the same term to describe Copeland's approach.[6] Certainly the two had much in common both in theory and practice, although Copeland was neither a student nor a disciple of Mitchell's. Still, Mitchell clearly had an important influence on him.[7] I have described Copeland's brand of thought as "institutionalism from a natural science point of view" partly to register his independent provenance, but also to indicate a different emphasis in their approaches to institutionalism. Copeland has been more explicit than Mitchell in spelling out methodologically just what would be required to make economics into the "evolutionary science" Veblen called for, and he has placed more stress upon the "qualitative" side of scientific economics than Mitchell did. The phrase "quantitative institutionalism" does not bring out either of these important aspects of Copeland's thought. These are important distinctions for a clear understanding of Copeland's economics, but they are nonetheless distinctions of degree and not of kind. Copeland and Mitchell clearly belong to the same broad branch of institutionalist thought, and they have been parallel influences in the development of a more quantitative and scientific economics.

COPELAND'S METHODOLOGY

Copeland's contribution to economic theory, as defined by the profession, has not been as great as his talent for theory would lead one to expect. His main contribution has been to methodology rather than to theory proper, particularly in spelling out the implications of an evolutionary natural science point of view. The methodological strictures he has proposed apply mutatis mutandis to the other social sciences as well, for economics and the other social sciences represent, in Copeland's view, "a branch of that part of zoology concerned with man, a branch of functional anthropology."[8] Human physiology and psychology deal with the other aspects: the functions of the various organs and the functioning of the human organism as a whole. The social sciences are, then, sciences of group behavior. Propositions about individual motivation, preferences, and so forth, like those about DNA, the circulation of the blood, or the physiology of the human brain, lie outside the boundaries of social science. Moreover, if "economics is a branch of zoology, it seems reasonable that economists should look more to biologists than to physicists for methodological guidance. Certainly Veblen did."[9]

Copeland takes the division of labor as the key feature of the economy as opposed to other social structures. The institutions that work to define and articulate specialization of production are, therefore, the special concern of the economist, and economics as a discipline may be distinguished from sister social sciences to the extent that institutions themselves have become specialized in the course of cultural evolution.[10] The distinction is as arbitrary as any operational definition is, but it contains no hidden metaphysical significance and suggests that the various disciplines merge as one moves back in history, or laterally to simpler contemporary societies, into a single field of anthropology.[11] Copeland defines economics "as the study of economies," which "has the advantage over several others that have been proposed in that it does not seem to confine the subject to economies in which institutions such as money and the price system play prominent parts."[12]

Institutionalism for Copeland is the "counterpart in the field of group behavior" to behaviorism in the study of individual behavior. He developed what he calls the *"natural science creed"* in the early 1930s. The rationale for working out methodology in terms of psychology and economics simultaneously is self-evident, given that a primary objective was to highlight the methodological distinction between orthodox economics and institutionalism. He stated, in part:

> The behaviorist and the institutionalist are particularly concerned that their formulations shall conform to two important canons: (1) that they shall be consistent with hypotheses in other fields, especially with the natural-evolutionary hypotheses in geology and general biology; (2) that they shall leave the door open to the solution of all psychological [and social] problems by methods of scientific observation and scientific reasoning.[13]

Copeland's definition of institutions and his conception of the way they function in human societies imply neither approval nor disapproval of institutions. He does not employ Veblen's phrase "imbecile institutions." An institution is "an established practice or customary behavior pattern or set of behavior relationships that is characteristic of the life and culture of a country or society."[14] For good or ill, economic institutions serve to organize and articulate economic activity. Although certain "noneconomic" institutions, such as the family, the kinship system, or monogamy, have economic implications, the contemporary industrial economy relies primarily upon money, exchange, price, wage, and accounting systems and other specialized economic institutions for the organization of economic activity.

For the economist, institutionalism involves description of the way institutions organize economic activity in particular societies, past and present, and it of course includes investigation of the way institutions have come to operate the way they do in these societies. Institutionalism has, then: "two main phases: one concerned with the process of cultural evolution; the other with the here and now."[15] The process of cultural evolution presumably requires eras, periods long enough for institutions such as exchange or the system of pecuniary incentives to become so well entrenched that they appear as "invisible" and "natural" stimulus-response patterns to the culture bound. Copeland cites Veblen's concept of "genetic processes of cumulative change," as illustrated by consideration of the Veblen's cultural incidence of the machine process, as an example of an institutionalist treatment of the process of cultural evolution.[16]

The "here and now" phase of institutionalism takes place in a time period too short for significant changes in such fundamental human institutions. The questions institutionalists should pose in this shorter run are, according to Copeland: (1) how does economic activity get organized in any particular society? (2) how well do economic institutions perform the functions implied? and (3) how might contemporary institutions be improved upon so as to accomplish certain agreed upon ends, or to avoid commonly accepted evils? The here and now phase of institutionalism is not restricted to examination of contemporary economies (although the third question would ordinarily be so restricted), and it necessarily involves the economist as economist in matters of appraisal either as a kind of institutional pathologist or as an expert in describing a means to or formulating a generally accepted end, such as full employment or peace.[17]

The here and now phase and the cultural evolution phase of institutionalism cannot, of course, be sharply separated from one another. Two studies that Copeland has praised highly involve elements of both. Copeland has called the theory of cumulative expansion and contraction of business activity that Mitchell developed in *Business Cycles* "the first triumph of the empirical natural science method."[18] And he described Clark's *Economics of Overhead Costs* as "much the greatest institutionalist contribution" to "realistic microeconomics."[19] Both studies assume as a premise the historical relativity of economic truths. Mitchell saw the business cycle as a relatively recent development in business societies, and Clark traced the historical rise in the significance of overhead costs as part of his analysis of their effects. In these and other respects, these two studies satisfy Copeland's criteria for scientific investigation.

Copeland has been quite explicit about the requirements scientific hypotheses must meet in economics:

(1) Hypotheses or descriptive generalizations in economics should be "capable of empirical test. Scientific theories should not be mere truisms, or be so abstract as to be incapable of factual disproof."

(2) Economics "deals with certain aspects of our social system not sharply marked off from the aspects with which other social sciences deal." Its "generalizations must somehow make peace with the general theory of biological evolution. They can only be true of and relevant to some definitely specified periods of social evolution."

(3) "The biological sciences do not confine themselves to description. They are normative as well as descriptive."[20]

It goes without saying that much contemporary orthodox economic theory fails to satisfy these criteria, but the same holds for certain branches of institutionalism as well. Much of contemporary orthodox economic theory, particularly of the mathematical model-building variety, apparently does not aspire to empirical test. Even applied econometricians seem often to prefer to reject their statistical models rather than challenge the theory when they come up with the "wrong sign" for a fitted parameter.

Much of contemporary economic theory fails to meet the criterion of "empirical definiteness"[21] (point two above). Indifference analysis, for example, is not empirically definite. It "fits the way people have behaved after the fact, but it fits any hypothetical past behavior that did not actually take place equally well."[22] It is doubtful, in fact, that indifference analysis (or utility analysis) can be restricted as an explanation to any subgroup of sentient beings.[23] Even much that passes for economic history and economic anthropology seems to have as its primary goal the application of timeless truths as historical explanations, that is, the avoidance of empirical definiteness. The so-called law of diminishing returns provides another example of lack of empirical definiteness.[24]

Finally, regarding criterion three above, confusion of statements of "what is" with statements of "what ought to be" is plainly evident in the apparent conflict between the claim to value-free position and praise for Pareto optima.

Copeland's methodological stance does not imply rejection of orthodox economic theory in toto, but it does imply rejection of a significant portion. The attempt to build up theory on the basis of individual preference functions and individual choice strategies obviously does not square with Cope-land's division of labor between psychology and the social sciences. More-over, certain branches of psychology have made great strides since Cope-land first wrote on this topic in the late 1920s, particularly in the way of scientific description of human motivation, decision making, and abnormal behavior, all of which have been completely ignored by economists who specialize in questions of human choice.[25]

Consequently, a great deal of what comes commonly under the heading of microeconomic theory requires extensive reformulation if it is to meet the canons of science according to Copeland. Macroeconomic models that rely extensively, or exclusively, upon behavioral equations that are based upon rationalized behavior, that is, upon profit and utility maximization rather than upon fitted data, fail to measure up. As more and more contemporary macroeconomic texts focus upon the "microfoundations" of macroeco-nomic models and devote increasing space to stability conditions for general aggregate demand and supply equations, it is fair to say that macroeconom-ics is regressing with respect to the requirements of scientific method.

COPELAND'S METHOD IN PRACTICE

Further discussion of methodology proper will be less illuminating than an examination of samples of Copeland's practice. Although he has devoted recent years to the "process of cultural evolution phase" of institutional-ism, studying the origins of the money economy and other topics in prehis-tory,[26] Copeland's main concern over most of his career has been with the "here and now" phase. Three areas in particular have occupied him exten-sively: (1) development of an empirical, largely statistical basis for econom-ic analysis, especially within the framework of social accounting systems; (2) understanding business cycles, especially the way money and financial institutions fit into and contribute to these phenomena; and (3) evaluation of and improvements in the way economic institutions organize economic activity in the United States.

At Mitchell's suggestion, Copeland was invited in 1944 by the National Bureau of Economic Research (NBER) to undertake an exploratory study of moneyflows in the United States. The choice was far from casual. Cope-land's career to that point made him a logical candidate. With the encour-agement of Stewart he had become "intensely interested" in business ac-counting as a graduate student.[27] His interest in money and in empirical testing led him in the late 1920s to seek to determine the direction of caus-ality in the equation of exchange, and this first attempt to define and test empirically the "money circuit" left him with grave doubts about the economic content and conceptual usefulness of the equation of exchange approach.[28] Employment both before and during World War II with various government agencies responsible for compiling and analyzing economic data had afforded Copeland wide knowledge of the kinds of nature of available economic statistics, and he had himself contributed to improvements in the conceptualization and presentation of national income accounts. Moreover, Copeland was prepared to devote the time required to solve the sheer technical problems involved in the creation of a new social accounting system — perhaps because of his methodological conviction that the analyst ought to know as much about the data as those who collect and prepare economic statistics.[29]

Exploration of moneyflows represented a high point in Copeland's career in several senses. Not only did it draw upon the extensive knowledge and experience he had acquired over more than twenty years of practice, the project also afforded him an opportunity to conduct a large-scale research operation in accordance with his methodological principles. The published version of his report, *A Study of Moneyflows in the United States,* stands as an example of the way Copeland believes economic science ought to be conducted. With the exception of a brief summary introduction, the volume opens with a technical explanation of the derivation of the various sectors and sector accounts. An analysis of his findings begins on page 211 and is entitled: "Some Tentative Interpretations." A third section on sources and methods is appended and runs in excess of two hundred pages. The structure of the book thus reflects Copeland's commitment to the conduct of empirical studies in such a way that a second investigator may replicate the findings. Although few who aspire to a scientific economics could complain about it, Copeland's presentation of his research, methods, and results may have been counterproductive by tiring less scientifically inclined readers before they reached the analysis and conclusions. In this respect, Copeland's study of moneyflows may not have been "well-packaged" for maximum impact.

Be that as it may, the money flows system of social accounting became the fourth and youngest of the systems that have been pioneered in this century. It is now maintained by the Federal Reserve Board as the Flow-of-Funds, and it has been widely imitated in other advanced economies. The four social accounting systems: national income, balance of payments estimates, input-output, and moneyflows, may very well prove to be the most lasting and influential contributions of the profession in this century. With the possible exception of input-output analysis, upon which the Soviet experience in planning has some degree of impact, these systems represent peculiarly American contributions to twentieth century economics.[30] Interestingly, institutionalists had a great influence upon the development of all but input-output too. National income and flow of funds accounting systems, in particular, provide conceptual schemes designed to reveal order in the complex, interrelated, seamless web of economic transactions in a modern pecuniary-industrial economy. They have influenced the way in which we conceive, measure, and analyze economies, and even Keynes's contribution of a new "macroeconomic model," for example, in its fullest sense, must be attributed in part to the concurrent development of social accounting.[31] In addition, Keynes's desire to wed monetary and "real" analysis in *The General Theory* is in fact realized more fully and consistently within the framework of the moneyflows accounts.

Our concern with moneyflows here is principally the way in which the study reflects Copeland's brand of institutionalism and his intellectual concerns as an economist.[32] Copeland's study of moneyflows may be viewed as a full-dress, full-scale battle with the equation of exchange, one for which his articles of the late 1920s were preliminary skirmishes. The "main money circuit" that emerges from the system of moneyflows represents an alternative to the equation of exchange as a formulation of the nature and volume of "money work" in the economy. Moreover, it leads to a conceptualization of the relationship between adjustments in the ordinary transactions sphere (that is, transactions in goods and services plus net transfer flows) and in the financial sphere (that is, net money obtained, returned, or advanced) that is antithetical to most versions of the quantity of theory of money and especially to all that suggest an hydraulic analogy for the nature of money work.

In a broader sense, the system of moneyflows provides an empirical basis for conducting analyses of changes in the level of economic activity in terms of simultaneous adjustments in ordinary and financial transactions. The accounts provide a much richer basis for macroeconomic analysis than Keynes's single-asset model could, and they make it possible to explain the way expansions and contractions of economic activity are financed and the way money and the banking system fit into the picture. It is lamentable to note that at this late date our most popular macroeconomic textbooks perpetuate misleading, or incorrect, explanations of where "the money comes from" to finance general economic expansion as well as of "where the money goes" when business contracts — despite Copeland's empirical demonstration of more than twenty-five years ago and an ongoing system of flow-of-funds accounts. Many still commit, or imply, actual algebraic error, for example, by treating increases in the money stock as "sources of funds" to nonbank transactors (taken as a whole). When algebraic error can persist for so long in a field that pays large rents to mathematically oriented economists the underlying bias must indeed run deep!

At bottom, this bias appears to be a conception of the main money circuit of the economy in terms of an hydraulic analogy. An increase in the money stock is visualized as an "opening of the spigot," increasing the flow (of money) to nonbank transactors. Implied in this conception are a number of pernicious notions for analyzing moneyflows: a) that there is a significant lag between a turn of the spigot and the receipt of funds; b) that the relevant money circuit is one in which goods flow one way and money the other; c) that inflation is essentially no more than a situation in which "too many dollars are chasing too few goods"; d) that new money can enter the circuit at the discretion ("injection") of a single transactor such as a central bank; e) that "hoarding" behavior somehow takes cash "out of circulation," that is, that cash hoards and increases in cash hoards are somehow not available to finance the economic activities of others.[33]

The moneyflows accounts reveal that these implications of the hydraulic analogy, individually or severally, are incorrect and misleading. As an alternative based upon what he calls the "five key features" of the main money circuit, Copeland proposes an electrical-circuit analogy. Money flows more like electricity than like a fluid because there are no lags between payment and receipt and because money as an asset is inseparable from its existence as an equal dollar debt (e.g., of the banking sector taken together with the monetary divisions of the Treasury). Moreover, the accounts of each transactor must always balance in the current period as well as ex post. And moneyflows transactions always involve a second party, one that ordinarily must agree to them. These features all clash with the implications of money conceived as a fluid.[34]

Unlike national income accounting, the moneyflows accounts assume no ultimate sectors in the economy. A system that accords an equal footing to all sectors clearly harmonizes with Copeland's scientific outlook and the clear distinction between measurement and appraisal that he sought. The accounts have three implications with respect to the discretion of the sectors for which moneyflows are charted:

1. nonbank transactors may vary their individual cash balances through management of their loanfund balances (and similarly for the banking sector with respect to its "negative" cashbalance), but even so, expansion (or contraction) of total nonbank cash balances requires the cooperation of both parties;

2. although transactors have little discretion over the "active" cash balances required to cushion short-term discrepancies in the time shapes of their receipts and disbursements, they have a degree of discretion over total "idle" balances of cash, which allows the transactor to vary his ordinary outlays more or less independently of his current receipts;

3. transactors ordinarily have less discretion with respect to receipts than with respect to expenditures.[35]

A "discretionary hypothesis" relating to the expansion and contraction of general economic activity follows immediately from these implications of the system of moneyflows. Some transactors are afforded discretion by virtue of cash balances or access to loan and security markets to increase or decrease their ordinary expenditures, despite the budget constraint imposed by current receipts. Copeland labeled those who draw down cash balances and other loanfunds to increase spending relative to receipts as "bulls." "Bears" are defined conversely as those who "stint and hoard." Transactors who neither spend nor stint aggressively are "sheep," for changes in their ordinary expenditures follow changes in their ordinary receipts (as in the consumption function for households). Whether aggregate income increases or decreases depends upon whether bulls or bears predominate, and the behavior of "sheep" helps to explain the cumulative aspect of business expansions and contractions.

Copeland stresses that the volume of transactions in any given period represents a "readjustment of the previous volume, a readjustment that arises from the mutually conditioning choices of bulls, bears, and sheep."[36] This readjustment involves, in Copeland's view, simultaneous, interacting spheres. One is the sphere of ordinary transactions; the other involves readjustments in the loan and security markets as well as in flows of (net) money through financial channels. This conception is related to but distinct from the familiar notion of simultaneous supply and demand adjustments in the "goods" and "money" markets of standard intermediate texts. The readjustment involves more than

> merely a readjustment between supply and demand. Taxes, contractual commitments, and public purpose payments are involved. And governments can initiate changes in their receipts [too]. . . .
>
> In the financial readjustment process lenders and investors in securities and borrowers, issuers of securities, and those who wish to liquidate portfolios must get together on terms. . . . But . . . [this] . . . is not the whole story. . . . [There is the rest of the world]. . . . And there are changes in sector cash balances to consider.[37]

Banks' ordinary expenditures and receipts are a negligible factor, but they may influence the spending plans of others in the capacity of financial intermediaries. The discretion of the banking sector is also asymmetrical in that banks may call or refuse new loans on their own but require borrowers, or transactors seeking to expand the cash portion of their portfolios, to expand bank credit outstanding.

Copeland's discretionary hypothesis, then, attributes the main motive force in business fluctuations to variations in aggregate demand. Asymmetry in the discretion of the various parties provides an institutional and empirical foundation for an analysis that treats aggregate supply and aggregate demand as not coordinate in the short (cyclical) run. In other words, the discretionary hypothesis directs attention to changes in aggregate demand as the main source of business fluctuations, and it supports fully the neglect of aggregate supply that neo-Keynesians have tried so hard to remedy in Keynes's *General Theory!* Copeland once described Keynes's *General Theory* as "an expurgated version" of Mitchell's theory of business cycles.[38] The system of moneyflows accounts allows for a revised, unexpurgated version of the theory, one that accords priority to no sector a priori and one that analyzes simultaneously the interrelated changes in ordinary and in financial transactions. The understanding that emerges emphasizes the primacy of aggregate demand and the importance of money and other pecuniary institutions for explanations of business fluctuations in our kind of economy.

COPELAND'S IMPACT ON
ORTHODOX AND INSTITUTIONAL ECONOMICS

Institutionalization of moneyflows as quarterly flow-of-funds accounts represented a widening of the empirical, social-accounting basis of contemporary economic analysis, and this may well turn out to have been Copeland's most important and lasting contribution to the profession from the standpoint of orthodoxy. Although his discretionary hypothesis seems to underlie much of current business forecasting and the type of advice the Congress and the President receive from their economic advisors (other than the monetarists, of course), it is obvious at the same time that formal reasoning about business fluctuations has been dominated by much simpler and much more rigid models. The thrust toward the creation of a macromodel based squarely upon social-accounting equations and fitted behavioral equations, to which Copeland's discretionary hypothesis pointed, has been blunted in recent years. In fact, a new kind of division of labor seems to have developed between those who seek to make empirical forecasts of aggregate economic activity and those who seek to build neat, deterministic macromodels in which economic behavior is specified in terms of utility and profit maximization and in which aggregate demand and supply submodels are assumed to be coordinate in the determination of the level of income and employment. These latter models tend to be more concerned with Walras's Law than with social-accounting equations. Copeland's discretionary hypothesis has not been found wanting as a construct. Rather, it simply has not succeeded in the competition for the minds of academic macromodelists who continue the quest for determinism and mathematical precision and prefer conventional supply and demand analysis.

That Copeland was not unaware of these trends at the time he proposed the discretionary hypothesis is plain from a series of lectures he gave in India in 1951 entitled "The Keynesian Reformation."[39] From the title alone it is clear that Copeland intended the essays as a corrective to Klein's *the Keynesian Revolution*.[40] Copeland does praise Keynes in these lectures, particularly his handling of time (expectations), his implicit definition of equilibrium as a concept not requiring the clearing of all markets as a necessary condition, and the push he gave toward including more exogenous variables in economic models. However, as Copeland has pointed out elsewhere, one clear effect of Keynes's *The General Theory* was to dampen institutionalist criticism of neoclassical model building.[41] In this sense the effect was counterrevolutionary, and the changes Keynes introduced represented modifications of neoclassicism, not its rejection. Hence, "reformation" is more description than "revolution." Even this more modest appraisal may turn out to be an overstatement. In the late 1950s Copeland frequently suggested in his graduate courses at Cornell that Keynes "was being brought back into the neoclassical church." If popular intermediate macroeconomics texts provide a reasonable test, the process is essentially complete today.

Copeland's discretionary hypothesis, unlike moneyflows as a social-accounting system, did not "sell" to the profession as a whole. Given a strong and continuing conservative trend in the profession, it was inevitable that Copeland's conception of the way economic theory ought to be written would not square with the preferences of mainstream economists. If Copeland has not made a substantial dent in economic theory proper, then, the reason is that much of what passes for theory in orthodox economics does not meet the methodological criteria of a scientific economics. Moreover, the kinds of theory that do emerge from Copeland's scientific stance must seem to the orthodox "to be lacking logical precision; certainly they smack of 'imperfect approximation.' "[42] It should be noted, however, that Copeland never proposed jettisoning the whole of standard economic theory, and his stance in this respect, particularly with regard to microeconomic theory, has apparently also puzzled and confused certain other institutionalists at times.

Copeland frequently described the neoclassical theory in his graduate classes, as "an older form of science," and what he had in mind was, no doubt, Veblen's distinctions between "sufficient reason," "efficient cause," and "genetic processes of cumulative change" as alternative (actually, sequential) bases for scientific work.[43] As Copeland pointed out a few years ago: "insistence . . . on explaining consumer demand and saving . . . in terms of the rational behavior of individuals, each maximizing his own utility, is an insistence that the only satisfactory way to account for human conduct is to find a sufficient reason for it."[44] Even so, Copeland argues that it would be a mistake to reject the whole of neoclassical theory because: "Up to a point it makes for precision of economic concepts and for accuracy of reasoning. . . ."[45]

He has been prepared to accept the neoclassical apparatus insofar as it may be treated as a "body of propositions," as a source of hypotheses suitable for testing or fruitful as conceptual frameworks. His insistence upon theory as hypothesis sets him apart from most orthodox theorists, and his tolerance of the neoclassical apparatus as an "older view of science" has estranged him from certain of institutionalists among whom the language of neoclassical analysis is proscribed. Copeland has been set apart from several brands of institutionalism as well by his lack of animus toward pecuniary institutions as such. From the very outset of his career Copeland has taken a decidedly "reformist" view of pecuniary institutions, a stand clearly evident in his 1924 article, "Communities of Economic Interest and the Price System." After exploring three nonpecuniary alternative standards of social appraisal — technological, psychological, and socioorganic — he concluded that none provided a satisfactory alternative to pecuniary measures:

> The pecuniary measure has certain obvious advantages: It is a definite affair, capable of statistical and accounting treatment. It is sufficiently objective so that different observers should get comparable results. Since price plays a central part in the incentives to economic performance and in the apportionment of men and the non-human factors among the several lines, to state a community of interests in pecuniary terms should throw considerable light on the methods by which such a community might be achieved.[46]

The problem becomes one of specifying the community of interest and of rectifying the system of pecuniary incentives so as to approximate the harmony of interests the neoclassical analyst assumes at the outset.

It is not always clear in writings of some institutionalists whether criticism is directed at the neoclassical analysis as an unsatisfactory scientific description of the way our kind of economy works or whether criticism is aimed at pecuniary institutions themselves. Copeland's approach to institutions as a scientific investigator and his conception of the way they function could not lead him to describe them as "imbecile."

Insofar as the community of interest may be stated in pecuniary terms, steps toward reform based upon it "should be in the nature of an attempt to preserve and improve upon the various pecuniary incentives which now function imperfectly in exchange coordination. Property rights, contract forms, social organization, and so forth, should be altered so as to make individual gain more closely reflect service rendered."[47] That this is more than a statement of political preference may be seen in the context of a more recent statement:

> But it is in order here to insist that starting with a clean slate is not an alternative that is open to us. . . . Anyone who would change our economic system must start with the *status quo* and specify just what changes in it he wants to propose — statutory changes, changes in executive policy, and other specific changes.[48]

What kind of economic system one prefers is a matter of personal taste, but it should be capable of objective description and recognize the historical fact that revolution as well as reform must begin with concrete reality and cannot dismiss "carryover variables" out of hand.

An economist's conception of and attitude toward the "pure competition" model of free enterprise has always served as a touchstone among the heterodox as well as the orthodox for distinguishing friend and foe. The question arises, therefore, of the extent to which the adjustments in the system of pecuniary incentives that Copeland lays the groundwork for would lead to an approximation of a laissez-faire economy. It is clear that Copeland finds a degree of "truth in laissez-faire." He does not assert that the pure competition model represents an accurate description of the way the United States' economy works. But there is, he believes, a substantial resemblance to the model in the way pecuniary incentives influence economic behavior. "The truth in laissez-faire is that anything that would weaken the stimuli this set of pecuniary incentives gives and anything that would affect the way these incentives guide productive activities . . . [adversely] . . . is to be avoided." It does not follow, however, that government manipulation of economic levers is wrongheaded or bad: "On the contrary, it leads us to the conclusion that some government actions are good and desirable. . ."[49]

CONCLUSION

Although there are others whom Copeland respected and admired as economists, notably Stewart and Clark, it seems safe to say that Copeland's
brand of institutionalism is closest of all to that of Mitchell. Like Mitchell,
Copeland has spent the greater part of his career seeking to make economics
a more scientific discipline, and a great deal of this effort has been devoted
to expanding the statistical basis of modern economic analysis. There is also
a similarity in their approaches to orthodox economic theory. Much like
Mitchell, Copeland is something of a connoisseur of orthodox theory.
Mitchell called traditional value theory "qualitative" economics and forecast its displacement by quantitative methods.[50] Hence the appropriateness
of Gruchy's description of him as a "quantitative institutionalist." Copeland uses the term "qualitative" differently to refer to scientific questions
that cannot be answered by quantitative methods. These include, for example, issues in law and in labor relations as well as descriptions of socio-
genetic processes of change and the description and appraisal of the way
economic institutions function in the "here and now." Quantitative institutionalism would be a somewhat misleading label. I have, therefore,
described Copeland's brand as "institutionalism from a natural science
point of view." This is not meant to exclude Mitchell, however, if only
because Copeland himself recently described Mitchell as writing "everywhere from a natural science point of view."[51]

Mitchell was more optimistic than Copeland is about the possibilities for
the development of more scientific methods in economics. Copeland has
pointed out that the problems institutionalists were addressing so successfully in the 1920s and 1930s have not disappeared, but that nonetheless
much less "has been heard from the institutionalists" since, and "it is not
because they succeeded in selling a major part of their platform. They did
not."[52] These words were written in 1951 at what was probably the high
point of his recognition by the profession, just after his *Study of Moneyflows in the United States* had appeared, and the situation has not changed
materially since.

Copeland has suggested several explanations for the failure of institutionalism to sell its program. The acceptance of Keynesian economics certainly helped to undercut institutionalist criticisms of the lack of realism of
orthodox theory. *The General Theory* also generated an enthusiasm for
empirical work on behavioral functions that doubtlessly deflected critical
attention away from the weaknesses of the behavioral assumptions underlying microeconomic theory. Aggregate economics and the development of
econometrics also helped to make some macroeconomic models more realis-

tic, with the same effect.[53] Thus, although institutionalists did not sell their program, the profession did seem to be moving for several decades in the direction many institutionalists preferred.

Veblen was obviously an important influence upon Copeland's thought, and Copeland cites him, along with Mitchell and Commons, as those in whose steps he has sought to follow.[54] Even so, Copeland's essay on Veblen implies that he was influenced more by Veblen's desire to make economics into a science and by the suggestion that economists ought to look "more to biology than to physics" than by Veblen's actual practice of the profession. As Mitchell implied, Veblen could be as speculative and unscientific at times as any of those he criticized.[55] Veblen liked to leap to large conclusions without taking all the steps required to make them scientifically sound.

Even today, the various schools of institutionalism agree more on what they do not like about orthodox economics than on what needs to be done to make economics more scientific. Institutionalism has not yet succeeded in coalescing behind a single, consistent methodology. Ayres complained at times in class that "institutionalism" was a poor choice of label for his thought. He preferred "instrumentalism," and it would indeed be a much more apt description for his conception of institutions and their relationship to technology. By contrast, Copeland's brand seems suitable to be called institutionalism. Insofar as the practice of science is a form of instrumentalism, Copeland is obviously an instrumentalist; however, unlike Ayres, Copeland has never suggested that the human mind, human value, and individual choice are somehow also instrumentalist in character.

Copeland's approach has been to adhere closely to the natural science point of view, that is, to insist upon scientific procedures, operational definitions, and the avoidance of any other dogma:

> To be scientific an observation must have relevance to some part of the scientific faith in which the observer is concerned as one of the high priests; it must have relevance to a scientific hypothesis. There is nothing inevitable about the truth of a scientific observation. It is true merely because the mores of science prescribe belief in those revelations which are made according to the ritual of scientific observation. . . . The mores of scientific observations are no less current mores for being understood as such. And as mores they are enforced by a penalty . . . excommunication. As a devout mos-fearing behaviorist I subscribe to the scientific creed, respect the ritual of observation, and claim membership in the cult of science.[56]

This unrelenting stance has put Copeland at variance with certain other branches of institutionalism quite as much as with standard economic theory. Students of Copeland will recall that his seminars were "Socratic" in the extreme. He never, to my knowledge, agreed "to explain" an economic concept. He merely asked questions, questions that, to be sure, probed deeply and critically into the received theory, questions that some of us are still trying to answer. Copeland did not believe in answering his own questions for us, presumably because he expected students to have the same confidence in their own mental powers that he felt in his and because he believed in the importance of having his students arrive at conclusions independently — in the importance of avoiding mere recitation of dogma.

ENDNOTES

1. Note, for example, the subtitle of his collected papers: Chandler Morse, ed., *Fact and Theory in Economics: The Testament of an Institutionalist, Collected Papers of Morris A. Copeland* (Ithaca, N.Y.: Cornell University Press, 1958). Hereafter this work will be cited as Morse, *Collected Papers*.

2. The fact that he was elected president of the American Economic Association in 1957 represents an important qualification to this statement. He was also associated with the National Bureau of Economic Research during the period of its greatest influence: 1944-1959. What one perhaps ought to say is that Copeland has had a very successful career as an economist despite the reluctance of the orthodox to accept his criticisms.

3. Allan G. Gruchy, *Modern Economic Thought* (New York: Prentice-Hall, 1947).

4. Allan G. Gruchy, *Contemporary Economic Thought* (Clifton, N.J.: Augustus M. Kelly, 1972).

5. I shall not deal with Copeland's career in government service. He joined the New Deal as executive secretary of the Central Statistical Board in Washington, D.C., in 1933, became director of research for the Bureau of the Budget (1939-40), and served subsequently as chief of the munitions branch of the War Production Board, 1940-44. See *Who's Who in America, 1976-77*, vol. 1 (Chicago: Marquis Who's Who, 1976), p. 654.

6. Gruchy, *Modern Economic Thought*, pp. 247-333.

7. Walter W. Stewart and John Maurice Clark were his teachers. In a recent letter to me, Copeland wrote: "The book by Mitchell I refer to much the most frequently is *Business Cycles — The Problem and Its Setting*. But it was not through what he wrote that he influenced me most. A number of times when I was in New York I went to call on him at his house on West Twelfth Street to ask his advice on things I was working on" (October 30, 1977).

8. Morris A. Copeland, "On the Scope and Method of Economics," in Douglas F. Dowd, ed., *Thorstein Veblen: A Critical Reappraisal* (New York: Cornell University Press, 1958), p. 58.

9. Ibid., p. 59.

10. Morris A. Copeland, *Our Free Enterprise Economy* (New York: Macmillan, 1965), pp. 15-18. There is an interesting parallel between Copeland's notion here and that developed by Karl Polanyi in his essay "The Economy as Instituted Process," in George Dalton, ed., *Primitive, Archaic, and Modern Economies* (New York: Anchor Books, 1968), pp. 139-74. There are a number of very substantial methodological differences, however, between Copeland and Polanyi.

11. Copeland, "On the Scope and Method of Economics," in Dowd, *Thorstein Veblen*, p. 72.

12. Copeland, *Our Free Enterprise Economy*, p. 16 and note 1, p. 16.

13. Copeland, "Psychology and the Natural Science Point of View," in Morse, *Collected Papers*, p. 12. Brackets added.

14. Copeland, *Our Free Enterprise Economy*, p. 289.

15. Copeland, "Institutional Economics and Model Analysis," in Morse, *Collected Papers*, p. 54.

16. Copeland, "On the Scope and Method of Economics," in Dowd, *Thorstein Veblen*, p. 69.

17. The role as pathologist arises from the institutionalist's description of the "functions" of institutions: " 'Function' in this sense is to be distinguished from purpose. The function of an organ, for example is a result that the observing scientist expects the organ 'normally' to bring about and in terms of which he appraises its behavior. It is not an end that guides or influences behavior." Copeland, "Psychology and the Natural Science Point of View," in Morse, *Collected Papers*, p. 19.

18. Copeland, "Economic Theory and the Natural Science Point of View," in Morse, *Collected Papers*, p. 50.

19. Copeland, "Institutional Economics and Model Analysis," in Morse, *Collected Papers*, p. 66.

20. Copeland, "Psychology and the Natural Science Point of View," in Morse, *Collected Papers*, pp. 38–39.

21. The phrase is Copeland's: "On the Scope and Method of Economics," in Dowd, *Thorstein Veblen*, p. 61.

22. Copeland, "On the Scope and Method of Economics," in Dowd, *Thorstein Veblen*, p. 64, note 12.

23. Copeland explicitly excluded indifference analysis as an "explanation" of heliotropism in, for example, sunflower "behavior" in a seminar on J. R. Hicks at Cornell sometime in the late 1950s.

24. "There are various senses for diminishing returns. In the sense in which universal validity can plausibly be claimed for this 'law' it would appear to be a proposition in physical science. But I am not aware that any physical scientist has claimed it to be a physical law." "On the Scope and Method of Economics," in Dowd, *Thorstein Veblen*, p. 61.

25. On this Copeland wrote in 1958: "Many economics texts written during the past decade, like their predecessors, offer as an 'explanation' of consumer demand a purportedly general theory of individual choice that is obviously a refinement of Bentham's felicific calculus. It goes without saying that as a general theory it has no standing whatever among modern psychologists. Logically the economists who adhere to it should feel embarrassed, but somehow they do not seem to." "On the Scope and Method of Economics," in Dowd, *Thorstein Veblen*, p. 60.

26. Two essays have been published recently: Copeland, "Concerning the Origin of a Money Economy," *American Journal of Economics and Sociology* (January 1974): 1–17; and Copeland, "Foreign Exchange in the 4th Century, B.C.," *American Journal of Economics and Sociology* (April 1977): 205–16.

27. Morris A. Copeland, *A Study of Moneyflows in the United States* (New York: National Bureau of Economic Research, 1952) p. xiii.

28. See, for instance, the somewhat abbreviated version, Copeland, "The Equation of Exchange: An Empirical Analysis," in Morse, *Collected Papers*, pp. 95–107.

29. Copeland, "Statistics and Objective Economics," in Morse, *Collected Papers*, p. 75.

30. Technically speaking, Leontief's input-output table is not closely related to the other three systems because it divides up business establishments by type of product and thus abstracts from actual economic transactions and business accounting records.

31. For a different conclusion see Don Patinkin, "Keynes and Econometrics," *Econometrica* 44 (November 1976): 1091–1123.

32. For a description of the way the flow-of-funds accounts are currently set up, see "A Quarterly Presentation of the Flow of Funds, Saving, and Investment," *Federal Reserve Bulletin* (August 1959):828; and "Revision of Flow of Funds Accounts," *Federal Reserve Bulletin* (November 1965):1533.

33. This summary of implications of the hydraulic analogy is based upon Copeland's "Note on the Quantity Theory," in *A Study of Moneyflows,* pp. 367–79.

34. Copeland has supplied a diagram of the money circuit conceived as an electrical diagram to substitute for the standard circular flow diagram. It may be found on p. 245 of Copeland, *A Study of Moneyflows.* He also provided "a less technical and rather less precise alternative statement . . ." from which the following extracts have been taken (pp. 322–23):

> They sat up in an ivory tower and watched the circuit-flow;
> So quick and fast the dollars passed they scarce could see them go.
> The Carpenter was much perplexed, and broached this argument;
> "I say! That's queer, but all the time some chap holds every cent."
> The Walrus sighed as he replied, "We must investigate,
> If there's no money in the land left free to circulate!"
> . . . .
> And so they studied money to sate their curiosity,
> Read books about its quantity and circulate velocity,
> Read books on the equation of exchange. "This means," they read,
> "That cash flows like a limpid stream." They wondered if instead
> It flowed like electricity, and they found a chart by Sahm
> That explained the money circuit in a wiring diagram.
> "If money flows with more than lightning speed," the Walrus said,
> "No wonder folks can hold their cash until their bills are paid."

35. Copeland, *A Study of Moneyflows,* pp. 237–38.

36. Ibid., p. 313.

37. Ibid., pp. 313–14. Brackets added.

38. Copeland, "The Keynesian Reformation," in Morse, *Collected Papers,* p. 328.

39. Morris A. Copeland, *The Keynesian Reformation* (Delhi: Ranjit Printers and Publishers, 1952).

40. Lawrence R. Klein, *The Keynesian Revolution* (New York: Macmillan, 1947).

41. Copeland, "Institutional Economics and Model Analysis," in Morse, *Collected Papers,* p. 59ff.

42. Copeland, "Statistics and Objective Economics," in Morse, *Collected Papers,* p. 81.

43. Thorstein Veblen, *Instinct of Workmanship* (New York: B. W. Hvebsch, 1918), pp. 326–27.

44. Copeland, "On the Scope and Method of Economics," in Dowd, *Thorstein Veblen,* p. 64.

45. Copeland, "The Keynesian Reformation," in Morse, *Collected Papers,* p. 330. Copeland goes on to say at a later point in the essay (p. 331):

> If the neoclassical . . . model analysis . . . has made economics develop like a science in several respects, there are others in which it has been more like a religion. It has not been intolerant of new ideas, to be sure, but it has been intolerant of ideas not couched in the language of the neoclassical apparatus.

46. Copeland, "Communities of Economic Interest and the Price System," in Morse, *Collected Papers,* p. 228.

47. Ibid., p. 246.

48. Copeland, *Our Free Enterprise Economy,* p. 60.

49. Copeland, *Our Free Enterprise Economy,* p. 58. Brackets added.

50. Wesley C. Mitchell, "Quantitative Analysis in Economic Theory," in *The Backward Art of Spending Money* (New York: McGraw-Hill, 1937, especially pp. 23–26.

52. Copeland, "Institutional Economics and Model Analysis," in Morse, *Collected Papers,* p. 58.

53. See Copeland's discussions in "Institutional Economics and Model Analysis," "Statistics and Objective Economics," and "The Keynesian Reformation," all in Morse, *Collected Papers.*

54. Copeland, *Our Free Enterprise Economy,* p. vii.

55. Lucy S. Mitchell, "A Personal Sketch," in Arthur F. Burns, ed., *Wesley Clair Mitchell: The Economic Scientist* (New York: NBER, 1952), pp. 95–96.

56. Copeland, "Psychology and the Natural Science Point of View," in Morse, *Collected Papers,* pp. 35–36.

III PLANNING

Problems of Managing

the Industrial State

10 HUMAN CAPITAL AND ECONOMIC PROGRESS IN EASTERN EUROPE
A Veblen-Ayres Perspective

Anthony Scaperlanda

Within the general perspective of institutional economics is embodied the technology-institutions dichotomy.[1] The aspect of the literature on this subject that is explored in this paper is the process by which technological developments influence institutional change. This relatively applied focus builds on Gruchy's observation that "Ayres does not ignore issues and policies, but he seems somewhat impatient with them. . . .There is no discussion of planning techniques or procedures. . . . Nor is there any discussion of the planning experience of such western democratic countries as France, Holland, Norway and Sweden. . . . His failure, however, to enlarge upon his views in this connection is a serious limitation of his instrumental economics."[2]

This paper is intended as a partial remedy for this "limitation." Here the focus will be on East European socialist experiences rather than on those of the United States or other western democracies. This focus continues to provide a test for the Veblen-Ayres explanation of the process of economic progress.[3] Second, and possibly most important here, it emphasizes the strategic importance of the development and deployment of human capital in linking technological change and institutional adjustment. Finally, it does provide implications for adaption of economic institutions both in Eastern Europe and in western democratic countries.

For Ayres, economic progress involves the process of coming "to enjoy greater economic abundance, full employment, greater economic freedom and equality and an economic life of higher quality."[4] Using Gordon's synthesis of the Veblen-Ayres model, economic progress is a function of (1) the positive, forward thrust of technological change, (2) the negative, institutional resistance to the dynamic forces inherent in the process of accumulating technical knowledge, and (3) the availability of resources appropriate to the prevailing technology.[5] If one assumes a relatively open international economy, resource availability can be assumed. Therefore, the fundamental forces influencing economic progress can be aggregated as being either technological or institutional.

Although Ayres's model is essentially dynamic, it can be adapted for analytical purposes to a comparative statics framework. In this context, one could use the quantity or quality of technology to identify various stages of economic progress. Movement from a lower to higher stage could be accomplished either by increasing the quantity of the same quality technology or by improving the quality of technology while the quantity remains sufficient to prevent a net decrease in output. In the East European context Selucky has termed the former "extensive technological change"; the latter "intensive technological change."[6] Either variety of technological change will result in economic progress only if society's organizational framework adapts, thereby permitting the optimal utilization of the new technology. In other words, a given technological base will be best utilized in an environment of compatible institutional arrangements. If the technological base changes, its optimal utilization will require that the economic organization of the society adjust.

When "testing" the Veblen-Ayres model, the most relevant data are found in the vicinity of points of adjustment, either precipitated by dramatic technological progress or by explicit awareness that institutional change must be made to accommodate existing technology. In the East European set of cases these points of adjustment are clustered in the mid-1960s, although some related changes were being discussed as early as 1958. Forces encouraging institutional adjustment as well as those opposing them are most clearly recognized at these turning points. Thus, they are emphasized in this paper. For reasons that are elaborated upon below, the analysis is also narrowed to East Germany and Czechoslovakia.

The economic sluggishness that began to manifest itself in most East European countries in about 1960 is generally regarded as the reason institutional adjustments (usually labeled reforms) in the economic planning process were undertaken. Bergson, Brubaker, Kaplan, and Shaffer are but a few of the scholars who have either presented data in support of this position or have reached this conclusion.[7] In searching for the cause of this growth decline, it seems rather certain that a drop in investment was not at fault. On the contrary, the proportion of total resources devoted to investment had increased.[8] Bergson, for example, expressed the opinion that further increases in the capital stock could not serve as a primary engine of growth without being "inordinately burdensome."[9] Most generally, it has been argued that the reason for the decline in the rate of economic growth was the increasingly complex, industrial economy that was developing in each of the countries in Eastern Europe.[10] Put differently, new investment was being used less efficiently. As Table 10-1 illustrates, the incremental capital-output ratio rose between the last half of the 1950s and the first half of the 1960s for all six of the countries included. The most noticeable increases took place in Czechoslovakia and East Germany.

As Selucky has argued:

> The decline of the effectiveness of capital and adequate growth of the capital output ratios . . . has been most pronounced in the industrially most advanced countries which, already in the mid-1950's, exhausted the other extensive resource—the free availability of the labor force. It might seem that the very fact of the exhaustion of the sources of available labor would automatically force a change of the extensive type of growth to an intensive one. But it did not happen, either in Czechoslovakia or in the German Democratic Republic (G.D.R.). What did change in both these countries was merely the manifestation of the extensive type of growth: Available labor having been exhausted, capital became the only source of growth. Thus, in the 1960–65 period, the increase in the incremental capital output ratios was highest in both Czechoslovakia (C.S.S.R.), and the German Democratic Republic. Both countries were forced to cancel their economic plans (in 1963, . . .) and to prepare economic reforms through which the traditional command economic system was to be adjusted to the requirements of intensive growth and of the technological revolution.[11]

These developments could have been predicted using the Veblen-Ayres model; however, the reform movement in Czechoslovakia and East Ger-

Table 10-1. Incremental Capital-Output Ratios: Selected Countries and Periods

Time Period	Soviet Union	Bulgaria	Czecho-slovakia	East Germany	Hungary	Poland
1950–55	1.77	1.86	2.61	1.28	4.04	2.75
1955–60	2.53	1.92	3.14	2.70	2.84	3.68
1960–65	3.83	3.89	14.28	6.02	3.65	4.62

Source: Selucky, *Economic Reforms,* p. 3.

many did not advance as rapidly as might have been expected. An inquiry into the "reform experiences" of these two countries is very instructive as to the role of institutional resistence in economic progress. Further, during the post–World War II period the technical skills of the populaces were utilized differently in the two countries. This provides important insights regarding the transmission of technical change through the human capital component of technology to promote institutional change.

In the GDR after World War II institutional conditions were favorable to continued technical progress. First, the transition to a Soviet command system was not large, given the previous German experience with the command system of the Third Reich. Secondly, the Soviet military administration in East Germany did not destroy the existing hierarchic division of labor within industrial enterprises. Nor was there much effort to force wage equalization in the GDR (relative to other East European countries). And small craft industries were not nationalized.[12] In general, the relatively small changes minimized the postwar transition problems of economic administration. And the fact that the technical experts were not purged set the stage for the economic reforms of the 1960s. These conditions were reinforced by the fact that East Germany was given access to the markets of the European Common Market through the Federal Republic of Germany.[13] It is very important to the argument of this paper that the GDR has thus had a direct contact with technological developments in the West.[14]

As I have argued elsewhere, in East Germany one endogenous and three exogenous forces can be identified as having retarded or prevented the implementation of reforms in the first decade and a half after World War II. These four forces were the short-run economic success experienced in East Germany, national unification efforts, Russian-German interaction, and the prevalence of Stalinist dogma.[15] The East German economy's performance was strong for most of the 1956–1960 period. Since progress was dynamic, little attention was devoted to institutional adjustment. But in 1961 and 1962 progress, although strong by some standards, substantially lagged behind the experience of the recent past. The deteriorating economic performance provided an indication that the relative technical complexity of the East German economy could not be efficiently organized through the existing command institutions.

Also, it can be asserted that East Germany did not fully accept an identifiable Soviet-type economy until possibly as late as 1958. This lag was caused by uncertainty as to the most desirable political route to follow. Should East Germany reunify with West Germany, or should a Soviet-type economy be established? Although the latter eventually was accepted, the distraction caused by this debate interfered with the full implementation of the Soviet-type command economy. This lag, in turn, pushed back the time when economic planning reforms were needed.

A third factor that might be identified as a distraction or a set of frictions slowing institutional change came as a result of post–World War II German-Russian interaction. Germany had lost a significant amount of manpower in the war, but the experiences of the postwar period heightened the manpower loss. Many productive and talented people migrated from East to West Germany, for example, and East Germany was left with a disproportionately large percentage of relatively dependent persons. Another example of the effects of Russian occupation can be found in the reparations that the Russians demanded and extracted. Further — and not incidentally — the East Germans were forced to pay the cost of sustaining the Russian army of occupation. The cumulative effect of these factors was to reduce substantially the labor and capital endowments below what they otherwise would have been. (Generally, these burdens were either eliminated or lightened on January 1, 1954.)

The final factor retarding East Germany's earlier adoption of market-type planning techniques was the influence of Stalinist dogma. "While the dictator with the authority of an infallible leader was still alive, any attempt at changing the state of affairs . . . was tantamount to attempting suicide." Thus, it is not surprising that East Germany adopted and retained planning techniques very similar to those employed in the Soviet Union.[16] Perhaps unwisely, this more technically advanced nation adopted for ideological reasons the institutions of a less-advanced nation. Regardless of the desirability of such a move, there is little doubt that the ideological force did delay planning experimentation in East Germany, since it should have developed earlier for economic reasons.

The East German experience, in summary, can be said to provide a good example of how the cumulative effect of several factors can shape the pace and form of institutional adjustments. Forces retarding technological progress cannot long exist if an increase of the rate of economic growth is to be pursued, for regardless of the immediate forces at work — assuming the existence of this goal — there exists fundamental pressure to reform the institutions of the economy. The pressure will increase as available technology is more widely applied or as technological advances are made. Regardless of the nature of the technological advance, the more individuals who are involved directly with technology, the greater becomes its political prominence. Therefore, over time, as more and more individuals find their vested interests tied directly to technological advance, there will be increasing pressure to confront and change those forces retarding such an advance. Stated differently, the pressures for changes in the planning institutions of socialist countries will increase as the number of technocrats increases. Baylis has made this point in connection with economic reforms in East Germany.[17] In addition, the influence of technocrats will be felt sooner and stronger the longer they are a stable (not politically disrupted) "group."

The Czechoslovakian experience provides a contrast to that of East Germany. Given the twenty-year experience as a democratic republic before World War II (1918–1938) and the three-year experience with democratic socialism afterwards (1945–1948), the imposition of a command economic system was a much greater shock in Czechoslovakia than it was in East Germany. In Selucky's view, for Czechoslovakia the command model was essentially "an alien system."[18]

After the communist party seized power in February, the initial five year plan (1949–1953) emphasized consumer goods. In February 1950, however, the plan's targets were increased substantially and priorities were shifted to investment goods. Under Korean War pressure a year later, the Soviet Union insisted on a near doubling of the already inflated rates of growth of heavy industry. Great imbalances developed in the economy as a result. Consequently, a Soviet command economic system was formally imposed in 1951. From the perspective of this paper, more important than the imposition of the command economy was the impact on technocrats. As Selucky has recorded:

> The Soviet command system . . . was introduced in full and at once, at a time, moreover, when political trials were unleashing a wave of political terror and when forcible liquidation of private crafts and businesses was accompanied by forcible collectivization. Neither the population nor the Czechoslovak economy as such were even remotely prepared for such changes. Along with an unsuitable restructuring of branches (for instance, Czechoslovakia became a steel power without owning any iron ore), a bureaucratic command system was abruptly introduced. This destroyed . . . the rationality of the previous management . . . Over 350,000 workers' cadres assumed managerial positions in the state and economic apparatus and replaced the technocrats and managers. The Communist Party of Czechoslovakia leadership quite deliberately forefeited the economic potential of the middle classes.[19]

The second five-year plan (1953–1958) aimed at restoring balance in the economy. The resulting relatively improved material well-being of the populace forestalled the need for reform; however, by the end of the second plan the incremental capital-output ratio had begun to increase. This encouraged (1) adjustments to improve medium- and long-term planning, (2) partial decentralization, and (3) action by producers to avoid overfull-filling a low target output in favor of optimizing output. Otherwise, the command system was left in place. This is one reason the three types of adjustment failed within three years. A second reason is that the plan placed undue emphasis on extensive investment in heavy industry. Another unbalancing development resulted from the especially harsh winter of 1962–1963. Also, export demand was substantially altered as a result of changes in industrial emphases in the Soviet Union. The Sino-Soviet political split resulted in the cancellation of Chinese orders. These changes in export demand resulted in considerable confusion in the quantitative, material links among Czechoslovakian industries and consequently made the plan less meaningful. On top of this, tens of thousands of technocrats were purged, many for the second time after working themselves back into the system after their removals from managerial positions in the early 1950s.[20]

The purging of technocrats reduced their influence within the country and thereby lessened the chances for successful institutional adaptation to utilize the prevailing technology. In addition, it reinforced the experience that it was politically risky to be entrepreneurial. Thus, technocrats who retained their positions were less likely to encourage or experiment with future reforms until they were officially sanctioned.

With the technocrats in a position of reduced influence, the reform proposals developed during the 1964–1968 period under the leadership of Sik had little chance of success despite the fact that the command system was effectively inoperative below the ministry level. Farmers did not support the reform because they had not been part of its formulation. Uncertainty as to the future of the reform proposals, together with insufficient gains in social prestige and income to compensate for risk taking, kept former small, private producers from supporting the proposals. The concept of self-administration did lead the workers to support the idea of a market-type reform.[21] Without a full complement of technocratic managers supporting the reforms, however, the political support in their favor was no match for the political bureaucrats of the Communist Party. "Particularly after 1965 . . . the official interpretation . . . blunted the proposed changes and tried to preserve as many elements of the old command system as possible." Thus, the political power center "never allowed the reforms to become institutionalized or legally anchored" in Czechoslovakia.[22]

In summary, Czechoslovakia had the political-cultural experience necessary to utilize market-type signals in the planning process. Further, its technological level was so advanced that a command system without a component of market-type institutions prevented optimal economic progress. Finally, the introduction of market-type institutions was continually thwarted primarily because the channel by which technological forces could influence institutional change was repeatedly closed. The purging of technocrats from positions of influence in the early 1950s and again in the early 1960s effectively broke the link and prevented institutional adaptation.

It is clear that the Veblen-Ayres theoretical framework is useful in analyzing economic reform (institutional adjustments) in socialist countries. The evidence is strong that the stock of technology and its sophistication dictate the economic institutional requirements if physical capital is to be utilized efficiently. However, even though the technology embodied in the physical capital is necessary, it is not sufficient. In order to be sufficient to promote institutional adjustment, the human capital technological component must be politically strong.

The political strength of technocrats might develop somewhat as follows. Physical capital developments require more technically capable management. If this technocratic management is not periodically purged, there will develop over time an ascendancy of technical, economically rational solutions at the expense of ideological-political ones. If this process continues for a sufficient period, the technical experts will become first a part and later a more powerful and influential part of the power (party) elite. As implied, resistance to such changes will be strong, but if technocrats do become important in the political process, the institutional adjustments required will be implemented much more easily. An important lesson, especially from the Czechoslovakian case, is that institutional resistance that undercuts or disrupts the human capital component of technology is most effective in preventing the institutional change that will permit more rapid economic progress.

The ascendancy of scientific technically oriented decision makers will be easier and smoother if the process begins within an environment of intelligible institutions; for example, an aspect of the institutional change in the GDR involved the amalgamation of enterprises. Since the concept was similar to the earlier German Trusts, the change was more easily accepted by enterprise management.[23] Also, the transfer of decision-making power from the ministries to the enterprise amalgamations met with little resistance because the new entities were conceptually familiar. Given this previous similar experience, the German change could be viewed as part of a minor institutional adjustment aimed at introducing market forces into a command system. Finally, the argument that the reforms are only minor adjustments in the command economy that will strengthen the party over time minimizes resistance to them.[24]

In contrast, the Czechoslovakian people expected more from socialism than was being realized under the Soviet system.[25] Thus, the reform proposals of 1964–1968 were not considered minor adjustments in the command economy but instead have been said to represent, "the most thorough attempt to date at a humanistic interpretation of Marxist socialism.''[26] With sentiments such as these pushing reforms forward and with political support from technocrats minimized, it is not surprising that the political resistance to reforms prevailed with harsh consequences in Czechoslovakia. Ideally, if effective reforms were the goal, slower implementation of the changes might have evoked less harsh reprisals. Put differently, if reform proposals had originated to a larger degree with technocratic management, they might have been slower in developing, but both the slower pace and the concomitant growth of technocratic "political" support for the changes would have enhanced the chance for the successful implementation of reforms. Thus, some short-run institutional resistances can be viewed as necessary to a smooth transition to new economic organizational structures. These resistances are less necessary the less alien is the institutional environment within which the changes are transpiring.

Insofar as they are pertinent to the Western countries, the experiences of the German Democratic Republic and Czechoslovakia strongly suggest that efforts should be made to strengthen and improve the market mechanism within any planning context. Whereas Ayres viewed the ideology of financial capitalism as retarding the market perfection that would be possible in the United States if available technology were utilized fully and efficiently, the data herein identify the ideology of a centralized command economy as playing a similar "economy-distorting" role.[27] Regardless of the system, if Ayres's values of economic abundance, equality, freedom, security, and excellence are to prevail, market instruments of planning must be incorporated into the overall process. Such use of the market must not be manipulated by technocrats for efficiency reasons. Substantial, well-informed consumer sovereignty is the key.

This last point emphasizes the potential, continuing conflict between producer-oriented decision makers and those who are consumer-oriented. There is a strong possibility that a production process dominated by technocrats may not serve consumers any better than when ideologically oriented decision makers are dominant. As Selucky has observed regarding Eastern Europe:

> Thus, faith in the omnipotence of technocratism is not substantiated. It could achieve substance only under one condition; that technocrats become the absolute rulers of society, that they take over the party, the state, and all of its apparatus, including the economic one. At that moment, of course, they would cease to be technocrats and would have become politicians and party officials. In other words, they would become transformed into a bureaucracy, ruling absolutely and controlled by no one. Nothing much would change in the system itself; perhaps a somewhat irrational dictatorship would be transformed and better educated but

not necessarily more tolerant or humane. For this reason, the technocratic concept of reform appears fallacious and, from a humanist point of view, unacceptable. While in its rudimentary form, it may have a positive effect at least in the direction of rationalizing the system and pluralizing the power elites, in its final form, it represents nothing but absolute manipulation and a pragmatic, cold dictatorship, scientifically organized and, therefore, perfect and difficult to dislodge.[28]

If he is right, a calculating technocratic regime, rationally using market instruments in the planning process may be less successful in achieving the values espoused by Ayres than a nontechnocratic, yet benevolent one.

Stated differently, institutions will always be present in society. From the Veblen-Ayres viewpoint, the greater the scientific-technocratic influence in prevailing institutions the more likely is technological and therefore economic progress; however, if technocratic producers become so dominant as to eliminate the process of "continually, objectively and intelligently reevaluating its rules and norms," the assimilation of technology will be stymied with the result that economic advancements will be slowed.[29]

Rather than maximizing just the political power of technocratic management, an optimum can be achieved if institutions can be strengthened or created that promote more scientific choices by consumers. Regardless of the political system, Ayres's values can be attained only if informed consumers dominate. With sufficient scientific analyses of alternatives, consumers ultimately can best judge which of available technologies best enables society to improve its way of life. Society should and does assimilate new technologies selectively.[30] And, since improvement in the human condition should be the criterion for selection, the consumers of the output must not allow themselves to be dictated to by technocratic producers. Technically competent consumer decisions will encourage more rapid technical change on the part of producers. Because all new technology will not be assimilated, a consumer-dominated system will stimulate competition among producer-technocrats. If genuine, this competition should maximize technological innovation.

The emphasis on informed, technically competent consumer decisions provides a Veblen-Ayres focus to an otherwise neoclassical-sounding position. This is so because the interdependence of technology and consumer preferences is explicitly recognized. The optimal organization of society may, therefore, involve the institutionalization of the scientific review and evaluation of alternative products and services that are available for purchase. Assuming that the consumer alternatives are evaluated and publicized by "individuals who are representative of the sciences and the arts, . . . the kinds of goods that are priced and sold in the private markets would also be the types of goods that would meet his (Ayres's) technological or scientific standard."[31] And if competition exists among several scientific product (and services) review agencies, the chances of consistently obtaining high-quality analyses and recommendations is enhanced.

In summary, from a Veblen-Ayres viewpoint an optimal technocratic society is one where the technocratic influence is important in both producer and consumer decisions. Crucial is the deployment of the human capital component of technology. Production management must be sufficiently scientific to guide the assimulation of new technology based on efficiency criteria. Scientific expertise must likewise be available to consumers, so that consumption decisions are truely rational. Such a world, regardless of country-specific political systems, would depend heavily on a perfected market mechanism as an important instrument in the economic planning process.

ENDNOTES

1. For a summary of an important part of the relevant literature, see Warren J. Samuels, "Technology Vis-à-Vis Institutions in the JEI: A Suggested Interpretation," *Journal of Economic Issues* 10 (December 1977): 871-95.

2. Allan G. Gruchy, *Contemporary Economic Thought: The Contributions of Neo-Institutional Economics* (Clifton, N. J.: Augustus M. Kelley, 1972), pp. 131-32.

3. James R. Elliott and Anthony E. Scaperlanda, "East Germany's Liberman-type Reforms in Perspective," *Quarterly Review of Economics and Business* 6 (Autumn 1966): 39-52; and Anthony E. Scaperlanda, "The Political Economy of Liberman-type Reforms," *Journal of Economic Issues* 5 (March 1971): 77-85.

4. Gruchy, *Contemporary Economic Thought*, p. 106.

5. Wendell Gordon, *Economics from an Institutional Viewpoint* (Austin, Texas: University Stores, 1973), p. 5.

6. Radoslav Selucky, *Economic Reforms in Eastern Europe: Political Background and Economic Significance*, Z. Elias, trans. (New York: Praeger, 1972), p. 4.

7. Abram Bergson, "The Current Soviet Planning Reforms," in Alexander Balinky et al. *Planning and the Market in the U.S.S.R.: The 1960's* (New Brunswick, N. J.: Rutgers University Press, 1967), p. 59; Earl R. Brubaker. "Embodied Technology, the Asymptotic Behavior of Capital's Age and Soviet Growth," *Review of Economics and Statistics* 50 (August 1968): 304; Norman M. Kaplan, "Retardation of Soviet Growth,"*Review of Economics and Statistics* 21 (April 1970): 458-84; Harry G. Shaffer, "Economic Reforms in the Soviet Union and East Europe: A Comparative Study," paper discussed at the joint meeting of the Midwest Economic Association and the Association for Comparative Economics, Detroit, April 23-25, 1970.

8. Kaplan, "Retardation," pp. 295-96.

9. Bergson, "Current Soviet," p. 61.

10. Ibid., p. 57; Kaplan, "Retardation," p. 302; Shaffer, *Economic Reforms,*

11. Selucky, *Economic Reforms,* p. 98.

12. Ibid., pp. 58-60.

13.   Werner Feld, *The European Common Market and the World* (Englewood Cliffs, N. J.: Prentice-Hall, 1967), p. 41.

14.   Selucky, *Economic Reforms,* pp. 70–71.

15.   Elliott and Scaperlanda, "East Germany,"

16.   Selucky, *Economic Reforms,* p. 32.

17.   Thomas R. Baylis, "The New Economic System: The Role of Technocrats in the DDR," originally in *Survey* (October 1966): 139–152 and reproduced in G. R. Feiwel (ed.), *New Currents in Soviet-type Economics: A Reader* (Scranton, Pa.: International Textbook, 1968), pp. 534–547.

18.   Selucky, *Economic Reforms,* p. 80.

19.   Ibid., p. 81

20.   Ibid., pp. 83–84.

21.   Ibid., pp. 85, 89, 100, 108–109. Many ex-small producers were not enthusiastic about reform because they were already producing for the black market. Legalization of "free" markets would undercut black market profits.

22.   Ibid., pp. 85, 88.

23.   Ibid., p. 63.

24.   Ibid., pp. 62–65.

25.   Ibid., p. 109.

26.   Ibid., p. 110.

27.   Gruchy, *Contemporary Economic Thought,* p. 105.

28.   Selucky, *Economic Reforms,* p. 67.

29.   Gordon, *Economics,* p. 16.

30.   Ibid., p. 23.

31.   Gruchy, *Contemporary Economic Thought,* p. 105.

11 INCOME DISTRIBUTION IN THE WELFARE STATE
Consequences of a Loss of Consensus in Britain

Walter C. Neale

A major problem for the industrialized nations in this half of the twentieth century is how to manage the welfare state. In greater or lesser degree, some sooner and some later, with myriad national variations, the western democracies evolved welfare states during the first half of the century. Inflation, balance of payments difficulties, and demands for higher wages are not new phenomena, but they are certainly characteristic of these last thirty years during which welfare states have reached maturity. Few indeed of their most loyal proponents would deny that welfare state policies directed toward full employment, income maintenance, income redistribution, and increased education and medical care have contributed to inflation and balance of payments deficits and insistent demands for higher wages. What the opponents of the welfare state have charged — that inflation must be the inevitable result of welfare state policies — became a nagging worry of its supporters and now, finally, a fear.

The purpose of this essay is to suggest that a major but as yet not fully appreciated cause contributing importantly to the magnitude and intractibility of these problems has been the loss of consensus about what does and what ought to determine relative incomes. While it is my belief that consensus on these questions has been or is being lost in all the western democracies, the illustration upon which the argument here will rely is the case of Britain.

The current lack of consensus — the "loss" will be discussed below — becomes evident whenever policies of wage and price restraint — under the Conservatives in the early sixties and early seventies; under Labour governments in the late sixties and late seventies — have given way to periods of rapid increases in wages, culminating in a wage explosion of 30 percent during 1974–1975. It shows up when miners demand a higher wage (1971, 1973–1974, 1977), when the government considers setting up an income "Relativities Commission" (1974), when the firemen strike (1977), and each spring and summer since 1975 when the issue of proper policy for the next "stage" of wage restraint arises. Miners' work is dirty and dangerous; they should get paid more on this account, but how much more than whom? Skilled workers should be rewarded for their greater skills and responsibilities, but how much more than what other group? Firemen encounter great if intermittent danger; they are skilled and should always be on call. How much are these things worth? In each case, one way or another, a "settlement" results from the negotiations. But each "settlement" is unsettling. So soon as miners are satisfied, workers in the electricity supply industry ask for "equal treatment," and once they have achieved something like what they regard as equal treatment, some third group *and* the miners feel they have been overlooked if not actually mistreated.

What those in Britain (and increasingly all of us) face cannot be accounted for by that eternal trait of man that goes under so many names: greed, self-betterment, looking after number one, or seizing opportunities as they arise. Of course, this trait is always involved — but unless there has been genetic change in the species since the last century, this explanation is insufficient. The trait has been as operative in times of secular decline in prices (e.g., 1873–1896) as in times of secularly rising prices (e.g., 1848–1873, 1896–1919) — as true in the 1920s as in the 1970s.

Certainly full employment — defined not as some specific rate such as the British aim of 3 (or maybe 2) percent (or the American aim of 4 or maybe 5 percent) but as the high priority given by modern governments to reducing unemployment whenever it rises much above such rates — full employment and modern monetary policies have a potential for inflation that was lacking when full-employment was not a major aim of governments and when "sound money" and the restraints of the gold standard severely limited national governments and central banks. But it would be far from true to assert that governments today are indifferent to inflation, that they are satisfied with, or even resigned to, the "wage leapfrogging" of group after and over group. On the contrary, the demands for incomes policies and the attempts to implement them, the electoral fears of parties that preside over inflation, and the acceptance in the mid-1970s of levels of unemployment that were unacceptable in the fifties and sixties are ample evidence that no one is satisfied with the present state of affairs.

If neither greed nor Keynes are fully satisfying, neither is the increasingly common view that *the* problem of welfare states is the high level of government expenditure. Speaking of Italy (whose current problems are worse than Britain's, and often said to be much the same), Friedenberg commented in a vein that reflects this common view:

> In the past four years Italy, the world's seventh ranking power, has gotten into more economic trouble than any other country in the West. . . .
>
> The consensus is that the root causes are two: The high cost of labor and, linked to it, *high public expenditures for social services and pensions.* [Italics mine.]

This makes it appear that the cause can be stated objectively and that the troubles are an inevitable consequence: the economic equivalent of the germ theory of disease. The view either misconceives the problem or slips over the crucial issue. What is "high"? One really must assume it is "too high"; it could not mean "just high enough." Bacon and Eltis have the matter right:

> Almost all the civilized activities of a modern society are wholly or largely non-marketed. Both Covent Garden and Glyndebourne cover only a fraction of their costs by selling tickets, and universities, schools, art galleries, libraries and hospitals produce outputs which are almost entirely non-marketed. Defense is also non-marketed. . . . It can almost be said that a country with a larger non-market sector than another similar country will be either militarily stronger or more civilized, but it must be able to afford to maintain its large non-market sector. If its people are prepared to give up marketed output to the government on the necessary scale it will manage this. . . .
>
> There would, of course, be no adverse response to a diversion of resources of this kind if the increased social spending was a direct and exact response to workers' preference for this.[2]

If civilized people must be willing to support a large nonmarket sector, so also must civilized people find ways of accommodating each other's desires for fair shares in the national product. So far the British have not found a way to do this.

It is often suggested that people do not know what to do about the situation, that the profession of economists lacks a proper theory. It seems implied that if there were a proper theory of current inflation, there would also be a solution to the problem. That a satisfactory, even logically unassailable, theory is also an actual solution in the real world was belied years ago by the failure of Ricardo and his classical colleagues to persuade the world outside the United Kingdom that free trade was the policy to adopt. But we all try. Within ten years after its publication British economists had great hopes that the time had come when Keynes's prescriptions in *The General Theory of Employment, Interest, and Money* could be administered to the economy with happy results. Fifteen years later American economists were enjoying the same hope. But whether one calls the policies "demand management" or "fine tuning," the hopes have become wishes no longer accompanied by faith. Robinson's predictions of forty years ago look more like being an accurate description of a Keynesian world than do the expectations of postwar Chancellors of the Exchequer or of Heller's Council of Economic Advisers.[3] Monetarists claim that they have a solution, both theoretical and practical, but whatever the intellectual merits of their position — their appeal to the logical, orderly mind — no government or central bank has yet seen fit to risk the consequences of following the advice of the monetarists, nor are a majority of economists clearly at one with them on the validity or appropriateness of their recommendations. While those who do not accept the monetarist position often feel that they can explain particular inflations, or assert that they can say much of relevance about the current situation, it is probably fair to say that economists do not have a generally acceptable solution, theoretical or practical — at least, not a solution both intellectually elegant and politically attractive.

It is not my purpose here, however, to argue the shortcomings — if that they be — of current theory or to propose a new theory. I have dealt briefly with arguments about the state of current theory only to allow myself to say that my readers should not be tempted to interpret what follows as a critique of or a contribution to recent disputes over full-employment and monetary policies. What follows bears not upon the rights and wrongs or the ins and outs of these disputes but upon the nature of the world to which any fiscal or monetary policy must apply.

CONSENSUS: THE WORLD BEFORE 1914

The world that has emerged in the last fifty years has lost a consensus upon what does or what ought to determine a person's income, but before 1914 there was such a consensus. It was not a result of agreement on why the world was as it was, nor on whether it should be as it was or would always remain as it was. Rather, the consensus was the result of different understandings and perceptions, sometimes quite inconsistent and contradictory, but which nevertheless led to common acceptance. There was an almost universal recognition that the world worked in such a way as to determine incomes and that, at least in any near term future of next month or next year, all were going to live in and with that world. It was the world in which "market forces," "supply and demand," "value and productivity" — what was offered to the worker or saver, which he could take or leave (if he could figure out a way to leave it without starving) — determined the incomes of most.

Smith accepted a world of markets, explained it, and admired it: "That's the way it is; it must work that way; and aren't we lucky it does work that way." By Ricardo's time it did not seem so lucky a world, but it was still accepted and explained. Already there were protests against that world, but there were no denials that Smith's world of markets become Ricardo's "the world one lived in." Protest took various forms. Luddites violently rejected the present for the past. Chartists demanded peaceful political revolution. Owenites wanted a revolution in the nature and spirit of men and women. Whatever the variations in form and aim, all protests had in common a demand for a radical change in the system of politics or of property or of society. All accepted that the system worked as it did and would not produce different incomes — only radical change could alter relative shares. While never much followed in Britain, Marxism epitomized the protests: Ricardo was right about the nineteenth century world — it was this world which was unacceptable. It was perhaps first Mill who accepted this world, explained it, and then suggested that it might slowly be changed for the better. Eleven years before Darwin it would not have meant much had Mill called for an "evolutionary economics," but twenty-five years after Darwin, Fabians could both accept the Victorian world for themselves and start to work within the system to evolve a new and better world for the next generation. But for Fabians in 1884 as for Mill in 1848, and for Ricardo in 1817 as for Smith in 1776, the market determined today's wage and old age's nest egg. Two decades were to elapse after *Fabian Essays* of 1889 before a Liberal government began to intervene to alter the distributional effects of markets, and not until 1919 did the Labour Party explicitly adopt the Fabian suggestion that there should be common ownership of the means of production. Even twenty years later Bevin was still insisting that the community's powers of ownership of London Transport should not be used to alter the consequences of the discipline of the market for fares or services or wages.

From the 1850s trade unions were trying to alter the distribution of income in favor of their members, but trade unionists did not argue that members should be paid according to criteria other than some version of what their members' productivity was worth on the market. Certainly there is a sense in which "free collective bargaining" was seen as a search for a just wage, but it was still bargaining and not justice that determined the wage.

From the Poor Law Reform of 1834 until 1914 (or maybe 1939) there was consensus that the income of a person depended on the market. There were those who approved of the system and either devoutly hoped or devoutly believed that its will, like His will, was, is, and will be forever and ever. Others — many others — did not like the system but accepted it, as people accept tides and earthquakes. So, whether the Unseen Hand stroked you or struck you, shoved you or guided you — whether the Providence to which it was likened was presided over by a benevolent or by a meanly indifferent Being — it was agreed, "That's the way it is, son. Love it or hate it, take it, because you can't leave it — and there is nothing you can do that will make any difference tomorrow or next summer."

This consensus has been lost: not all at once, but slowly. It was there in 1914; it is not here now. The radicalism of the Liberal Party in the decade before the Great War was insufficient to prevent the rise of an overtly socialist Labour Party to the position of second largest party. But both short-lived Labour governments of the interwar period fell in attempts to preserve the basic structure and rules of the pre-1914 period. Actually no political party has announced that it is resigning from the consensus and going into opposition. Until late 1977 "free collective bargaining" — certainly a rhetoric (if not properly an element) of pricing by productivity in the market — was as virtuous in Labour as in Tory eyes.[4] Both parties — and the solid frame of civil servants — make "productivity" the centerpiece of justification for wage increases (and some mighty peculiar bargains are made acceptable by the use of the term).[5] But even if the wordings used in public reflect many private perceptions, and even if they imply a consensus about the way in which incomes are and should be determined, nevertheless, the responses of people, both as individuals expressing feelings and as groups setting forth aims or demands, are inconsistent with the referent ideas. For instance, there is no way that one can consider the present weekly wage of about £70 for miners at the coal face consistent with their worth or productivity *and* think that the National Union of Mineworkers' demands for £135 are proper.

The lack of consensus need not be between groups or between different sets of standards, each of which is consistently articulated. The same people can hold quite mutually inconsistent ideas, using them as standards in differently perceived situations. The emergence of the "poverty trap" *and* its continued existence after widespread recognition that it existed illustrate the point. The poverty trap occurs when the income granted by the government to an unemployed person (with a wife and a child or two) — an income hardly overgenerously computed on the basis of a consensus about the minimally decent standard of living due anyone — is as much, sometimes even more, than the weekly wage the unemployed person could earn in employment. What we are getting are answers to two different questions: (1) How much should anyone living in the United Kingdom get to live on? and (2) How much should a worker be paid? Since Mill economists have known that the answers to these two questions need not be the same "in principle" — but economists have not — no more than have statesmen or lawyers or civil servants drafting legislation — yet figured out a way to legislate and administer — to institutionalize — a stable system in which the numerical answer to question 1 is higher than the numerical answer to question 2.

Ideologically, there has always been an opposition to the idea that what the market pays is the right amount. The continuous denial that the market system achieved justice has certainly been influential in breaking down the consensus. The more doubt the critiques raised about whether what the market offered was just, the weaker must have been the consensus. Probably more importantly, the greater the doubt aroused that what the market offered *had* to be one's income, the weaker the consensus. The doubt, the intellectual basis for a rejection of the market's valuation of productivity, was conceived and nurtured by socialist thought. But, rightly or wrongly, market valuations could continue to be the criteria for distributing incomes because, before 1939, situations seldom arose in which the criteria — or the belief that the criteria applied — could not be employed to explain (and, for many people, to justify) the incomes paid.

Before 1939 — before the subtle but nonetheless real direction of labor during the war and before the growth of public sector employment since 1945 — most wages were paid by private concerns operating within the commercial restraint of a market according to that rule that could not be evaded, that receipts must exceed outlays, and therefore that the wage paid must "pay for itself." To the question — "How much should policemen be paid?" — the answer was: "Their wage in alternative employment." Their values, and hence by a not quite complete argument, their productivity, could be measured by their alternative cost. Offer what was necessary to attract enough men with the needed talents (brains, physique, sense of responsibility) to fill the desired positions on the police force, and one had the market wages for policemen. The number of jobs offered to policemen

— and to firemen and to teachers and to sanitarians — was so small a proportion of the total number of jobs in the commercially organized sector that the productivity — and therefore the worth — of people in such public employment could be assumed to be, or could be treated as if it were, their alternative productivity in the private sector. For the system to work it was not necessary to ask the impossible-to-answer questions (e.g., what is the marginal social value of a policeman just responsible enough or just quick enough to hush a drunk early on a Sunday morning?). A system that works — not perfectly, not fairly, not with total logical consistency, but which manages to carry on from day to day and from decade to decade — does generate its justification, does persuade or bully its dissidents, and does continue to work. And it would not be wrong to say that the market did determine the wages of policemen and other public employees.

Since 1939 (or 1945) the British world has been a different one. The number of employees in the public services has risen enormously. The demands of the government, derived from the programs for defense, education, development, health, public welfare, as well as from the older demands for policemen and firemen, are now so large that the demands of the private, commercial sector no longer set a going wage independently of the wages and salaries offered by government. Furthermore, the large government demand is not subject to the commercial rule that the employee's pay must pay for itself. Certainly, it is hoped that the productivity in social good and human happiness is at least as great as the wage paid the policeman or the social worker or the teacher of English to the child of Jamaican immigrants, but there is no *numerically* objective way to establish, *or* to disprove, to the correctness of the hope.[6] Whatever arguments can be made that public employees could conceivably be paid at a going rate established in the private sector, they have become largely irrelevant to people who have actually experienced or seen incomes determined by quite different criteria.[7] Where once the criticisms were that people did not get their just desserts — because of inequality of bargaining power between employer and employee, because all value is produced by labor, because there are monopolies and monopsonies, because there is inherited wealth — now there is added an habituation to an everyday world of matter-of-fact where lobbying and law, sympathy and fear and ministerial decision, strikes and working-to-rule, appeals to public standards of justice and fairplay — and the idiosyncrasies of the histories of particular trades as well as just plain luck — appear to have as much effect upon a person's income as his productivity. In a world where bankruptcy meant shutting down the plant, the plea that "we can't afford it" carried weight. In a world in which the National Enterprise Board takes over a financially failing British Leyland

and in which the government pays £20 per week per worker in subsidies to maintain employment in depressed areas, the plea loses its force.[8]

The result is that there are no commonly accepted criteria for wages or for income. Decent minima, danger, skill, responsibility, talent, essentiality and custom are all respectable criteria for setting a wage. In the general way, most people in Britain would now agree that all are somehow relevant to the determination of incomes. But the agreement remains "general and somehow." How much danger is the equivalent of how much skill? Is the responsibility of a social worker faced with strains and frustrations worth how much more or less than the essentiality of a skilled manual worker in electricity generation?

It is not the problem of quantification that causes the trouble. Even if we could quantify skill or danger or responsibility, we would still face the problem of equating these quantities to flows of money paid out in wages and salaries. Conversely, societies have answered such questions without quantifying "units of contribution" before the fact — willy-nilly, serfs and lords accepted their shares in William I's kingdom, the British support the royal family in the appropriate style, and the kill in the Kalahari gets divided fairly among the members of a hunting group of Kung bushmen. So too does the money and the roast and the milk and the beer get divided fairly in America among husband, wife, mother-in-law, son, and daughter. Perhaps mother-in-law, wife, or a child will not feel that the division is all that fair — but in none of these cases is there the complaint: "but there is no quantification!" Rebelliousness or dissatisfaction is felt in all these cases about what happens, not about the absence of numbers.

One of three conditions must prevail if the division of the crop or the distribution of money incomes (or of the Kungs' kill or of the family's roast) is to be accepted. First, there may be a general agreement that the division is fair. Second, it may be felt that the division can no more be changed than can the weather. Third, there may be agreement that the process that determines the division is just, or at least so good or so necessary as to make the preservation of the process more desirable than an alteration in the division would be.

The first may be true not only of the Queen but of most of her subjects. The second was probably — at least, I have no urge to disagree — the foundation of the 11th century serf's consent to his share, and of the Manchester millhand's consent to his share in the 1870s. It is perhaps the third that most often leads to acceptance in modern democratic societies. It was what led — or what they say led — Governors Faubus and Wallace to accept integration of schools and universities. It accounts for our acceptance of damages assessed by courts. With some disgruntled murmurings, it is why people accept the salaries paid to MPs and to ministers (and to Congressmen and to governors). It contributes to the cheerfulness toward which every family strives.

There has not been agreement for thirty years on what is fair in the realm of wage determination. As between miners and electricity supply workers, or as between school teachers and doctors resident in hospitals, there is no agreement upon what, precisely, a share should be. Even where there is agreement that one group should be paid more than another — as there probably is between toolmakers and those who clean up the plant — there is nothing like enough precision to permit a mutually satisfactory settlement. Recent disputes between employees and employers, between the shopfloor and the leaders of the TUC, between the TUC and the government, between the ministry of health and the younger doctors in hospital service, constitute persuasive argument that agreement upon the equitable is not in the immediate offing. The first condition does not exist in Britain today.

Neither does the second condition. Nearly everyone is convinced that he or she does not have to accept the present distribution of income. The same events that make clear the lack of agreement on what is fair are the evidence that each group thinks that it can do something about the distribution of income. And in a liberal democracy the government is hardly in a position to use the force and violence that might persuade them otherwise.

Which leaves the third condition: agreement on the process. And recent events leave little doubt that agreement about or even acquiesence in any process is lacking. Trade unions and much of the Conservative Party reject arbitration. When the TUC and the government have agreed on a wages policy for a year in advance — as they did in July of 1975 and July of 1976 — the strains created by general adherence to the policies for two years made it impossible for the TUC to enter a similar "social compact" for a third year. If the TUC and the stewards representing shopfloor workers will not accept decisions by a Labour government, a fortiori they will not accept parliamentary processes for wage determination when the Conservatives govern. The rhetorical agreement on the process of "free collective bargaining" amounts to no more than a rejection of any form of wage determination — for there is no agreement that the result of a "free collective bargain" will be binding upon the third parties; and if third parties will not accept the relative shares in income implied by the bargain there has been no determination of real incomes beyond that short period that it takes for third parties to alter the actual, substantial content of that "free collective bargain" that all say they want.

What should Britain do? I do not know. In any case, it would hardly be suitable for me to say. It is not my country and they have not asked my advice. Rather than trying to answer the question, let us consider where the argument has led so far and what its implications are.

AN EMERGING CONSENSUS?
THE PROSPECT FOR FAIR INSTITUTIONS

Thus far the argument implies a rather cheerless or at least an unstable and confusing future. Some, in more dismayed moments, may be inclined to predict that an authoritarian state must emerge to force compliance with its decisions upon all. No one who has spent some portion of his life on this planet since 1930 can dismiss such a prediction out of hand, but human attitudes, unlike Euclidian shapes, change. Despite a deeply ingrained fear of inflation, it has not been definitely established that a civilized, industrial society cannot live in a state of perpetual inflation with quickly shifting relative incomes. Certainly many of the legal instruments of property — the standard mortgage, bond, savings account, or insurance policy — cannot survive in such a world. But we are already thinking up many forms of indexation. If democratic, liberal societies could survive the period 1929–1945, they must certainly have a resilience that could — of course, not necessarily will — allow them to adjust and adapt to chronic inflation. Instead of a heart attack or a coronary, the medical analogy may turn out to be the common cold, or even the morning-after hangover.

Quite aside from the authoritarian and the "if you can't get what you want, want what you get" possibilities for a new consensus, there remains the possibility of changes in attitudes. The idea that a common view of precisely what income each role is worth will emerge can be classified as wishful thinking. Different people in different situations will always view the positions of others and the nature of the whole differently. But, as indicated above, there does seem to be some agreement already on broadly stated principles: that in some as yet unspecified degree, danger, skill, responsibility, and essentiality should be rewarded. Perhaps also people will begin to view willingness to put up with boredom as a trait to be rewarded. Given some consensus on the characteristics worthy of reward, there are probably many ways in which a generally acceptable process might be institutionalized. To argue for the model that charms one today is a road to utopian foolishness, but suggesting elements that might (or might not) contribute to the process may indicate that there can be roads to real places too.

Commissions of all sorts could weigh evidence and set rates. "All sorts" includes the elected and the appointed; the representative and the delegatory; the expert and the man on the street; the parliamentary, the extra-parliamentary, and the subparliamentary. "Evidence" might embrace anything from industrial injury statistics to legal briefs to opinion polls to systems of preferential voting. How the British — or any other people — might put these and many other elements together, I do not know. The belief that it is possible need not be founded upon a persuasive argument for this or that possible set of institutions, but it rests upon the fact that institutionalized ways of doing things have emerged, been invented, and been restructured by the species since the fifth millenium B.C., perhaps since Olduvai Gorge. Mention of a current example may illustrate the point. Modern industrial nations have tax systems of enormous complexity. Legislatures, lobbyists, revenue services, administrative courts and boards, negotiators, assessors, referees, and appeals courts play roles almost, if not totally, impossible to disentangle. No single principle governs; no specifiable set of six or sixteen or any number of principles can be identified as governing (although some principles may clearly be more important than others). And these tax systems work — not in all nations, but in some. The processes are accepted. Year after year some results of the processes are felt to be "wrong," to be less desirable than some other results that seem possible or at least worth a try. The processes are then amended.[9] If tax systems can be run in such disorderly fashion, then there is no a priori, unavoidable, ineluctable reason why systems for fixing incomes cannot emerge, grow, and change in disorderly but morally and politically acceptable ways.

Whatever the solution to inflation (including learning to live with it), in one of five or ten years' time, two remarks can be made about the prospects. The first is that it is very unlikely that policies of fiscal or monetary management alone will succeed in controlling inflation. Just as all policies do, they depend for their success upon a widespread acceptance of the results they produce. Neither fiscal nor monetary policies, certainly as currently conceived, even begin to answer questions about who should get how much for what, let alone provide generally approved solutions. That they do not determine relative incomes has been one of their supposed virtues, and it could be regarded as a virtue if — but only if — there was consensus that the relative incomes determined elsewhere in the system were proper. In the absence of such consensus, fiscal policy will almost certainly always tend to be inflationary. The monetarist cure is no more than an attempt to revive with a new terminology one of the elements of the pre-1914 consensus. But with that consensus lost, the consequences of monetarist policy will be unacceptable and each episode of strong monetary restraint will be abortive. Which is not to say that there cannot be roles for either fiscal or monetary policy.

Secondly, we can remark that new institutional arrangements must (and will) emerge to make it possible to reach a widely and mutually acceptable system for distributing income. It will be within such a new context, but not until such a new context has evolved, that the policy guidelines of Keynes and of the monetarists, the directives and decisions of the Bank of England, and the budgets of Conservative and Labour chancellors will find effective but more limited roles.

ENDNOTES

1. Walter Friedenberg (Scripps-Howard staff writer), "Italy's Anguish," Part 1, *Knoxville News-Sentinel* (February 5, 1978: p. 1, and other Scripps — Howard newspapers of that date, I assume).

2. Robert Bacon and Walter Eltis, *Britain's Economic Problem: Too Few Producers* (London: The Macmillan Press Ltd., 1976), pp. 31, 100.

3. Joan Robinson, *Essays in the Theory of Employment* (Oxford: Basil Blackwell, 1947, c1937), pp. 1–28, and esp. pp. 6–17. If this chapter ("Full Employment") had not been published in 1937 it would make an original and perceptive article in a journal today.

4. In late autumn of 1977 ministers in the Labour government began making remarks — rather off-handedly, perhaps in the spirit of what Americans call "trial balloons" — indicating that they thought some other system of wage determination ought to be found and made permanent. The trade unions, however, are showing no inclination to go along.

5. I do not mean here to deny that increasing productivity should be a prime aim of British policy, certainly so long as Britain is so tied in as it is to world markets and to the free trade area of the EEC. The point is that "productivity" is a referent that need not be justified because it is not questioned — as opposed to, say, being a part of an argument that for the moment foreign market dictates must be heeded until it is possible to sort out some other, better way in a better ordered world.

6. This certainly does not mean that the hope is wrong, or meaningless, or that the British should not employ more social workers, or that bad mistakes are being made. It is not necessary that one be able to say "86" in order to be able to say that an act is kind or good or better, or nasty or foolish.

7. Commissions appointed to fix the salaries of higher level civil servants at the market equivalent of "top salaried" private executives — of course allowing for differences in security of tenure and fringe benefits — are obviously designed to find such a going rate. Comments upon the going rates discovered (and adjusted) indicate that, whatever is conceivably possible, the commissions do not arrive at clearly acceptable or justified rates — at least one issue out of four of *The Economist* (the weekly journal of modern social science commentary that still badly wants to believe in the beneficent efficiency of markets) has nasty comments to make on the pay of civil servants.

8.   While these facts are taken by many as obvious criticisms of British policy, I do not cite them here in that spirit. In fact, I think the British government would have been crazy to shut down Rolls Royce or British Leyland — at least as crazy as would have been an American government that sold the Penn Central's track and rolling stock for scrap.

9.   The reader who thinks that this presentation owes a large intellectual debt to Commons is quite right.

12 SOURCES AND SYMPTOMS OF MONETARY INSTABILITY

Thomas Havrilesky

PROLOGUE: AN INSTITUTIONALIST MONETARY THEORY?

Monetary theory is not exactly a haven for institutionalists. Yet an institutionalist perspective can help illuminate the penumbra of controversy that confounds the field. Monetary theorists continually join battle over Keynesian versus monetarist views regarding the structure of the economy. This paper proposes, first, that the distribution of income and political discordance influence the stability of monetary policy and, second, that the stability of monetary policy in turn influences the structure of the economy, Keynesian or monetarist, that will be observed and estimated. Therefore, the relationship between the polity and the economy, one of the elemental interests of institutionalism, is also of considerable relevance for contemporary monetary economics.

I am grateful to John Adams, Martin Bronfenbrenner, Ronald Rogowski, and Joseph Spengler for helpful comments. Some of the ideas developed in this paper were spawned in an inflation seminar that I led for Pieter Korteweg at Erasmus University in Rotterdam in 1977.

Positing a connection between the monetary and the political, this paper defends the case for monetary stability and explores appropriate strategies for advancing it in a milieu of unremitting pressures for politically expedient "easy money."

THE STABILITY OF STABILIZATION POLICY

Economists typically see stabilization policy as a constrained maximization problem. In the most naive form of this view the policymaker is assumed to maximize an assumed fixed and independent preference function subject to an assumed fixed and independent hypothetical structure of the economy.

For decades discussion of stabilization policy has been dominated by this simplistic vision. The image, conjured up for generations of students, has been one of hardheaded policymakers, their preferences molded by democratic mandate, nimbly adjusting the controls of an economic machine labeled Money Supply, Interest Rates, Autonomous Government Expenditures, and Tax Rates. Schooled in the mathematics of classical mechanics applied to the fancied workings of this economic machine, the learned have regaled their students with tales of the vast bounty of output and employment that could be "multipliered" and "acceleratored" out of it by skillful policymakers. Economists' celebrations of this paradigm have reached such delirious proportions that alternative approaches to stabilization policy have virtually disappeared from the principles textbooks. Lost to most students, except for the few who went on to a painful unlearning in advanced courses, was any connection between this vision and the constrained choice and learning process of individuals and related efficiency criteria taught in courses in basic price theory.

Then, in its hour of greatest popularity and triumph, the vision began to fail. From the mid-1960s to the mid-1970s, the performance of the economy grew worse. Steadily increasing inflation was replaced by steadily increasing unemployment, which was followed, in turn, by steadily increasing inflation *and* unemployment. What went wrong? The stabilization policy paradigm allowed economists only two explanations: either the preferences of the policymakers had changed or part of the underlying economic structure had shifted; either the policymakers had wavered in their resolve to bestow low inflation and low unemployment on the nation or else something was seriously amiss inside the economic machine.

Certainly a cogent case could be made that changes took place in the preferences of the policymakers. For years critics of the Federal Reserve System had pointed out that it had never fully specified its own economic objectives. Could it be that Federal Reserve officials recognized that an apparent poor performance could always be rationalized by ex post adjustment of the weights that they said they applied to different objectives?[1] The shifting of policymaker preferences moved from the realm of possibility to that of reality when statistical evidence was uncovered to suggest a gradual decay in the Federal Reserve's antiinflationary militance during the 1964–1972 period[2] and, perhaps, again in the 1976–1978 period. In addition, some observers claimed that sound monetary policy suffered when Arthur Burns assumed the Chairmanship of the Board of Governors of the Federal Reserve System in 1970 and collapsed in inflationary chaos when Richard Nixon, desperate to secure his grip on the Presidency, stimulated the economy drastically before the 1972 election.[3] Growing numbers of economists are attracted to the notion that a business cycle is initiated by Presidential incumbents who can woo myopic voters by more or less deliberately exciting the economy prior to election years and contracting it afterwards.[4]

Persuasive indeed are the arguments that quantum revisions have occurred in policymakers' preferences in the past decade. Equally compelling, however, are the contentions that the structure of the economy has changed profoundly over the same period. Econometric studies reported a shift in the demand for money in the early 1970s.[5] And, structural variations were probably not confined to money markets. If any *two* of the several garden varieties of the Phillips curve had obtained empirically in the past decade, labor markets would also have experienced rather drastic turnarounds in behavior.[6] Moreover, if the long-run Phillips curve has actually assumed the exotic upward tilt recently proposed by Friedman, then labor markets have gone through more alterations than Jackie Gleason's wardrobe.[7]

TWO TYPES OF INSTABILITY

Thus there is considerable evidence that neither the pattern of preferences of the policymaker nor the structure of the economy has remained fixed over the past decade. This implies that the paradigm of stabilization policy itself may be suspect. Of what use is the conventional approach to stabilization policy if the policymakers' objective function and the constraining economic structure are rapidly changing?

Consider first the problem of structural change (ignoring, for the time being, the volatility of the preference function). In operational models of the economy, no parameters are known with certainty. Moreover, it is widely recognized that parameter estimates will be modified from time to time. The implicit conventional understanding is that structural change is driven by slow and steady motivating forces, such as technological innovation. Therefore, structural change is not perceived by the vast majority of economists to be an insurmountable problem for the conventional stabilization policy paradigm. Experience combined with scientific progress is assumed to be capable of reducing the random components more rapidly than technological change can do the reverse.

Unfortunately, we appear to be living in a world where the structure is not only shifting fairly rapidly but one in which this is accompanied by alterations in the preferences of the policymaker. The presence of two types of instability should arouse more skepticism toward the stabilization policy paradigm than would the existence of purely gradual and independent structural changes. How should the approach to policy be revised if there is reason to believe that preferences *and* structure will continue to shift together in the future?

For an answer to this question, a broader perspective will be helpful. Institutional economics has always been concerned with the adaptation of market behavior, reflected in the estimated structure of the market economy, to changes in values, reflected in this case by the shifting preferences of the monetary policymaker. In addition, institutional economics has traditionally been concerned with the impact of social changes (transmitted in the present case through the behavior of the monetary policymaker) upon the structure of the economy. In particular, an institutionalist vantage point will provide insight into the debate between Keynesians and monetarists by illuminating how monetary policy is influenced by the political discordance over the distribution of income and how monetary policy, in turn, influences observed structural (market) relationships in the economy. Such a perspective has unsettling implications. For if political considerations help to determine which theory of the structure of the economy will more closely approximate reality, then *the choice between Keynesian and monetarist theories is really an epiphenomenon, a mere reflection of anterior processes.*

THE NEW CASE FOR A STABILIZATION RULE

In order to examine theories regarding the structure of the economy and the policies that influence that structure, it will be useful to examine the frontiers of conventional thought regarding monetary stabilization policy. Proudly poised on that frontier is what has come to be known as the rational expectations hypothesis.[8] This hypothesis suggests that economic agents will not discard, a priori, any means of generating information that may prove useful in developing more accurate expectations regarding the future. Among the many means of developing more accurate expectations is investment in ways of predicting policymaker behavior. Thus, the behavior of individual economic agents, as estimated in the behavioral relations of a hypothetical model of the economic structure, may actually reflect expectations regarding the objectives of policymakers.

Thus, according to the rational expectations hypothesis, changes in the structure of the economy may not be unrelated to changes in objectives of policymakers.[9] If the economy is in equilibrium and if changes in monetary policy objectives are anticipated, then economic agents will adjust their behavior so as to minimize the effect of anticipated monetary stabilization policy on their desired allocations; equilibrium values of real variables and the estimated structure will be relatively stable over time. If, for example, given a fixed preference function, any monetary policy action is perfectly anticipated by the public, then (assuming wage-price flexibility) changes in money supply growth rates will affect only nominal wages and prices and can have no effect on real wages and the allocation between labor and leisure and hence on output and employment. Only unexpected shifts in policymaker preferences, resulting in surprise variations in money supply growth, can generate unanticipated inflation, temporarily alter the perceived real wage and interest rates, thereby change the structural responses of labor suppliers, labor demanders, and asset holders to observed inflation, and consequently affect output and employment temporarily.

Thus in the long run, with all policy actions fully anticipated, the estimated structure is relatively stable. In the short run, if all policy actions are not fully anticipated, unless estimators have accurate knowledge of how behavioral responses to unanticipated policy actions are formed, the estimated structure will not be so stable. The systematic interdependence between preferences and structure virtually eliminates the ability of policymakers to affect output and employment in the long run and, given the state of current knowledge, greatly diminishes their ability to predict the effects of imperfectly anticipated policy actions on output, employment, and prices in the short run. Thus, the rational expectations hypothesis casts considerable doubt on the usefulness of the constrained maximization paradigm as it has typically been applied to monetary stabilization policy.

Recent papers have contended that control theory, a popular variation of standard thinking on stabilization policy, is not likely to result in optimal policy actons.[10] Fischer argues that under the rational expectations hypothesis current public decisions depend upon expected future policy and "there is no mechanism" (in control theory) "to induce *future* policymakers to consider the effect of their policy on current decisions of the public.''[11] In other words, current changes in policymaker preferences will affect current public expectations, which will create changes in the estimated structure, which will, in turn, require future changes in policy and affect current public expectations.

Under the assumption that the only goal of stabilization policy is to have predictable effects on macroeconomic variables and thereby promote efficiency in the economy, these considerations imply that any stabilization policy action that instigates structural change should be avoided unless those structural changes are so small or so distant as to be easily discounted.[12] Therefore, only a regime of stabilization rule would be acceptable; *only a rule would be perfectly anticipated and thereby minimize policy-induced structural changes.*

THE STABILITY OF PREFERENCES
AND THE TYPE OF ECONOMIC STRUCTURE

The preceding analysis suggests a systematic connection between the stability of the preference function of the policymaker and the structure of the economy. The rational expectations hypothesis indicates that a regime of stable and hence perfectly anticipatable policy actions will generate a stable structure in which policy actions have no effect on output and employment — a neoclassical world — and a regime of unstable and hence imperfectly anticipatable policy actions will generate an unstable structure in which policy actions have some, generally unpredictable, effect on output and employment and prices.

Another connection between preferences and structure may exist if an unpredictable policy environment persists over long periods of time. This would tend to foster greater uncertainty in the behavior of economic agents. Pervasive uncertainty about future prices, wages, and interest rates generates inelastic price, wage, and interest rate expectations, and it is these inelastic expectations that are the root cause of the highly wage-elastic labor supply, highly interest-elastic money demand, and highly interest-inelastic expenditures relations that characterize a Keynesian economic structure. Inelastic expectations impede the ready adjustment of prices, wages, and interest rates to economic perturbations, that is, they result in "sticky" wages and prices. In the face of excess demand, market decision makers will not know the "correct" market-clearing prices for goods, services, and productive factors. Consequently, they will adjust the *quantities* they exchange rather than the *prices* at which equilbrium quantities are exchanged. In this fashion, an economy becomes more prone to quantity adjustments of production and employment to exogenous shocks.[13]

The same crippling uncertainty helps to explain those volatile "animal spirits" — that is, unstable expenditures and money demand relations — that permeate the world view of unreconstructed Cambridge (England) Keynesians.

Thus, an unpredictable stabilization policy tends to result in quantity adjustments to "surprise" policy actions and, if persistent over longer periods, results in the pervasive uncertainty that "Keynesianizes" the structure of the economy.[14] If uncertainty is the philosopher's stone of Keynes's world view, then an unpredictable policy environment is the crucible in which it is refined. Conversely, a predictable monetary environment tends to generate a neoclassical structure of ready price adjustments to predictable policy actions and, over longer periods, of relatively elastic price, wage, and interest expectations that result in wage-price flexibility.

This leads to the question: May there not be a systematic pattern in the way the structure of an economy behaves over time? There is considerable evidence that as *macro*economic policy activism creates a Keynesian structure, it is complemented by *micro*economic policies that tend to help preserve that structure. As an example, we have already discussed how unstable macroeconomic policy leads to inelastic (or adaptive) expectations in the labor market. This results in a negatively sloped, perhaps even flat, long-run Phillips curve. Humphrey has argued that this type of Phillips curve, in turn, can be and has been used to rationalize a wide array of microeconomic government interventions in the market, ranging from wage-price guidelines and controls (to "root out" inelastic expectations) to manpower policies (to shift the Phillips curve into a "more favorable" position).[15] As another example, macroeconomic policy instability can be shown to lead to high nominal market rates of interest arising from anticipated inflation and greater risk premiums. Such high interest rates serve, in turn, as the primary justification for a wide variety of microeconomic government interventions in the credit market ranging from ceilings on deposit rates of interest and regulations on mortgage rates of interest to restrictions on the assets and liabilities of financial intermediaries and even direct credit allocation by government.

It is, therefore, rather ironic that government interventions in labor and credit markets tend to perpetuate the kinds of price, wage, and interest stickiness upon which they are often predicated. Moreover, some of this stickiness can perhaps be allayed to the uncertainty generated by stabilization policy. *Consequently there seems to be a remarkable complementarity between the unstable macroeconomic policy environment that generates a Keynesian structure and the concomitant microeconomic policy actions that follow from that structure and, at the same time, help to perpetuate it.*

THE INFLATIONARY CONSEQUENCES OF THE IMPACT OF DISTRIBUTIONAL CONSIDERATIONS ON MONETARY POLICY

Having argued that complementarity between microeconomic and macro-economic policy actions will help perpetuate an economic structure, let us now examine the source of macroeconomic policy instability. What accounts for the apparent shifts in the preference function of the policy-maker? In addition to the conventional problems of inflation, unemployment, and exchange rates, factors such as the funding and refunding of the government debt, union contract negotiations, oligopolistic price increases, and the behavior of natural resource pricemakers seem to have sporadic impacts on monetary policy. During the early 1970s, for example, Federal Reserve officials claimed that the strength of the oil cartel made traditional antiinflationary militance even more untenable. At other times, during the late 1960s, they said that the size of the federal deficit, and a related crisis in the housing sector, or excessive nominal wage increases required an accom-modating monetary policy.[16] One is drawn to the conjecture that the apparent erratic element in the behavior of the policymaker, and hence the instability that bedevils the economy, arises from the effect of these excep-tional forces on the behavior of the monetary authority. Moreover, it appears that these "special" circumstances have a common thread running through them. They reflect the systematic importance of distributional con-siderations in monetary policy deliberations. Whenever the monetary au-thority has altered its preferences, changed its conventional reactions to the state of the economy, and relaxed its commitment to a specific money growth target, it seems to have done so because of pressures on the economy or sectors of the economy arising ultimately from attempts by groups to improve their position in the distribution of national or world income.

A good example of how distributional considerations impinge on mone-tary policy involves the relation of the government budgetary process to ostensible shifts in the preference function of monetary policymakers. For many economists the budgetary process is viewed as a sequence of delib-erate, cost-benefit calculations. This perspective does little to illuminate the actual relationship between the government budgetary process and monetary policy. The manifestly destabilizing monetary policies of many western economies in recent decades could hardly have been grounded in ultrarational governmental budgetary deliberations. A better perspective on monetary policy can be gained if, instead, both government expenditures and the taxation process are viewed as outcomes of a complex array of distributional pressures, wherein the costs and benefits are perceived only after long lags.

Let us first outline, rather impressionistically, the roles played by elected officials, voters, and bureaucrats in the determination of the size of government expenditures. The evasiveness of elected officials on the proper allocation of national income between public and private expenditures is legendary. Politicians seem to win office on the basis of their promises to deliver governmental largesse, not on pledges regarding how these services will be financed; This rule of thumb is caricatured by the old maxim for politicians "never vote for a tax or against an appropriation." Opinion leaders in the press and communications seem to applaud, somewhat ingenuously, activism in government, often with little regard to future outcomes. The present ambience of domestic and international ideological struggle heightens a government's tendency to overreact to real or imagined crises. Voters tend adamantly to support particular spending programs from which they benefit while remaining only vaguely opposed to "excessive government." The archetypical bureaucrat often seems to have precious little incentive to do anything other than promote the growth of his domain.

The result of these incentives facing elected officials, voters, and bureaucrats is that information regarding the costs and benefits of government programs is likely to be unreliable or inefficiently utilized until after a lengthy lag. In such an environment it is naive to regard the allocation of income between public and private uses as the upshot of stolid, ultrarational, cost-benefit deliberations. Moreover, the ultrarational viewpoint provides little insight into the related problem of monetary instability.

The ultrarational conception of the budgetary process seems even less credible when it is extended to the financing of government expenditures. Given the size of government expenditures, it is often contended that consideration of administrative and tax avoidance costs of various modes of taxation determine how the expenditures will be financed. Once again, this disposition cannot easily explain the interrelation between the budgetary process and monetary instability.

Consider a world in which there are two kinds of taxation, conventional income taxation and taxation from fully anticipated inflation. There will be a marginal cost relation associated with each type of taxation, and a cost-minimizing mix between the two types of financing may ideally be attainable. Now assume that there occurs a "temporary" increase in the desired size of government. It is commonly argued that massive boosts in conventional taxation are costlier to collect and generate a greater private investment in tax avoidance than increases in taxation from inflation.[17] Even when the welfare burden of the inflation tax is considered, which it seldom is, it is often said that this form of taxation is less costly than its alternative.[18]

INFLATION AND THE MARKET SYSTEM

From the perspective of monetary theory, this ultrarational explanation of inflation is not particularly appealing. Too many of the costs associated with inflation are too easily ignored. Recent experience shows, for example, there will be sizeable private expenditures in avoiding the tax from anticipated inflation by finding substitutes for cash. Some instances of capital expenditures in this area are investments in credit card technology, point of sale terminals, and electronic funds transfer systems. Some examples of current expenditures are outlays to manage more closely a cash position and to search for and provide more credit, including trade credit. Other costs include the cost of gathering information in order to anticipate inflation more accurately, i.e., to avoid any tax from unanticipated inflation, as well as the cost of changing money prices. Another important class of costs associated with anticipated inflation stems from the observation that high rates of inflation distort relative prices and increase the instability of money prices about their trend.[19] This, together with the uncertainty created by inflation, reduces the information content of any price and may generate considerable costs of searching for additional price information and avoiding the risks of inflation. The added uncertainty may also shorten the time horizon of the capital investment decision and result in lower rates of private capital formation. In short, the more rapid the inflation the greater the rate of depreciation of price information. Thus, inflation not only reallocates resources away from individuals who make frequent price searches, but it also reallocates resources away from productive activity to forecasting and risk transferring.

Many other sources of inefficiency and redistribution associated with high and highly variable rates of inflation can be adduced. Suffice it to say that most of these arguments imply that persistent inflation damages the market-exchange subsystem of our social system. As the market diminishes as a social organizer, the domain of government involvement in the social system increases. Therefore, the persistence of monetary instability must be of concern to those who would preserve the market exchange system.[20]

A stable monetary environment allows the market to operate more efficiently. Unless one is ideologically compelled, as by acceptance of the Marxian dialectic, to embrace the notion that the success and efficiency of the market are incompatible with human progress, one may recognize that a stable monetary environment has considerable advantages even for planned economies (especially but not necessarily those economies with significant market sectors).[21] Private and public decision makers alike should be better able to forecast and therefore operate more efficiently in an environment that is relatively free of unexpected monetary perturbation. Not only would market-determined prices and wages be more predictable, but there would be less susceptibility to error in decision making arising from liquidity crises and recessions that are the product of an unstable monetary environment. Even if one believes that the domain of market allocation should be supplemented or even displaced by planning, it may be wisest to carry out such a transformation in a relatively stable monetary environment, such as exists in modern Switzerland or West Germany, rather than to sabotage the economy spiritually and materially through erratic monetary policies—such as have persisted in Great Britain or Italy—and then to proffer more "planning" as the "only hope."

The purpose here is not to make a case for or against planning, rather it is to show that a good deal of governmental activism is doomed to failure because it is enacted in an atmosphere of economic despair and inefficiency generated by destabilizing monetary policy. It is unfortunate that stabilization policy decisions in many countries are influenced by individuals who either ignore the long-run structural consequences of monetary activism or even applaud them, perhaps covertly, as consistent with the destruction of the market. In these cases intervention leads to a plea for planning as the private sector ironically finds itself increasingly reliant upon government to restore the certainty that its "stabilization" policies have eroded.[22] And this backwards and unintentional movement into planning is hardly the proper means of determining the desired amount and type of planning nor does it ensure any sort of long-run view of or control over where the economy is moving.

THE FORMULATION OF MONETARY POLICY

The preceding considerations make it appear unlikely that high inflation rates, similar to those experienced in western economies in recent years, could be the outcome of careful, well-informed policy deliberations. Moreover, the ultrarational approach to inflation cannot easily explain the variability of inflation rates, including intermittent attempts at deflation. It seems more reasonable to view the inflation associated with government spending as arising from the multiplicity of distributional considerations that influence the growth rate of government expenditures. In cases where governments (democratic or not) are confronted with resistance to higher taxes, the deficit financing of these expenditures grows rather persistently. The monetization of large and growing deficits introduces a proinflationary shift in the preference function of the monetary authority. As the costs of inflation become more fully perceived, the monetary authority will once again be induced to shift its preferences, this time to slow the inflation and thereby bring about recession by reducing liquidity and disappointing inflationary expectations. Thus, rather prominent swings in the preferences of the monetary policymaker underlie the inflation-recession process associated with the growth in government spending.

Let me be more specific. The growth in government deficits is, at least partly, motivated by distributional considerations. One consequence of this growth in an economy near full employment is upward pressure on market rates of interest and a crowding out of private by public expenditures. Even for an underemployed (inflexible nominal wage) economy, it has been shown that a bond-financed government deficit can exert far greater pressure on market rates than standard textbooks usually allow.[23] For fully employed (flexible wage) economies, of course, crowding out will generally be complete, regardless of how government spending is financed. A squeeze on credit is a direct consequence of an increased government deficit. Thus it is hardly surprising that monetary policymakers will often find themselves under pressure to mask the distributional and allocational effect of government deficits on interest rates by increasing the money supply. For example, in 1978 there were widely publicized appeals, coming from Congress and the President, to Federal Reserve officials to hold interest rates down. Increased liquidity will reduce market rates of interest as individuals use newly created money balances to acquire financial assets. The decline in interest rates will be temporary, however, because lower rates of interest will be inconsistent with the full-employment equilibrium level of output. The lower market rates will stimulate private expenditures and, in a fully employed economy, cause an increase in the general price level. The higher price level will reduce the real value of nominal financial wealth and cause market rates to rise to their initial levels.

If monetary policymakers continue to find themselves under pressure to do something about the distributional effects of "tight money," the money supply will continue to increase in the above manner, period after period, and any resulting liquidity effect of money on interest will, period after period, be wiped out by consequent increases in the price level. It is in this willy-nilly fashion, rather than through ultrarational deliberations, that government opts for inflationary financing and creates an unstable monetary environment. Upon discovering the true costs of inflation, public pressure may induce the monetary authority to curtail the money supply growth rate, whereupon the reduction in liquidity will temporarily drive interest rates even higher. The credit crunch will itself reduce aggregate expenditures and generate at least temporary underemployment.

This should not suggest that other problems of income distribution do not also impinge on monetary policy preferences. Consider, for example, either the effect of a wage settlement wherein nominal wage increases exceed productivity gains, or consider the effect of an international conflict whereby the price of an imported raw material rises. Either of these factors will increase costs to domestic business firms. Assume that these firms raise their prices in order to shift, in inverse relationship to the elasticity of demand, part of the cost on to consumers. There then ensues a general upward movement in nominal wages and prices as individuals endeavor to circumvent the loss in real income. The resulting increase in the general price level (the acceleration in inflation) would, ceteris paribus, reduce the real value of financial wealth in the economy and thereby drive interest rates upward and aggregate demand downward. The decrease in aggregate demand is likely to persist until, depending on the source of the initial increase in costs, either nonunion wages or prices and wages in industries other than that of the imported raw material fall. The attempt by certain groups to attain a higher income can, in the short run, reduce real aggregate income in the economy as a whole.

In this situation the monetary authority has a choice: it can wait for a corrective reduction in the price level (a deceleration in inflation) to its full-employment equilibrium level (rate of change) or, alternatively, the monetary authority can validate the new price level (the new rate of inflation) by increasing the money supply growth rate. While the latter "accommodating" alternative foregoes the necessity of a corrective adjustment in the economy, if part of a persistent policy, it results in an acceleration of inflation and ultimately the cyclical processes described above.

Monetary validation temporarily conceals the redistribution of income that is taking place. By increasing the money supply (or its rate of growth) the monetary authority may prevent an absolute decline in any nominal wages or prices and thereby temporarily (and partially) mask the decrease of certain relative wages and prices. We conclude that while the accommodating alternative is fruitless in the long run, because it cannot prevent the loss in real income that must occur in certain (nonunion or nonimported materials) sectors, it has two advantages in the short run: it ameliorates swings in real aggregate demand and it conceals the redistribution of income.

In the case of the growing bond-financed government deficit the monetary authority has a choice. It could allow interest rates to rise, consistent with a new equilibrium, or, in order to ease the squeeze on credit and cover up the redistribution that is taking place, it could try to sustain lower interest rates in the short run at the cost of further inflation and higher interest rates in the long run. In each instance, the monetary authority has in recent decades tended to resolve these choices on the side of more inflation in the present and episodic antiinflationary binges in the future.

AN INSTITUTIONALIST THEORY OF MONETARY INSTABILITY

Monetary officials often assert that the shifting distributional considerations that hamper their proper stabilization activity stem from the failure of elected officials, union leaders, and business men to resolve distributional conflicts effectively and realistically. On the other hand, individuals and organizations learn from experience that the central bank will try to protect the economy from the adverse short-run impact of their actions on production, interest rates, and employment and mask the redistribution that they are engineering. Given such an assessment, economic agents are generally willing to "bet" on more inflation in their decisions. They obviously believe it highly unlikely that the monetary authority could refuse to monetize a whopping deficit or validate a sizeable and significant wage-price hike without strong Congressional or Presidential support. In addition, public and private decision makers apparently perceive that the monetary authority, as a bureaucracy, can be expected to be notably eclectic in its reflexive willingness to appear to be able to "fine tune" the economy in response to shocks, including those arising from distributional problems. The monetary authority has apparently arrived at the conclusion that increased monetary ease can, at times, mollify distributional conflict.

It would be equally fanciful to suppose that elected officials, union leaders, and business men can regularly reach "noninflationary" decisions. Their bargaining is often the focal point of ideological and social antagonisms that make "fair" and "realistic" resolution difficult. Consequently, the monetary authority can often serve as a convenient scapegoat for their failures. Still, to drag the monetary authority further into the distributional morass usually widens the impact of the distributional conflict, impedes the economy, damages the market system, and tarnishes the legitimacy of the central banks as an institution.

From a static point of view, abstracting from social change, it is apparent that the Federal Reserve should reduce the degree to which it hedges the risk of parties to distributional conflicts; that is, it should attempt to sustain some semblance of "independence." From an evolutionary vantage point — a disposition that would regard distributional conflict as a reflection of underlying social and technological change—it may be fruitless to argue for a resolutely independent central bank with a perfectly stable preference function. As has been demonstrated in this paper, when redistributive problems mount, the central bank will yield to political pressures and cannot remain strictly independent. *A realistic outlook would be to develop a theory that recognizes that the distributive issues that give rise to monetary instability are concomitants of social change.*[24]

Social transformations and consequent income redistributions threaten the property and power bases of incipiently declining social classes. These groups then must tend to use their political power to resist change or else, because of weakening alliances, they will be subject to cooptive efforts and bargaining pressures from other groups. A redistribution of income would therefore tend to result in a marked increase in political discordance from groups threatened by the redistribution. When we attempt to measure the monetary policymaker's sensitivity to redistribution-induced discordance, there is evidence that recent U.S. monetary policy has been more erratic during periods when efforts are being made, privately or through government, to redistribute income.[25] As discussed earlier, rapid money supply growth *can* be used as a cosmetic to cover up redistribution, for example, from nonunionized to unionized labor, from property income to labor income, from raw material exporters to raw material importers, and from the private sector to the collective sector. It is my conjecture that rapid money supply growth *will* be used in this way to the extent that groups threatened by a redistribution can utilize political power to resist it.

Monetary stability historically tends to occur in social systems where either the amount of redistribution is relatively small, where the government is corporatist or authoritarian, or where groups that are threatened by a redistribution have little power in government. Under these conditions redistribution gives rise to relatively little discordance.[26] In contrast, where redistributive measures are sizeable and give rise to considerable discordance, monetary instability will result. These situations seem to arise historically where one group has gained political power and is able to press for a redistribution on its behalf but where the government (coalition) is too weak or dependent to allow the income of other groups to be overtly reduced. In these cases, rapid money supply growth is used to cover up temporarily the redistribution that is going on.[27] Circumstances such as this were present in Central Europe following World War I when new democratic regimes gave power to working class parties but could not afford to antagonize upper-and-middle-income groups. They were also present in post–World War II Latin America where many regimes came to power on the basis of urban and rural lower-class support but could not take resources away from upper-income groups. To some extent Jimmy Carter's coalition suffers a similar weakness—one of being pledged to help some groups while being politically unwilling to alienate others.

The modeling of social systemic processes is not the usual domain of the monetary economist. It is especially not the forte of central bankers and their advisors. Nevertheless, monetary stability simply seems to have more to do with social change, redistribution, and the resulting discordance than many economists usually care to admit.

Ideally, in order to understand monetary instability in an evolving social system, monetary economists should be armed with workable theories of the evolution of the economy and the polity.[28] We should want to know more about social change and its relationship to the redistribution of income and the redistribution of political power. Specifically, we would like to be able to predict the trade-off between the redistribution of income and political discordance. Is this a stable relationship or does it reflect a differential between the redistribution of income and the redistribution of political power? To the extent that the central bank cannot isolate itself from redistributive discordance, such knowledge would help us to anticipate erratic money supply behavior. To the extent that this cannot be predicted, monetary instability will continue to perturb the economy and policy-induced economic disturbances will continue to be one of the more acute vagaries of social change.[29]

SUMMARY

There is a great deal of evidence that neither the preference function of the policymaker nor the structure of the economy has been stable in the past decade. This casts considerable doubt on the standard view of stabilization policy: maximization of a fixed and independent preference function subject to a fixed and independent economic structure. The rational expectations hypothesis, since it suggests a relationship between changes in the policymakers' objective function and changes in the estimated structure, leads to the endorsement of a stabilization rule because such a rule would minimize policy-induced structural changes.

This paper contends that there is correspondence between the instability of the monetary environment and the type (Keynesian or neoclassical) of economic structure. It argues that there exists a remarkable complementarity between the macroeconomic policy activities that generate the economic structure and the concomitant microeconomic policy activities that follow from the structure and help to perpetuate it.

Finally, this paper argues that under certain circumstances the redistribution of income produces increased discordance that results in monetary instability. To the extent that political discordance is one of the unpredicted concomitants of the redistribution of income, monetary instability will continue to be one of its consequences.

ENDNOTES

1. Karl Brunner, "The Ambiguous Rationality of Monetary Policy," *Journal of Money, Credit, and Banking* 4 (February 1972): 3-12.

2. Central banks, usually acting as agents of central government, are supposed to be able to control the supply of money. Economists have estimated reactions of the monetary supply and other variables controlled by the monetary authority to the state of the economy as measured by the actual and predicted rates of price inflation, levels of unemployment, and other indices of economic well-being. The sign and direction of these monetary policy reactions roughly correspond to the implicit countercyclical mandate imposed on the central bank by government. Nevertheless, there is evidence that these reaction patterns are quite variable over time. Thomas Havrilesky, Robert Sapp, and Robert Schweitzer, "Tests of the Federal Reserve's Reaction to the State of the Economy, 1964-1974," *Social Science Quarterly* (March 1975): 835-852, reprinted in Thomas Havrilesky and John Boorman, *Current Issues in Monetary Theory and Policy* (Arlington Heights, Ill.: AHM, 1976).

3. Sherman Maisel, *Managing the Dollar* (New York: W. W. Norton, 1973).

4. C. Duncan MacRae, "A Political Model of the Business Cycle," *Journal of Political Economy* 85 (April 1977): 239-263.

5. Thomas Havrilesky and John Boorman, *Monetary Macroeconomics* (Arlington Heights, Ill.: AHM, 1978).

6. Thomas Humphrey, "Changing Views of the Phillips Curve," Federal Reserve Bank of Richmond, *Monthly Review* 58 (July 1973): 2-13. Reprinted in Havrilesky and Boorman, *Current Issues.*

7. Milton Friedman, "Nobel Lecture: Inflation and Unemployment," *Journal of Political Economy* 85 (June 1977): 451-472.

8. Thomas Sargent and Neil Wallace, "Rational Expectations and the Theory of Economic Policy," *Journal of Monetary Economics* 2 (January 1976): 3-37.

9. Sims and Lucas have argued that since expectations are at least partly rational, structural relations are functionally related to policy changes. Neftci and Sargent have tested for this dependence. See Christopher A. Sims, "Distributed Lags," in M. Intriligator and D. Ken-

drick, eds., *Frontiers of Quantitative Economics* (Amsterdam North Holland, 1974); Robert E. Lucas, "Econometric Policy Evaluation: A Critique," in Karl Brunner and Allan H. Meltzer, eds., *The Phillips Curve and Labor Markets* (Amsterdam: North Holland, 1976); and Salih Neftci and Thomas Sargent, "A Scrap of Evidence on the Natural Rate Hypothesis," Manuscript, 1976.

10. Finn E. Kydland and Edward C. Prescott, "Rules Rather than Discretion: The Inconsistency of Optimal Plans," *Journal of Political Economy* 85 (June 1977): 473-492.

11. Stanley Fischer, "Long-Term Contracts, Rational Expectations, and the Optimal Money Supply Rule," *Journal of Political Economy* 85 (February 1977): 191-206.

12. Edmund S. Phelps, *Inflation Policy and Unemployment Theory* (New York: W. W. Norton, 1972).

13. See, for example, A. C. Hines, *On the Reappraisal of Keynesian Economics* (London: Martin Robertson, 1971) reprinted, in part, in Havrilesky and Boorman, *Current Issues,* pp. 29-39.

14. A paper by Mullineaux indicates that uncertainty is greatest during periods of stabilization policy "surprises." Donald Mullineaux, "Inflation Expectations and Money Growth in the United States," Federal Reserve Bank of Philadelphia, *Research Paper No. 28,* (July 1977).

15. See Humphrey, "Changing Views."

16. See Maisel, *Managing the Dollar;* and Arthur Burns, "The Role of the Money Supply in the Conduct of Monetary Policy," Federal Reserve Bank of Richmond, *Monthly Review* 58 (December 1973): 20-23, reprinted in Havrilesky and Boorman, *Current Issues,* pp. 520-531.

17. Robert Gordon, "The Demand for and Supply of Inflation," *Journal of Law and Economics* 11 (December 1975): 817-836.

18. John A. Tatom, "The Welfare Cost of Inflation," Federal Reserve Bank of St. Louis, *Review* (November 1976).

19. See Benjamin Klein, "The Social Costs of the Recent Inflation: The Mirage of Steady, 'Anticipated' Inflation," in Karl Brunner and Allan H. Meltzer, eds., *Rochester Conference Series on Public Policy* (Amsterdam North Holland, 1974); and John Fleming, *Inflation* (London: Oxford University Press, 1976).

20. The link between the stability of (the value of) money and the success of the market is an ancient one. The famous Currency School versus Banking School or Mill-Attwood debate is replete with the pleas of the classicists for the importance of a stable (value of) money as a prerequisite for justice in contracts. John Stuart Mill, *Principles of Political Economy,* new edition, W. J. Ashley, ed., (1848; London: Longmans, Green, 1909), p. 552.

21. Extreme examples of monetary instability in a planned economy as well as Leninist ambivalence toward it can be found during the periods of War Communism and NEP in the early Soviet Union. See Alex Nove, *An Economic History of the Soviet Union* (Baltimore: Penguin Books, 1972), pp. 63-95. Other planners talk about once-and-for-all redistribution as a substitute for inflation. The Allende plan in Chile appears to have been an example of the latter. See, for example, Andrew Glyn and Robert Sutcliffe, *British Capitalism, Workers and the Profits Squeeze* (Baltimore: Penguin Books, 1975).

22. For another view of this process see Grant McConnell, *Private Power and American Democracy* (New York: Alfred Knopf, 1967).

23. Havrilesky and Boorman, *Current Issues,* ch. 12.

24. Clarence Ayres, "Beyond the Market Economy: Building Institutions That Work," *Social Science Quarterly* 50 (March 1970): 1055.

25. Similarly, monetary policy in earlier periods seems to bear a close relationship to distributional questions. Debate over various metallic monetary "standards" often appears, for

example, to have been predicated upon the desire of emergent mercantile interests for a money that was stable in value (and widely acceptable) in exchange in order to enhance trade, a money that could not easily debased by rulers.

As another example, controversies surrounding the quantity theory versus the commodity theory of the value of money arose largely from the desire of industrial and agricultural interests for ample growth in the supply of money (as a productive resource) while, at the same time, absolving it from responsibility for price level movements. In opposition stood international trading and banking interests who recognized the relationship between the quantity of money and its value.

26. See Walter C. Neale, "Income Distribution in the Welfare State, Consequences of a Loss of Consensus in Britain," ch. 11, above.

27. Discordance may be reflected by instability in formal electoral processes as well as by unruliness in nonelectoral modes of political "signaling." Because of the paucity of data in these areas we have developed and use an index of legislative turnover as a measure of political instability and use an index of man-hours lost per 1,000 workers because of strikes as a measure of unruliness. Preliminary work reveals a high positive correlation between these measures and monetary instability, as measured in the deviation of money supply growth rates from trend. For further development of this theory see Thomas Havrilesky, "A Theory of Monetary Instability," in Michael Cooley, Raymond Torto, and Herbert Kaufman, eds., *The Political Economy of Policymaking* (New York: Sage Publications, 1979). For some suggestive correlations see M. Panic, "The Inevitable Inflation." *Lloyds Bank Review* 16 (July 1976): 1–15.

28. For an alternative point of view on this matter, see Wallace C. Peterson, "Institutionalism, Keynes, and the Real World," *Journal of Economic Issues* 11 (June 1977): 201–228.

29. Technological change is not only the source of shifts in the structure of the economy, as explained earlier in this paper, but, through the social change and hence distributive discordance it spawns, it is also the cause of variations in the preferences of the monetary policymaker which, as described earlier, induces further shifts in the structure.

13 INSTITUTIONALISM AND MICROANALYTIC SIMULATION OF ECONOMIC SYSTEMS

Robert L. Bennett

Most of the institutionalist economists who are alive today learned from Gruchy's *Modern Economic Thought* what institutional (holistic) economics was all about and how it differed from orthodoxy. Particularly in the first and final chapters Gruchy provides a lucid and thought-provoking analysis of the fundamental differences between these two ways of defining and practicing economic science. The basic assumptions that set holistic economics apart are:

> The total economic system . . . (is) . . . a cultural process or going concern rather than a mechanism or equilibrium of stable economic relations.

> All economic behavior . . . (is) . . . social or collective in the sense that all individual economic acts are carried on within the total . . . organizational complex known as the economic order.

> Man is largely a creature of habit . . . by nature essentially a cooperative being, and . . . his reason is basically of an exploratory rather than a contemplative nature . . . . [1]

Great emphasis is placed on the inadequacy of orthodoxy's mechanistic, Newtonian view of the economy compared with the evolutionary, Darwinian view of the institutionalists.

172

Institutionalists usually emphasize the following ideas as fundamental in their approach to policy questions:

1. The economy should be studied as an evolving cultural system in which technological change is continually presenting the institutional arrangements with new situations requiring adaptation.
2. The parts of the economic system are sufficiently interrelated, interacting, and diverse that analysis of the parts in isolation is relatively unrewarding and, perhaps, misleading as a guide for policy.
3. Evolution and the emergence of new phenomena are so pervasive as to render static equilibrium analysis of the economic system virtually worthless as a guide for policy.
4. Policy recommendations should be based far more on empirical and experimental analysis than has been usual and far less on introspection and logical deduction from a set of possibly unrealistic assumptions.

The thesis of this paper is that microanalytic simulation of the economic system is a tool particularly well suited to the institutionalist methodology and its basic assumptions about the economy and economic decisionmakers. This tool, developed by Orcutt in the 1950s, is only one of several advances in macroeconomic science that have resulted from rapid development of computer, mathematical, and statistical technology and science in recent decades.[2] But whereas the other major advances are subject to the same disabilities that have drawn the fire of institutionalists for years, this is not necessarily the case for microanalytic simulation.

MICROANALYTIC MODELS

A distinguishing characteristic of microanalytic models is the depiction of economic activity as taking place through the explicit decision making of microeconomic units — individuals, families, firms, and governments. Each of these decision-making units is composed of a set of characteristics — such as age, occupation, skills, or assets in the case of an individual. A set of behavior rules describes the way in which the unit will respond to different circumstances. The physical embodiment of a microanalytic simulation model is data and a program available to a computer. The data give the characteristics of each of the decision units; the program describes their behavior rules and the timing of their individual decisions.

Simulated activity occurs as the decision units survey their characteristics and make their programmed decisions; these in turn may alter the characteristics that they and others will face in the next round of decision making. A particular individual, for example, may have the characteristics of a particular job skill, be unemployed, and have a job offer from a particular firm. A decision may be made to accept the job offer. In that case, the individual's characteristics of being unemployed and having that particular job offer, and the firm's characteristic of having the job opening, are changed for the next round of decision making.

A microanalytic model may be general equilibrium or general disequilibrium, depending on whether or not there is an attempt to attain a general equilibrium solution in a round of decision making.[3] It may be static or dynamic, depending on whether the simulation involves one or more than one round of decision making.[4] It may be deterministic or stochastic, depending on whether the probability is one or less than one that a specific set of circumstances will result in a specific outcome.[5]

INSTITUTIONALISM AND
MICROANALYTIC SIMULATION

Three aspects of microanalytic simulation methodology make it well suited to the institutionalist approach described above: (1) the possibility of its depicting the economic system as a dynamic process rather than a mechanism; (2) its focusing of attention on the actual decision-making process and actual characteristics of economic units; and (3) the possibility of its describing behavior rules for economic units with greater regard for realism.

The Economic System as a Process

The idea long emphasized by institutionalists that the economy must be studied as a process — as having a past, present, and future — fits very nicely in a dynamic general disequilibrium simulation in which the model moves through rounds of activities, continually evolving as new conditions emerge. The teleological problem of equilibrium systems — the danger that the model does what it is doing in order to attain an equilibrium — need not arise when the decision rules are formulated as reasonable facsimiles of the actual behavior rather than as rules designed to endure the possibility of attaining an equilibrium.

One might protest that a computer program in which all of the behavior rules must be written in advance of starting the simulation process is quite mechanistic — so much so that it is out of keeping with the institutionalist idea of economic activity as an evolutionary process. Consider for a moment, though, that economic models — whether institutionalist or otherwise — are concerned with predicting the results of alternative policies. When Tugwell recommended more social management, or Means recommended more national planning, or Commons recommended different bargaining procedures, they formulated an idea of the ways in which the economic process would be different as a result of incorporating their suggested institutional changes.[6] They considered that the responses of economic units to the changed circumstances were sufficiently predictable to warrant conclusions regarding the impact of the policy changes on the economic process. Thus, they implicitly predicted the decision rules for economic units faced with unfamiliar situations. The primary difference between the thought of the great holistic economists and the computer program of a microanalytic simulation is that in the latter the decision rules *must* be stated *explicitly*.

The issue is not whether the decision processes of economic units can be stated mathematically; the only issue is whether these decision rules can be predicted and, hence, stated explicitly. If the decision rules are predictable then they can be represented in the form "if A, then B," which suffices for the computer simulation. If the decision rules are not predictable with reasonable certainty, then even the great holistic economists are unable to foresee the consequences of changed policies.

Focusing on the Decision-Making Process

For microanalytic simulation the decision-making process is the heart of the model. The entire model, in fact, is the data on which decisions are based, the specific decision rules, and the sequencing of the decisions. Data gathering is thus focused on the behavior of individual decision makers — on identifying the data they use to make decisions, identifying precisely how they use those data, and identifying precisely the outcomes of this process. The types of data that are most useful are largely cross-sectional surveys of economic units and longitudinal studies that follow specific decision makers through time. The major creative effort in the construction and use of a microanalytic simulation model could well be designing the necessary surveys and experiments and even collecting the primary data.[7]

This contrasts sharply with the role of decision making in conventional macroeconomic empirical models. At the heart of conventional macroeconomic empirical analysis today is the large-scale simultaneous equation model used to forecast the future performance of the macroeconomy and to predict the effect of alternative public policies.[8] The basic components of such a model are the individual equations used to predict the value of dependent variables from the known or predicted values of one or more independent variables. Each of the equations is designed so as simultaneously to conform to the following rules; it must:

1. include a set of independent variables that adequately "explains" the variance of the dependent variable:
2. avoid violating the commonly accepted rules of statistical procedure;
3. conform with the other equations that make up the overall model;
4. require only data that are available already or that can be made available with reasonable dispatch; and
5. include only independent variables for which a reasonable microeconomic decision-making scenario can be described to link them with the dependent variable.

The microeconomic decision-making scenario is required in orthodox models to invest the equation with the legitimacy of being "theoretical" and, thus, to distinguish it from the results of a "fishing expedition" for independent variables, which might merely "explain" the variance of the dependent variable. In this conventional econometric model the scenario of decision making really performs only a veto function over the independent variables of the equation: a variable is eliminated if no believable scenario using it can be described or if some believable scenarios would specifically avoid its use. This peripheral role of the decision-making process in conventional macroeconomic models invites introspection in devising the scenarios rather than empirical investigation of the actual decision-making process, since the specification requirements for the decision rules are so modest.

Thus microanalytic simulation of the economic system has as a necessity that careful attention to the real world (at the expense of introspection), which has pervaded the practice of institutionalist economics from Veblen to the present.

Realism versus Computational Convenience

The difficulty of "solving" large simultaneous equation macroeconomic models has acted (1) to restrict the number of equations in the model and, hence, the number of parts of the economy that receive explicit attention; (2) to restrict the form of the equations and, hence, to limit types of relationships between the independent and dependent variables; and (3) to encourage the use of partial rather than general analysis since the general analysis is so complex. Each of these limitations moves the typical large-scale simultaneous equation model farther from the institutionalist ideals of realism and holism. But none of these limitations is necessarily applicable to microanalytic simulation.

The conventional econometric model of the economy is simultaneous rather than recursive—the equations are solved simultaneously rather than sequentially—because the effects of interactions among the parts must be considered before their equilibrium states can be determined. Currently, these models are usually solved each calendar quarter, largely because the data that are used to estimate the parameters of the models are available on a quarterly basis. During a quarter it is likely that economic units will make several of each of a number of types of decisions and, hence, will be influenced by the decisions of others that occur in the same data period. If a quarterly system were made recursive, much of the effect of this real world interaction would be either lost or badly miscalculated.[9] But this requirement of simultaneous solution is a major constraint on the number of equations and their complexity since computer storage capacity is limited.

When attention is focused primarily on decision making, a recursive system becomes more plausible and manipulable. The decision maker in fact is influenced only by events that have occurred prior to the time of the decision.[10] And no violence would be done to reality by making a sequence of a group of concurrent events if they do not affect each other. The microanalytic simulation can be designed so as to make the round of decision making (which is sequential and, hence, involves no interaction among the units) coincide with the periodicity of actual decision making rather than the periodicity of data from the macroeconomy.[11] In the purely recursive microanalytic model every decision made by every economic unit prior in time to the one in question can influence it, but no decision made later in time will affect it. Making the system fully recursive not only more nearly portrays the manner in which an individual economic unit behaves, it virtually eliminates the size of computer storage capacity as a restraint on the model, since at the instant of a particular decision only the data necessary for it need be in the computer.

Thus, not only does the microanalytic simulation methodology direct attention toward the empirical, experimental analysis of decision-making processes, but it also frees the analyst from the necessity of unwarranted simplification of reality in the interest of computational convenience. If the investigator finds that all individuals follow the same decision rule for some particular type of decision, then homogeniety can be assumed. On the other hand, if there is reason to suspect that individuals can reasonably be grouped into no fewer than a thousand categories, each of which follows a different decision rule, then that assumption can be accommodated. If the investigator finds that an enormous amount of information is brought to bear on a particular decision, that can be done in the microanalytic simulation.

As an illustration of the flexibility of microanalytic simulation in depicting a decision-making process, consider the following simple example designed to show how a consumer's tastes might be changed through advertising—a subject well known in institutionalist literature. Suppose a study of individual behavior indicates that (1) persons under twelve and over thirty years of age are influenced by television advertising but others are not, and (2) the specific nature of the influence is shifting .005 (one-half of 1 percent) of their weekly purchases of a particular type to products for which they have seen television advertising for twenty consecutive weeks at the expense of products for which they observed no television advertising. Product Sickies is advertising on program "Gross" that is seen weekly by 12 percent of the twelve to thirty age group. Product Healthies is the only product in the same category as Sickies that does not advertise on television.

Figure 13-1 is a flow chart of the weekly activities of each simulated person regarding a possible change in tastes for Sickies and Healthies. To make the decision for an individual requires current information on age (AGE), number of consecutive times "Gross" has been watched already (TIMES), and the usual fraction of this type of expenditure going to Sickies (PROPSICK) and Healthies (PROPHEALTH). Let us follow individual Joe through this process. If Joe is between twelve and thirty his tastes are not affected by advertising so the program exits. If Joe is in the susceptible age group, however, we determine whether or not he watched "Gross" this week by drawing a number from a uniform distribution table of random numbers between 0 and 1. If the number is equal to or less than .12 we say that Joe was in the 12 percent of the age group that watched "Gross." If Joe did not watch "Gross" this week, the program exits after setting TIMES back to zero, since his tastes would not be changed. If he watched "Gross" this week we update TIMES and exit if it is not exactly 20. If TIMES is 20 we add .005 to PROPSICK and subtract .005 from PROPHEALTH.

In this example the decision rules PROPSICK and PROPHEALTH are changed for a group of individuals in a specific age group who have exposed themselves to program "Gross" for twenty consecutive weeks. The study of individual behavior led us to program the possibility of different decision rules, and the specific rules for particular individuals developed from their engaging in a process of simulated economic activity.

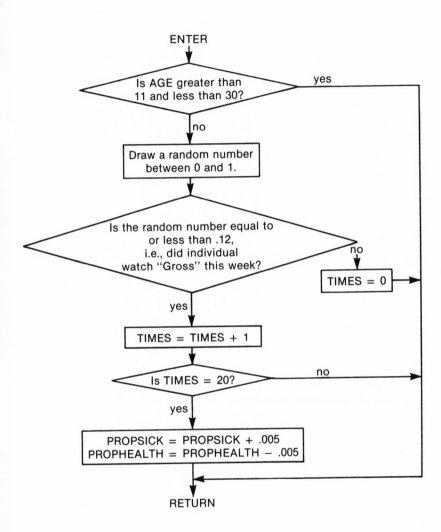

Figure 13-1. Flow chart illustrating change in consumer tastes by advertising

The fact that the microanalytic simulation methodology is so flexible in accommodating descriptions of reality makes it ideally suited to advancing the interest of institutionalists in basing policies on realistic, holistic predictions of economic behavior.

ENDNOTES

1. Allan G. Gruchy, *Modern Economic Thought: The American Contribution* (New York: Prentice-Hall, 1947), pp. 557, 563, 564.
2. Guy H. Orcutt et al., *Microanalysis of Socioeconomic Systems: A Simulation Study* (New York: Harper Bros., 1961).
3. An example of a general disequilibrium microanalytic model is Ebbe Yndgaard, *GDM: Computerization of Micro-founded Macro Econometric Models* (Aarhus, Denmark: Aarhus University, 1977). An example of a general equilibrium microanalytic model is the Adelman-Robinson model of the Korean economy developed in Irma Adelman and Sherman Robinson, *Planning for Income Distribution* (Palo Alto: Stanford University Press, 1977).
4. The Adelman-Robinson model is an example of the static type while the dynamic type is exemplified by that described in Robert L. Bennett and Barbara R. Bergmann, *A Microsimulated Transactions Model of the United States Economy* (forthcoming).
5. The various Orcutt models have been largely stochastic while that of Bennett and Bergmann is largely deterministic.
6. Gruchy, *Modern Economic Thought*, Chs. 3, 6, and 7.
7. This point was made forcefully by Barbara Bergmann in her 1974 presidential address to the Eastern Economic Association entitled "Have Economists Failed?," *Eastern Economic Journal*, supplement (July, 1975). In that address she recommended that even the so-called stars of the profession become involved in survey design and the data collection process and praised the activities of institutionalists along this line while castigating them for an inadequate theoretical structure.
8. An example of one such model is found in J. S. Duesenberry et al., *Brookings Quarterly Econometric Model of the U.S.* (Chicago: Rand McNally, 1965).
9. For example, assume that consumer spending in quarter $t(C_t)$ is a function that quarter's income (Y_t), and that current income is also a function of current consumer spending. Thus $C_t = f(Y_t)$ and $Y_t = f(C_t)$ among other factors. Simultaneous solution would allow for the interaction of these variable during quarter t, but recursive solution would require that one equation be solved and, then, that the solution value be used to solve the other equation. The use of quarterly data together with recursive solution would require saying either that $Y_t = f(C_{t-1})$ or that $C_t = f(Y_{t-1})$. One would predict the same Cs and Ys using these two methods only if C and Y did not change between the quarters in question.
10. Of course, these prior events may be used in the form of expectations concerning the future course of events.
11. For an elaboration of this point see Bennett and Bergmann, *A Microsimulated Transactions Model*, ch. 1.

IV PLANNING AND DEVELOPMENT IN THE THIRD WORLD

14

TECHNOLOGY, DEVELOPMENT, AND RESOURCES
Theory and Problem Solving in a Worldwide Context

Thomas R. de Gregori

Following World War II, great hope was expressed that something called technology could be harnessed to solve the problems of poverty in the world. The United States and, later, other governments carried out programs of technical assistance to further this vision. The United Nations created, or inherited from the League of Nations, agencies that provided technological aid in health, agriculture, and other areas of human concern. Three decades later, we view many outstanding achievements of these efforts, yet the initial promise is far from realized. In recent years, many have sought to understand the reasons for the failure of this promise. Some have blamed technologies; others have located the fault in the scale of the technology used or in its origins. We hear calls for new forms of technology: intermediate technology, appropriate technology, or indigenous technology. Rarely do any of the authors offer a definition of technology; it is assumed that we all know what the term means.

This paper will sketch a conceptualization of technology as problem solving. By this formulation all technology is appropriate by definition. This is not an attempt to dismiss a problem by the semantic legerdemain of defining it into nonexistence. Rather, it is an attempt to formulate a theory that allows us to define the nature of development more clearly and then to propose more effectively a technical means for its solution. In fact, many of the specific proposals of those who advocate intermediate or appropriate technology or indigneous technology have merit in certain circumstances. Without a clear conception of what technology is or can be, however, these theories are as subject to errors as those they are seeking to replace.

The institutionalist tradition in American economics, be it the theorizing of Veblen or Ayres or Commons or Gruchy, has always sought to understand economic processes in terms of larger patterns of technological change and institutional transformation. Nowhere is this perspective more virtually necessary than in the study of the Third World countries. It was said in the 1930s that all economists in Washington were institutionalists. A roughly similar statement could be made today, that most economists in the field in Third World countries are institutionalists. Making these statements about the 1930s or today, however, is more concealing than revealing. The statements seem to imply that all one needs to do to be an institutionalist is to abandon orthodox theory (or at least modify it at some points and be ready to abandon it at others) and be pragmatic and empirical. And they suggest a readiness, willingness, and ability to study the institutional structure and relate it to current and contemplated economic actions. These attributes may fit most institutional economists, but they also mean that any economist or social scientist could be an institutionalist merely by wanting to and by being open minded and eclectic. But this is not sufficient. Anyone with adequate intelligence can be an economist of any kind or an anthropologist or whatever, if he is willing to expend the time and effort to learn the body of theory and data necessary to accomplish the task. Being a institutional economist means having a particular mind-set and a mastery of a body of theory about technology and economic and institutional change.

It is precisely on this question of a theory change that institutional economics has the most to say about economic development problems in the Third World. For, as noted above, if an institutional economist were merely pragmatic and recognized the importance of technology and institutions, then almost everyone would qualify. In the colonial regimes and now in the independent nation states there was and is a widespread recognition that new technologies are needed to solve economic problems. Despite some significant, recalcitrant devotees of economic man, most persons dealing with development problems understand that there are social and cultural barriers — i.e., institutional resistances — that must be overcome for development to proceed. The recognition of the importance of technology in economic transformation is reflected in the emphasis that has been placed upon the introduction of new technology. But the very manner in which governments, be they colonial or postcolonial, have sought to introduce technology implies a deficient theory of technology. And the debates about appropriate technology or the scale of technology or the labor or capital intensity of technology indicate that pragmatism, in the vulgar use of that term, without theory, is woefully inadequate.

Looking at historic attempts to diffuse technology to Third World countries, one can reasonably infer an implicit theory of technology as gadgets. This is precisely the conception that Ayres and institutionalists sought to overcome. To Ayres, technology is a problem-solving process.[1] A tool must be adapted to the physical characteristics and skills of the user, whether it is a person using a different size or weight hammer or a baseball player using a different size or weight bat. Similarly, a tool must be adapted to a specific use. A nut of a certain size requires a wrench of the appropriate size, with questions of taste being irrelevant in this instance. A wrench is to solve a problem and its appropriateness is precisely the degree to which it does just that. The validity of tools is derived from the context of their use. Scientific principles of hypothesis testing are universally valid. These are equally the principles of technology. In fact, they may have arisen out of the observation of tool using. In one sense, then, technology as an ongoing process, as a set of principles for problem solving, is universally valid. In the accumulated body of tools and skills and knowledge that are the stock of technology is a cumulated heritage of inestimable value to all countries, developed or underdeveloped. But, to repeat, just as we select a specific tool from our tool boxes in terms of its fit, in terms of its ability so solve a problem, then similarly, tools must be borrowed and adapted to fit problems as they exist in less developed countries.

Throughout the twentieth century, colonial powers sought to transplant tools, machines, agricultural practices, educational systems, and so on, to their colonies. Agricultural practices from the temperate zones were attempted in the tropics and frequently led to crop failures and serious problems of soil erosion and destruction. Factories were introduced with little reference to the body of skills of the labor force. Small-scale replicas of the metropolitan countries' universities were established in the colonies. Teaching is predicated upon a number of factors, some of which are the previous learning and general cultural experiences of the students, the library and other accesible learning materials, and the needs of the students to enter a universal world of discourse and to enhance their ability to apply their knowledge to local problems. The diffusion of tools and ideas requires their adaption and integration into the entire ecology of the recipient peoples: their existing complement of tools, skills, and habits of mind, their institutions and their capacity for resistance, and the physical environment.

The economic failures of colonial schemes abound in the literature on Third World development. The primal cause of the failures was a fundamental misconception of the nature of technology. Specific tools, techniques, ideas, machines, and so on, were treated as absolutes, as the very essence and embodiment of all technology. But technology that was best for one area of the world was not necessarily that which would serve the purposes of another area. This would not, however, constitute a failure of technology as defined here. We are concerned with problem solving. Those areas of the world that had attained the highest level of technological achievement had in a real sense, because of their technological primacy, attained the greatest problem-solving capability. There were many instances throughout the nineteenth and twentieth centuries in colonial history of the establishment of research institutes that brought to bear advanced science and technology — modified, adapted, and cut to fit, so to speak, to the needs of colonial areas. Their successes are also legion and are all too frequently neglected.[2] Had these practices and the underlying conception of technology that they implied prevailed, the story of colonial and postcolonial development would have been different. The material elements of technology are tools, and tools are always tools, carrying with them potentials for problem solving. Whether or not they are technology depends upon the use to which they are put. The technology of tools is specific to their uses. But the nonmaterial aspects of technology, the instrumental-scientific method, are universal.

A number of areas and types of errors in technological diffusion can be identified. Agriculture is a broad area in which colonial regimes in Africa and elsewhere repeatedly made errors. Preconceptions about the nature of agriculture have haunted agricultural schemes in the tropics. Clean rectangular fields are the éclat of agronomy in the temperate zone and are predicated upon conditions of rainfall and soil structure that are not found in the tropics. Such fields also require tractors and fertilizers. Irregularly shaped fields with stumps and roots left in place to protect the soil were an adaptation to Africa's tropical climate and low use of fertilizer. The hoe cultivator, with more land than time, simply hoed the most productive areas.

The earliest attempt by colonial regimes to explain the failures of their tropical agricultural schemes was the claim that the soil was infertile or that the tropics were not suited to productive agriculture. (This type of explanation followed earlier European beliefs that the tropics were so rich and productive that the native inhabitants did not have to work. They merely had to lie around under the trees, occasionally stirring to harvest and consume nature's bounty.) Beliefs about the inherent infertility of areas on the periphery of a civilization and technology had a long and erroneous tradition. The Romans were convinced that Northern Europe (i.e., north of the Alps) was unproductive and destined always to remain so. Of course, in the areas that they had conquered, the Romans established the latifundia and attempted a Mediterranean-style agriculture in a region for which it was unsuited.

In the late seventeenth century and throughout the eighteenth century there were serious debates in Europe about the climate of the New World. It was argued that, because of climate, animal and vegetable life would be stunted in the Americas.

In terms of current technology, Northern Europe and North America are the most productive regions in the world for an array of vital food crops and for animal husbandry. If these lands are now productive, it is because of the agricultural use to which they are put and the sophisticated technology that evolved to exploit a set of unique environmental opportunities. "Appropriate technology" for these regions was a synthesis of some elements of indigenous technology and of an alien technology that was highly productive (for the times) in another environment. The key was the dynamic nature of the process in which this synthesis was merely the first step towards the evolutionary development of a new indigenous technology.

Health care has many parallels with agriculture. People have generally considered new areas to be unhealthy. Such notions eventually passed as migrants to these regions adopted changed life styles and adopted medical technology suitable to the new environmental circumstances. Again, since people in some of these former unhealthy regions now have some of the longest lifespans, we can see the way in which technological change transforms what was once an environmental constraint. Tropical Africa was long known as the White Man's Grave, which it was for a sizeable percentage of those who went there. Advances in tropical medicine, in most cases applications of modern science and an adaptation of modern medicine, have considerably reduced death rates, particularly those of locals and expatriates who can afford preventive medical care, including vaccines, good food, and medicine.

Much is heard today about the failures of western technology and the need for appropriate technology in the areas of agriculture and health care. But we can speak of failure only if we are willing to argue that Mediterranean technology failed in Northern Europe, and European technology failed in the New World. If we recognize the workings of the historical process of technology, however, then we see technological adaptation as the prime factor in appropriateness. A good deal of uncertain and unclear thinking on the subject could have been avoided had there been some greater understanding of the history of technology or even a modicum of awareness of the economic theories of Veblen, Ayres, and Gruchy — all economists who attempted to comprehend the nature of technological change.

There are many activities where advanced technology was used with only a minimum of adaptation. The educational systems, as noted above, were too frequently replicas of those of metropolitan countries. The development literature of the 1950s and early 1960s was replete with anecdotes about colonial (or former colonial) education systems where African students learned about their "Gallic ancestors" or studied the flora and fauna of England or France. My own experience at the University of Khartoum in the Sudan was comparable. The many fine empirical studies carried out during the colonial period on everything from birds and plants to soils and water were regularly deposited in the libraries in England but not in those of the University of Khartoum. Six years after independence these studies were still gathering dust in the closets of government ministries.

There have been parts of the world where colonial governments purported to account for cultural differences in their educational systems. Many of these were racist and patronizing, operating under the assumptions that underlay the concept of social dualism. It was argued that some people and cultures were fundamentally and inherently different and destined to remain so. Education was to help them along the natural trajectories of their cultural evolution but could not affect basic traits. Such education equipped the recipients only for subordinate economic and social roles. The colonial proponents of such schemes included the cynical as well as those with good but misguided intentions. A lingering operating manifestation of these beliefs is the apartheid system in South Africa. We will argue below that the concept of appropriateness of technology as propagated by Schumacher and others involves many of the same underlying beliefs as the traditional concept of social dualism.

One final problem in technological diffusion is important, since it is contemporary and not merely a colonial hangover. This is the issue of the scale of technology to be used in development, particularly in industry. The classic factors of production approach argues that labor is cheap and capital is expensive (i.e., scarce) in the Third World and, therefore, that a technology should be used that takes advantage of the more abundant factor — labor, — and economizes on the relatively scarce factor — capital. This analysis is inherently tautological and static. Essentially, what we mean by underdeveloped is that there are large numbers of poor people with inadequate means. This economic inadequacy involves a complex of factors, some of which are lack of sufficient technology (i.e., capital), lack of skills and education (now called capital after having been previously ignored by orthodox economists), and lack of decent health to allow them to do a day's work. The scarcity of the physical means of production (material technology) cannot entirely be divorced from the shortages of skills and the knowledge (nonmaterial technology) to use it. A material technology that fits the existing complement of skills is going to work, but it is not going to carry the economy very far. Quite clearly, new skills will have to be learned.

New skills imply new behavior, which in turn frequently conflicts with established practice. A strategy for the introduction of new advanced technology will seek adaptation that will minimize but probably not eliminate these difficulties.

The orthodox economics approach to development is static because it treats the world in terms of fixed categories: land, labor, capital, and entrepreneurship. Institutional economics, with its concept of technology, has tried to create a logic of economic change. Technology in development is not static; when successful, technology brings change, which is the basis of future change. The logic of choice among scarce factors provides little basis for understanding the long-run developmental implications of short-term policies. In refining the logic of choice, modern economists have erected an intellectual structure that is avowedly ahistorical. But we are trying to argue that a theory of development and technological change must be deeply rooted in historical understanding.

A number of romantic or mystical notions have arisen in response to the misconceptions and misuses of tools in failed development projects. If modern western large-scale technology has not helped people to lift themselves out of poverty, then what some think is needed is "small-scale" or "intermediate" technology or some type of improvement of "indigenous" technology.[3] Many of the writers, researchers, and implementors of these theories speak of "appropriate technology," which is a redundancy. By our definition, if it is not appropriate it is not technology. This would be to judge other peoples' use of language by our definition. The term does imply, however, a differing concept of technology because its implication is that it is possible to have an inappropriate technology. This leads back again to the implicit assumption that technology is material gadgets. If the gadgets fail, then the God technology has failed. The very terms used beg the question. Appropriate technology is appropriate to what? Intermediate technology is intermediate between what — that technology which is too big and that which is too small? And why is small beautiful? I read the book with that title, *Small Is Beautiful,* and I was no more convinced then than I am now that big or middle-sized or small is beautiful. And small or big is defined relative to what — that which already is, that which was, or that which is possible? Instead of a concept of appropriate technology, what is needed is a conceptualization of a theory of technology as a problem-solving process that thereby embodies the concept of appropriateness within it.

Whatever be the so-called failures of modern technology for Third World development problems, the failure of indigenous technology is by definition far greater. It is the indigenous tools and techniques that are the ones in use and are, therefore, the ones that have been inadequate in the task of raising the population from poverty. Indigenous technology has one overwhelming advantage over competing technologies. It is adapted to the specific environmental and cultural ecologies of the area. It is emotionally acceptable because it is part and parcel of the complex array of institutional practices and cultural traditions. As such, indigenous technology is difficult to replace and sometimes even to modify. Given its advantages, indigneous technology should be an important element of any strategy for the technological and economic development of a country or region. Indigenous technology should neither be ignored nor considered as the only possible technology. Unfortunately, institutional habits of mind in the form of commitments to one or another form of technology have dominated too much of the thinking on development. Whether indigenous or alien technology is used, it is almost inevitable that the technological processes of modification and adaptation will come into play. And if the process is to be successful, it will be because instrumental ways of thought govern the selection of relevant technologies.

Just as we cannot treat technology as an array of tools, neither can we view resources as either natural or having some fixed physical nature.[4] Now and again, throughout human history, has come the idea that we are depleting our resources and some day will have to pay the penalty and suffer some form of impoverishment. This old cry gained new strength in the late 1960s and continues to the present. In many ways it is a companion notion to the ideas of Schumacher and Illich. As Ayres and many others have argued, resources are not natural but a function of our technology. Looking at technology as a problem-solving process and concomitantly as a series of relationships between and among humans, ideas, and physical objects, then evolution of the totality of the relationships brings human beings into differing relationships with the physical environment. When certain of the raw materials (or immaterials as the case may be) of the universe have the capacity to be used by humans for problem solving, then we call this stuff a resource. The stuff of this planet or the universe acquires resource character when humans can use it for a problem-solving purpose, and it loses much (or all) of its resource character when changing technology (or discovery) makes other stuff more useful for some or all of these purposes. To convert ore into metal is a far greater act of transsubstantiation or transmutation than that sought by alchemists to create gold. By this conceptualization, resources are part of the problem-solving process we call technology. Some would have us believe that it is technology that is devouring and exhausting our resources, when it is in fact technology that has created them.[5] If we are using our tools and techniques to use or destroy nonrenewable (or difficult to renew) resources — such as petroleum or the soil, — faster than we are creating new ones, then we are at best solving short-term problems at the expenses of long-term ones. Since the conception of technology expressed here is one of a process, i.e., problem solving over time, sacrificing long-term solutions to immediate needs (or assumed needs) is not a use of technology but a misconception of it. The failure here, where there is one, is not in the machine or in the technology, but in the institutional patterns of thought that lead to the misuse of tools.

Many of the faddish ideas of Schumacher and others about appropriate technology are bound up with fundamental misconceptions about the nature of resources.

> The technology of *mass production* is inherently violent, ecologically damaging, self-defeating in terms of nonrenewable resources, and stultifying for the human person. The technology of *production by the masses,* making use of the best modern knowledge and experience, is conducive to decentralization, compatible with laws of ecology, gentle in its use of scarce resources, and designed to serve the human person instead of making him the servant of the machines.[6] [Italics in original]

The question here is whether Schumacher's gentle and humane technology exists. The key words in the quote are "the best of modern knowledge and experience." What is the criterion for "best"? And if we show parts of the earth whose productive potential has been greatly reduced or destroyed in the past or in recent times — by small-scale technology fitting his definition — can the reply be that people there were not using modern knowledge? Schumacher goes on:

> I have named it intermediate technology to signify that it is superior to the primitive technology of bygone ages but at the same time much simpler, cheaper, and freer than the supertechnology of the rich.[7]

There is no evidence in Schumacher's book that he is talking about any real known technologies. In reality, he is attributing to his technology all the characteristics that he would like to have so that it will be compatible with his idyllic conception of society. He does, however, make statements that are empirically testable and falsifiable. When he speaks of the technology of mass production, he must in fact be referring to what is generally called modern technology, if his statement is to have any meaning. And, as we have noted, technology creates resources. Offshore drilling for oil is not carried out by a technology of production by the masses. With modern agriculture and forestry have come advanced ideas about conservation. Ecology is a scientific discipline, part and parcel of modern science. It is not the fault of modern science that its knowledge is not always properly understood and applied, nor is it inherent in advanced technology that it may be destructively used. A retreat from modern science and technology does not solve the problem of gearing our *institutions* to the appropriate use of the means at hand.

Schumacher has a clear preference for small, decentralized social units. His theory of technology is derived from this conception and not the reverse. The ideas about primitive simplicity appeal greatly to those living in and enjoying the benefits of large-scale urban scientific and technological societies.[8] Rozak, in his introduction to the American edition of Schumacher's book, categorically states as an article of faith that bigness is bad.[9] Schumacher goes back to Aristotle to draw succor for the notion of the superiority of small-scale ownership. He further argues that no city should exceed a half a million in size.[10]

Like orthodox economists, Schumacher makes assertions that need to be tested against historical experience. Quoting Coomaraswamy, he argues that the difference between a carpet loom and a machine loom is that the former is a tool and the latter is a machine, which acts as a "destroyer of culture" because of the "fact that it does essentially the human part of the work."[11] He later speaks of modern technology replacing the "skillful productive work of human hands in touch with real materials of one kind or another."[12] Is Schumacher suggesting that life for those in textile production before the industrial revolution was easier and more rewarding than that of a worker in a modern textile mill? Does he mean that any sizeable number of these workers would willingly return to the hand loom if that were possible? Merely asking these questions provides the answer for all but the true believers of small is beautiful. And one of the central problems in introducing new technology to poor countries is that they lack the skills to use it. Contrary to popular mythology, modern science and technology have required a vastly greater array of knowledge and skills on the part of the workers than prior technologies. Schumacher's statement about diminution of skills is true only if it is meaningless. If skills are whatever Schumacher says they are, then he is right by definition. If the term has any objective meaning, then his conception can be readily and abundantly refuted.

To Schumacher, technology is a "foreign body" in modern society, and he sees evidence that it is about due for "rejection" (whatever that means).[13] It is generally recognized by anthropologists and other students of the subject that all humans have and use tools. Some argue that tools were a key factor in the evolution of human beings and human culture. Man is the tool maker. In order for technology to be a foreign body, a distinction must be made between tools and technology. Any time we have an assemblage of tools, we have technology and the dynamic possibilities of change. And when tools are combined and recombined, we eventually create compound tools and machines. As Schumacher admits, technology has laws of its own, but these laws are different than the ones set forth in his book.[14] These laws of technology are basically problem-solving ones, and they follow from human activity and aspiration toward this end. There is nothing humane about choosing less effective means for problem solving.

Schumacher concedes that his intermediate technology does not yet exist.

> Although we are in possession of all requisite knowledge, it still requires a systematic creative effort to bring this technology into active existence and make it generally viable and available.[15]

One wonders how so many virtues can be attributed to a technology that does not yet exist and, therefore, has not been tested against the problems it would be designed to solve.

Schumacher's concept of society is considered radical and utopian by many fervent followers of his system. It is based upon economics for the flower children of the 1960s who have now grown a little older. In point of fact, Schumacher's ideas are basically conservative if not reactionary. Much of his romantic reaction against the industrial revolution merely echoes literary criticisms of the last two centuries. In an article in *Psychology Today* published at about the time of his recent death, Schumacher argued that unemployment in the United States could best be solved by the local community or even by a smaller group such as the neighborhood.[16] In modern urban societies there is a tendency for people to be grouped economically as well as ethnically and racially. One of the implications of Schumacher's proposal would be that the rich would work through their neighborhood to solve their unemployment problem and the poor would do the same. Calvin Coolidge would have recognized the wisdom of this approach, but for Herbert Hoover it might have been a bit too conservative. To Schumacher, we need "guidance." It must come not from science and technology but from the "traditional wisdom of mankind."[17] He also advocates what he calls "Buddhist economics."[18] The institutional economics of Veblen, Ayres, and Gruchy argues that those societies most deeply committed to past binding traditions are the ones most deeply mired in poverty; it is those societies most nearly attuned to the principles of science and technology that have gone the farthest in eliminating poverty and many diseases. They have also done quite well in cultivating the arts and making them widely accessible. Institutionalists find little that is humane in a society, based on tradition, that has a strategy for the use of limitation of technology that is, in effect, a prescription for continued poverty.

ENDNOTES

1. For a detailed analysis of Ayres's theory of technology as problem solving, see Thomas R. de Gregori, "Technology and Ceremonial Behavior: Some Aspects of Institutional Economics and Modern Economic Problems," *Journal of Economic Issues* 11 (December 1977): 857–866.

2. To catalog the failures and successes of technology transfer here would be interesting, but it would also be a digression from our main argument. We will, however, outline in the discussion that follows some of the general types of errors that were made in the attempts to diffuse technology. For detailed empirical documentation of this theme of technology transfer failure, see my book, Thomas R. de Gregori, *Technology and the Economic Development of the Tropical African Frontier* (Cleveland: Case Western Reserve Press, 1969).

3. Among the proponents of appropriate technology, upon whose writing fame has recently smiled, are E. F. Schumacher, *Small Is Beautiful: Economics As If People Mattered* (New York: Harper & Row, 1973); and Ivan D. Illich, *Tools for Conviviality* (New York: Harper & Row, 1973); and by the same author, *Celebration of Awareness: A Call for Institution Awareness* (Garden City, N. Y.: Doubleday, 1970). Illich is also concerned with the use of technology in developed countries, as is Schumacher, but to a lesser degree.

4. Clarence Ayres, *The Theory of Economic Progress* (Chapel Hill: University of North Carolina Press, 1944), pp. 89, 113. In this discussion of resources, there is no pretense that we are modifying or improving Ayres's theory in any way. On this question we are merely applying it to current concerns.

5. Robert Solow, in combatting some of the fears of imminent resource exhaustion, gives the following U.S. government estimates for years of availability and crustal abundance for some of our minerals. Lecture, University of Houston, Fall 1976.

	Known Reserves	Ultimately Recoverable Reserves (with current technology)	Crustal Abundance
Coal	2,736 yrs.	5,199 yrs.	—
Copper	45	340	242.10^6 tns.
Iron	117	2,657	$1,815.10^6$
Phosphorus	481	1,601	870.10^6
Molybdenum	65	630	422.10^6
Lead	10	162	85.10^6
Zinc	21	618	409.10^6
Sulphur	30	6,897	—
Uranium	50	8,455	$1,855.10^6$
Aluminum	23	68,066	$38,500.10^6$

6. Schumacher, *Small Is Beautiful*, p. 145.

7. Ibid.

8. There is a note on the title page of *Small Is Beautiful* that "the text of this book is printed on 100% recycled paper." No mention is made as to whether it was printed with humane hand presses.

9. Schumacher, *Small Is Beautiful*, p. 4.

10. Ibid., pp. 31–32, 63.
11. Ibid., p. 52.
12. Ibid., p. 141.
13. Ibid., p. 139.
14. Ibid., p. 138.
15. Ibid., p. 146.
16. E. F. Schumacher, "Taking the Scare Out of Scarcity," *Psychology Today* 2 (September 1977): 16.
17. Schumacher, *Small Is Beautiful,* p. 281.
18. Ibid., pp. 50-58.

15 TAX POLICIES TOWARD MULTINATIONAL CORPORATIONS IN DEVELOPING ASIAN COUNTRIES

Edward Van Roy

This essay explores one dimension of the complex relationship between the multinational corporations (MNCs) and the developing countries (LDCs) — the welter of tax policies that have been brought to bear on these "guest" firms by their "host" governments. The discussion is based on a cross-sectional analysis of national tax policies with respect to MNCs in seven East and Southeast Asian and four South and West Asian LDCs.[1] The first section compares these countries' profit and dividend tax structures with respect to MNCs. The second section examines major modifications to these tax structures. Some further relevant issues and broad implications are considered in the third section.

PROFIT AND DIVIDEND TAX STRUCTURES

In the presence of a fluid international capital market the capacity of taxes to affect profits, and thus investment decisions, permits differing LDC

The views expressed in this essay are the author's and not necessarily those of any organization with which he is associated.

profit and dividend tax regimes to influence the magnitude of MNC capital flows from the developed countries to the LDCs as well as the composition of these flows among LDCs. Table 16-1 summarizes the basic profit and dividend tax structures imposed on MNCs in eleven Asian LDCs. Profit tax rates in these countries range from a low of 15 percent in Hong Kong to 60 percent in India, Pakistan, and Sri Lanka, with the remaining countries occupying a middle range of between roughly 30 and 50 percent. Several of these countries, in addition, base certain supplementary taxes on profits: India and Malaysia impose an excess profits tax; India and Korea impose a profit tax surcharge; and Iran, Malaysia, and Pakistan impose various profit surtaxes.[2]

Table 15-1. Basic Profit and Dividend Taxes Imposed on MNCs in Eleven Asian LDCs

Country	Tax Base	Tax Rate
East and Southeast Asia		
Hong Kong	profits	15%
Indonesia	profits	12% of first Rs 10 million
	dividends	45% of the balance
		20%
Malaysia	profits	40%
	profits	5%
	profits exceeding	
	25% of capital	5%
Philippines	profits	25% of first P 100,000
		35% of the balance
	dividends	8.75%
Republic of Korea	profits	20% of first W 300 million
		30% of next W 200 million
		40% of the balance
	profit tax[a]	5%
	dividends	25%
Singapore	profits	40%
Thailand	profits	20% of first Bhat 500,000
		25% of next Bhat 500,000
		30% of the balance
	dividends	25%

[a]For firms located in Seoul or Pusan.

Table 15-1. (cont'd.)

Country	Tax Base	Tax Rate
South and West Asia		
India	profits	55% of first Rs. 200,000
		60% of the balance
	profit tax	5%
	"chargeable profits"	25% of amount equivalent
	after deducting profits	to 5% of capital
	equivalent to 10% of	40% of the balance
	capital[b]	
	dividends	24.5%
	dividend tax	5%
Iran[c]	profits (various taxes)	13%
	profits net of above-	
	mentioned taxes	45.8% of first Rls. 50
		million[d]
		60% of the balance
Pakistan	profits	30%
	profits	30%
	dividends	20%
Sri Lanka	profits	60%
	dividends	33.33%

[b]"Chargeable profits" are net profits after profit tax and certain other downward adjustments.
[c]Structure for a "limited liability company"; a foreign-invested "joint stock company" faces somewhat different treatment.
[d]The effective rate at Rls. 50 million after summing a series of thirteen marginal rates up to 60%.

Taxation of dividends remitted to MNC parents shows greater uniformity among the eleven countries under review. Hong Kong, Iran, Malaysia, and Singapore impose no tax on remitted dividends.[3] For the remaining seven countries dividend tax rates range from 8.75 to 33.33 per cent. It should be noted that these nominal rates exceed the effective rates with respect to pretax profits to the extent that profit taxes intervene to reduce the MNCs' dividend payout capacities; in addition, MNCs can of course voluntarily reduce their dividend tax liabilities by lowering their dividend payout rates.

Profit tax progressivity occurs in six of the eleven countries examined. In United States dollar equivalents (at mid-1975 official exchange rates) the tax rate increments occur at $50,000 or less in India, Indonesia, the Philippines, and Thailand. In Iran the rate rises to 60 percent at $750,000, and in Korea to 30 percent at $600,000 and 40 percent at $1 million. With the exception of Iran and Korea, then, profit tax progressivity may be considered generally inconsequential to MNCs in Asian LDCs. It should be noted, however, that India and Malaysia impose additional profit taxes employing rate of return on investment as a component of the base. The intent in both cases is to penalize "monopoly" or "excess" profits, but concern over the potential detrimental effects of such taxes on economic efficiency and entrepreneurial initiative has dissuaded other Asian LDCs from employing them and has constrained their application in Malaysia to a low rate and in India to a narrowly defined "chargeable profits" base.

A useful means of examining the effects of these LDC tax structures on MNC profits, and thus by implication MNC investment decisions, is to trace out their impacts on representative MNC projects. Table 16-2 presents the results of such an exercise for two hypothetical MNC projects.[4] Both projects are assumed to be locally incorporated industrial joint ventures with half their equity provided by the MNC parent and the other half by local partners. It is further assumed that project A has a total investment of $2 million, a 20 percent pretax profit rate, and a 50 percent dividend payout policy, whereas project B has a total investment of $10 million, a 30 percent pretax profit rate, and a 75 percent dividend payout policy.[5]

In the case of project A the effective profit tax bite on pretax profits ranges from 15.0 to 62.7 percent with the mean at 42.2 percent. This compares with a range of from 15.0 to 63.9 percent with a mean of 45.4 percent for project B. The small difference between these two distributions reflects the absence of substantial progressivity in the tax structures examined. The widely differing magnitudes of these tax bites may be expected to have considerable influence on MNC investment decisions. In comparison with the magnitudes and range of profit tax bites, the bites taken out of pretax profits by dividend taxes would appear to be of subordinate importance in MNC investment decision making. For project A the dividend tax bite out of pretax profits ranges from 0 to 9.9 percent, with the mean at 3.9 percent. For project B, with a dividend payout rate one-and-a-half times greater, the range is from 0 to 13.1 percent with the mean at 5.5 percent. Deflated to the same payout rate as project A, however, project B's mean dividend tax bite is reduced to 3.6 percent, slightly lower than that of project A.

In combination, profit and dividend taxes reduce remitted earnings on project A by between 15.0 and 57.5 percent (mean 46.1 percent) and on project B by between 15.0 and 70.9 percent (mean 50.2 percent). With cor-

Table 15-2. Impact of Eleven Asian LDC Profit and Dividend Tax Structures on Two Hypothetical MNC Projects (percentages of pre-tax profits)

Country	Earnings	Project A	Project B
East and Southeast Asia			
Hong Kong	after profit taxes	85.0	85.0
	after dividend taxes	21.2	31.9
Indonesia	after profit taxes	56.5	55.2
	after dividend taxes	11.3	16.6
Malaysia	after profit taxes	55.0	54.2
	after dividend taxes	13.8	20.3
Philippines	after profit taxes	65.4	65.0
	after dividend taxes	14.9	22.3
Republic of Korea	after profit taxes	79.0	63.8
	after dividend taxes	14.8	17.9
Singapore	after profit taxes	60.0	60.0
	after dividend taxes	15.0	22.5
Thailand	after profit taxes	70.9	70.1
	after dividend taxes	13.3	19.7
South and West Asia			
India	after profit taxes	37.3	36.1
	after dividend taxes	6.9	10.1
Iran	after profit taxes	47.1	38.3
	after dividend taxes	11.8	14.4
Pakistan	after profit taxes	40.0	40.0
	after dividend taxes	8.0	12.0
Sri Lanka	after profit taxes	40.0	40.0
	after dividend taxes	6.7	10.0

porate income taxes ranging between 45 and 55 percent in most industrial countries, it would appear that profit and dividend tax structures on average do not constitute a major consideration in MNC decision making concerning investment in the home country as against investment in Asian LDCs. But with eight of the eleven LDCs under examination having total tax bites falling outside this range, it would appear that the profit and dividend tax structures prevailing in these countries do form an important variable in MNC investment choice among Asian LDCs.

MAJOR MODIFICATION

A considerable gap exists between the tax structures outlined above and the actual situations confronting MNCs in the eleven Asian LDCs under examination. In practically every instance the basic profit and dividend tax structure is considerably modified by a variety of fiscal instruments designed to induce private foreign capital inflows.[6] In certain cases these investment incentives apply to all MNCs in such favoured sectors as manufacturing, tourism, and finance, but in most instances they are restricted to projects in priority industries or meeting various functional economic criteria; the policy intent is thus to open the door to MNC projects, but not indiscriminately.

In most cases these tax modifications are elements of broadly conceived investment promotion programs that are in turn integral aspects of national development plans. As such, they do not form a regular part of the basic tax code but are implemented as addenda to it in the form of ad hoc legislation, presidential or ministerial decrees, or elements of investment promotion acts that may precisely define the magnitude and range of application of each tax incentive or leave such matters to the discretion of the competent authorities. These various tax incentives can be analysed cross-sectionally as profit and dividend tax exemptions, indirect tax exemptions, and profit tax deductions.

Profit and Dividend Tax Exemptions

The "income tax holiday" is perhaps the most important and certainly the most widely heralded tax incentive offered to MNCs by Asian LDCs. Though the tax holiday concept traditionally refers to a total exemption from tax liabilities, its meaning has been diluted in some countries to cover partial exemptions, and while the term was originally applied specifically to profit taxes it has been broadened by at least one Asian LDC to refer to various other taxes as well. To avoid the confusion necessarily arising from this increasingly ambiguous concept, it is preferable to consider profit tax exemptions as a general category of tax incentives inclusive of tax holidays, thus ignoring the popular treatment of tax holidays as an incentive sui generis.

The major profit tax exemptions available to MNCs in the eleven Asian LDCs here under examination are summarized in Table 16-3.[7] With the exception of Hong Kong and the Philippines all these countries offer profit

Table 15-3. Major Tax Exemptions Offered To MNCs in 11 Asian LDCs

Country	Base	Terms
East and Southeast Asia		
Indonesia	profit tax	full exemption for 2–6 years
	dividend tax	full exemption for 2–6 years
	import duties on capital goods	full exemption for 2 years
	sales tax on capital goods	full exemption for 2 years
Malaysia	profit taxes	full exemption for 2–10 years
Philippines	import and export duties	full exemption for 5 years, gradually declining to 10%, ending in 15th year
	import duties on capital goods	full exemption for 5–7 years
	sales and turnover taxes	full exemption for 5 years, gradually declining to 10%, ending in 15th year
Republic of Korea	MNC component of profit tax	full exemption for 5 years, 50% exemption for next 3 years
	MNC component of dividend tax	full exemption for 5 years, 50% exemption for next 3 years
	import duties on capital goods	full exemption
	sales and turnover taxes on exports	full exemption
Singapore	profit tax	full exemption for 5 years
	profit tax on exports	90% exemption for 5–15 years
	import duties on capital goods	full exemption
Thailand	profit tax	full exemption for 3–8 years, 50% exemption for next 5 years
	dividend tax	full exemption for 3–8 years, 50% exemption for next 5 years
	profit tax on exports	partial (variable rate) exemption
	import duties on capital goods and on inputs into exports	full exemption

Table 15-3. cont'd.

Country	Base	Terms
South and West Asia	sales and turnover taxes	partial (up to 90%) exemption for 5 years
India	profit taxes	exemption up to 6% of capital for 5 years, with 3-year carry-forward of unused portion
	dividend taxes	full exemption for period of profit tax exemption
Iran	profit taxes	full exemption for 5-10 years
	profit taxes on exports	full exemption
Pakistan	profit tax (30% only)	exemption up to 5-10% of capital for indeterminate period
	profit tax (30% only)	exemption (as rebate) up to 4.5% of profits for in-determinate period
	profit taxes on exports	25% exemption (as rebate)
	import duties on capital goods	exemption up to 100% (as rebate)
	sales taxes on capital goods, exports, and inputs into exports	full exemption
Sri Lanka	profit tax	full exemption for 8 years
	dividend tax	full exemption for 8 years
	import duties on inputs into exports	partial (variable) exemption (as rebate)
	sales taxes on exports and inputs into exports	full exemption

tax exemptions for multiyear periods. The specific MNC project character-istics required to take advantage of this tax incentive vary widely, however: Korea provides exemptions to all MNC projects (and unlike the other ex-emption-granting countries examined here excludes local partners from this privilege); Iran and Pakistan, among other cases, base eligibility on specific activities, locations, and other designated project characteristics; Malaysia and Thailand, among others, restrict eligibility to projects receiving promo-tional status, itself granted on the basis of specific project characteristics. With the exception of India and Pakistan (which limit exemptions to speci-fied rates of return on investment) and Korea (which exempts only the for-eign investment component of MNC projects), the exemption-granting countries provide full profit tax exemption where applicable.

Supplementing the profit tax exemption in India, Indonesia, Korea, Sri Lanka, and Thailand is the extension of exemption coverage to dividends. The inducement thereby given MNCs to remit rather than reinvest earnings makes this policy instrument of dubious merit, yet only Pakistan and the Philippines have not succumbed to its appeal (Hong Kong, Iran, Malaysia, and Singapore being excluded from consideration here because of their lack of a dividend tax). Adding the adverse impact of dividend remittances on the balance of payments to the public revenue loss arising out of the tax exemption of such remittances raises the social cost of this investment incentive to a point where its worth must be seriously questioned.

The impact of profit tax exemptions on two hypothetical MNC projects in the nine exemption-granting Asian LDCs is illustrated in Table 16-4.[8] Exemption provisions tend to be standardized in these countries during the first five years of project operations, but they begin to fade out at differing rates thereafter. For project A the mean posttax profit rate without tax exemption is 10.8 percent. With the profit tax exemption the mean rises to 18.6 percent during the first five years of operation, declining to 14.0 percent during the second five years. For project B the mean posttax profit rate without exemptions is 15.2 percent. With exemption it is 27.5 percent during the first five years, declining to 20.2 percent during the second five years.

The impact of tax exemption on profits thus seems to be substantial, providing prima facie evidence of the effectiveness of this policy instrument as an MNC investment incentive. It is particularly interesting that the application of this incentive eliminates Hong Kong's tax advantage relative to most of the other Asian LDCs examined here for the term of their tax holiday periods. On the other hand, variations in the impact of profit tax exemption among the Asian LDCs examined appear (with the exception of India and Pakistan) to be so small as to have little influence on MNC choice of host country.

A number of underlying issues nevertheless leave the merits of profit tax exemptions in the LDCs open to serious question. One problem relates to the possible public revenue losses accompanying tax exemption. Such losses occur whenever exemptions are granted to MNCs that would have entered irrespective of this inducement. The extent of such redundancy is unknown and probably unascertainable, but it undoubtedly exists to varying degrees in all exemption-granting countries. A second problem relates to the investment-phasing distortions introduced by tax exemptions having fixed termination dates. Prior knowledge that profits will become taxable following a certain date may well accelerate MNC investment turnover and lead MNCs to compress taxable earnings into the exemption period while postponing costs to the postexemption years.

Table 15-4. Impact of Profit Tax Exemptions on Two Hypothetical MNC Projects in Nine Asian LDCs[a] (percentages of investment)

Country	Project A profit rate			Project B profit rate		
	Without Exemption	With Exemption[b]		Without Exemption	With Exemption[b]	
		1–5 yrs.	6–10 yrs.		1–5 yrs.	6–10 yrs.
East and Southeast Asia						
Indonesia	11.3	20.0	13.0	16.6	30.0	19.3
Malaysia	11.0	20.0	20.0	16.2	30.0	30.0
Republic of Korea	15.8	20.0	17.1	19.1	30.0	22.4
Singapore	12.0	20.0	12.0	18.0	30.0	18.0
Thailand	14.2	20.0	17.7	21.0	30.0	26.4
South and West Asia						
India	7.5	13.7	7.5	10.8	16.8	10.8
Iran	9.4	20.0	9.4	11.5	30.0	11.5
Pakistan	8.0	14.0	14.0	12.0	21.0	21.0
Sri Lanka	8.0	20.0	15.2	12.0	30.0	22.8

[a] Assuming maximum standard exemption rates
[b] Annual averages

Indirect Tax Exemptions

In contrast to profit and dividend tax exemptions, exemptions from indirect taxes tend to magnify MNC taxable profits and thus increase profit tax liabilities. This perverse effect arises partly because indirect taxes may tend to reduce sales volume as a result of increased selling prices and partly because indirect taxes are ordinarily deductible as business expenses in calculating taxable profits. While the sales volume impact of indirect tax exemption can either increase or decrease profits depending on the elasticity of demand, indirect tax exemption generally tends to increase taxable profits as a result of the elimination of deductibles from computation of the tax base. The public revenue loss implicit in indirect tax exemptions is thus partly recouped out of increased profit tax revenues; by the same token the actual financial advantage of indirect tax exemptions to the MNC is reduced below their nominal value because of the resultant decrease in deductions applied in calculating profits for tax purposes.

Exemption from indirect taxes thus plays a substantially different role from that of profit taxation in MNC investment decision making as well as in development planning in LDCs providing this investment incentive. This distinction is reflected in the attitudes of most MNCs and Asian LDCs to the importance of these two types of policy instruments. Most of the countries here under examination relegate indirect tax exemptions to footnote status in documents advertising the advantages of investing in their economies, whereas they generally place great stress on profit tax exemptions. Among MNCs operating in these countries the distinction is even more marked, with most considering indirect tax exemptions worth little more than passing mention and some appearing wholly ignorant of their existence while dwelling on the financial advantages accruing from profit tax exemptions. Given the importance of indirect taxes in most LDCs' fiscal systems, this disregard would appear misguided were it not for the facts that they are generally distributed on a narrowly selective basis and their value is greatly reduced as a result of the ease with which they can be shifted by many MNCs.

The major indirect tax exemptions offered to MNCs here under examination were summarized in Table 16-3. An unwieldy number of assumptions concerning the structure of alternative types of MNC projects would be required in deriving quantitative estimates of the comparative impacts of such exemptions on profits. Rather than pursue such a conjecture-laden course, this essay will merely survey and subjectively evaluate these MNC investment incentives and their influence on MNC capital flows to the LDCs.

The significance of indirect tax exemptions as MNC investment incentives is, as Table 16-3 reveals, highly variable. Hong Kong, Malaysia, India, and Iran offer no consequential incentive of this sort. Of the remaining countries only the Philippines and Thailand offer exemptions against indirect tax liabilities of sufficient weight to make this policy instrument a significant variable in MNC investment consideration. The Philippines is exceptional in that a general "tax holiday" is provided against all indirect taxes for a multiyear period in lieu of exemption from profit and dividend taxes. In Thailand, the "business" tax, a turnover tax with a rate varying by industry, is sufficiently high in most cases that exemption, even if partial, can constitute a sizable financial windfall for eligible MNC projects.[9]

With these exceptions, indirect tax exemptions are of substantial incentive value only in selected MNC investment situations, such as import-dependent projects (which are in some cases exempted from tariffs) and export-oriented projects (which are in some cases exempted from sales taxes and tariffs). Capital-goods-importing MNCs are granted tariff and/or sales tax exemption in Indonesia, the Philippines, Korea, Thailand, and Pakistan.[10] Exemption from certain indirect taxes is offered to export-oriented projects by the Philippines, Korea, Thailand, Pakistan, and Sri Lanka. Not only are these exemptions restricted to MNC projects with these or other special characteristics, but in most cases they are further restricted to projects within those categories also receiving promotional status. As a result of this high degree of selectivity, indirect tax incentives have a smaller impact on the profits of most MNCs than is suggested by the summary provided in Table 16-3. The apparent ease with which indirect tax exemptions may be shifted by MNCs in the cost-plus pricing environments common in most LDCs' industrial sectors further reduces their potential impact as an incentive, generating perverse patterns of tax incidence among local factor suppliers and the consuming public.

Profit Tax Deductions

Although calculation of taxable profits is theoretically a straightforward accounting exercise consisting of the deduction of expenses from revenues, specification of the appropriate range and magnitude of deductions raises a variety of complications affecting this calculation and, consequently, tax liabilities and posttax profits. In contrast to the norm in the developed countries, where litigation has built up a solid body of judicial precedent to supplement the legislative core, these issues are not adequately treated in the law and supplementary regulations of Asian LDCs and are commonly resolved through case-by-case negotiation with individual MNCs. An important implicit modification to the profit tax structure confronting MNC projects in most Asian LDCs thus becomes the liberality with which each project may expect to be treated in handling such major expenses as depreciation on plant and equipment, depletion of resource stocks, and amortization of intangibles.

In addition to intercountry and interproject variability in permissible "ordinary" deductions ("ordinary" in the sense that they purportedly reflect expenses actually incurred), most Asian LDCs provide MNCs with selective "special" deductions as investment incentives. As in the case of indirect tax exemptions, the number of assumptions (e.g., the MNC's range of activities, composition of assets, size of labor force, location, and export orientation) required to quantify the impact of special deductions limits one to a mere summary and commentary on the special deductions offered to MNCs in the countries here under examination.

The major special deductions available to MNCs in these countries are classified in Table 16-5 into accelerated depreciation allowances, extra deductions, and carry-forward and deferral provisions. Accelerated depreciation is limited to the first year following asset acquisition in five countries. For plant and equipment (excluding buildings, for which the accelerated rates tend to be lower), the rates are 20 percent of the cost in Malaysia and India, 25 percent in Hong Kong, Indonesia, and Pakistan, and up to 80 percent in Sri Lanka. Accelerated depreciation over their full accounting lifetime permits eligible assets to be fully written off in three years in Singapore, in two to five years in Malaysia, and in one year in the Philippines, while India and Pakistan add accelerations of 50 and 100 percent of plant and equipment used on double- and triple-shift operations, respectively.

Complementing the accelerated depreciation allowance is the extra depreciation allowance. The former special deduction shifts the depreciation expense toward the earlier years of operations but does not increase the value of this deduction beyond asset cost. By contrast, the latter increases the depreciation allowance beyond 100 percent of asset cost with the provision of a special depreciation surcharge, usually in the first year after asset acquisition. Thus, Korea raises the depreciation allowance on eligible MNC assets to as much as 130 percent of asset cost; the Philippines raises the first year's depreciation allowance on MNC assets acquired out of reinvested earnings by as much as 100 percent; and Indonesia provides a special deduction equal to 20 percent of investment (spread over four years) to MNC projects not eligible for the profit tax exemption.

A variant of the extra depreciation deduction is the investment credit applied in several Asian LDCs. While the extra deduction reduces pretax profits, the investment credit reduces the profit tax liability itself. As its impact on posttax profits is more direct than special deductions, it avoids various potential perverse fiscal effects associated with extra deductions and is thus generally a preferable tax policy instrument, particularly in countries with progressive profit tax structures. Only a few Asian LDCs, however, have turned to this investment incentive: Malaysia's 25–40 percent investment credit (the rate depending on the firm's promotional status) and Sri Lanka's 20 percent tax credit for promoted projects are the only remaining cases since the termination in 1974 of India's 15–40 percent "development rebate".[11]

In addition to extra allowances against fixed assets, various extra deductions on other types of expenses are provided. India permits an extra 33.3 percent and Malaysia an extra 100 percent deduction on certain export promotion expenses. Malaysia and the Philippines permit certain extra deductions based on the value or the annual increase in value of export sales. The Philippines provides an extra deduction equivalent to 25 percent of local labor and materials input costs. And Thailand provides a 100 percent extra deduction on transport and utilities expenses for projects at preferred locations and an extra deduction of up to 20 percent on construction expenses. Such subsidies, though rather miscellaneous in terms of the MNC characteristics they aim to promote, can have a substantial impact on posttax profits where they apply.

According to general accounting convention, losses are deductible as an ordinary operating expense in the year following their incurral. Thus, the loss carry-forward provision is an anomaly in this discussion because specification of limited loss carry-forward serves not as an MNC investment incentive but as a restriction. It is one of the ironies of MNC investment promotion programs that such restrictions are commonly included as purported incentives. Recognizing this anomaly makes it apparent that the most liberal cases with regard to loss carry-forward are Hong Kong, Malaysia, Korea, Singapore, Thailand, and Pakistan, none of which specify any loss carry-forward limitation. An exception to this rule is Sri Lanka, which specifies full loss carry-forward and adds to it a provision that the deficit firm may increase its loss deduction by four percent of its depreciation expenses; Indonesia limits it to the first six years following investment and after that to four years per loss; Iran limits it to a maximum of 33.3 percent of annual profits in each of the first three years following the loss; and the Philippines limits it to six years per loss during the first ten years of operations.

Loss deferral extends the carry-forward privilege by permitting the MNC to delay deduction of losses to years when they will have a tangible impact on tax liabilities. In countries with progressive profit tax structures this would suggest deferral to high-profit years; in the Asian LDCs, however, the loss deferral privilege is most significant in permitting postponement of

Table 15-5. Major Profit Tax Deductions Offered as Investment Incentives to MNCs in Eleven Asian LDCs

Country	Accelerated Depreciation	Extra Deduction	Carry-forward (CF) and Deferral (DEF)
East and Southeast Asia			
Hong Kong	25% on plant and equipment and 20% on buildings in first yr.		
Indonesia	25% on equipment and 10% on buildings in first 4 yrs.	5% of investment in first 4 yrs.	Full loss CF during first 4 yrs; 4-yr. CF thereafter DEF on accelerated depreciation to end of profit tax exemption
Malaysia	20% on plant and equipment in first yr. 40% on all depreciables in certain cases	100% of export promotion expenses Increase for export firms based on export sales growth 25–40% investment credit	DEF on depreciation expenses to end of profit tax exemption DEF on losses to end of profit tax exemption to extent that losses exceed profits for period as a whole
Philippines	Up to 100% on plant and equipment	25% of local labour and materials expenses for 5 yrs. 25–100% in first yr. for reinvestment of profits for expansion 10% of export sales in first 5 yrs. Increase of certain deductions for certain export projects	6-yr. loss CF during first 10 yrs. DEF of loss CF to end of tax exemption

Country			
Republic of Korea		20% of depreciation expense on machinery and equipment, in some cases on total assets Up to 30% of depreciations expense on fixed assets, depending on share of export sales	DEF of loss CF to end of profit tax exemption
Singapore	33.3% on plant and equipment		Up to 10 yrs. DEF of extra deduction on construction
Thailand		100% of transport and utilities expenses Up to 20% of construction costs	
South and West Asia			
India	20% on plant and machinery in first yr. 50% and 100% for double- and triple-shift operations	33.3% of certain export promotion expenses	Full CF of depreciation expenses in excess of profits
Iran			3-yr. loss CF with maximum of 33.3% of each yr.'s profits
Pakistan	25% on plant and equipment and 15% on buildings in first yr. 50% and 100% for double- and triple-shift operations		
Sri Lanka	33.3–80% on various types of assets in the first yr.	20% investment credit	Full loss CF with 4% annual increase on depreciation CF

loss write-off to the conclusion of the profit tax exemption period. This is the case in Malaysia, the Philippines, and Singapore, but is not so in other profit tax exemption countries on the grounds that such deferral rewards inefficiency and tends to retard project phase-in. Deferral privileges can also be accorded to expenses other than losses. In Indonesia and Malaysia, for instance, depreciation expenses are deferred to the end of the profit tax exemption period, and in Thailand the extra deduction for construction expenses may be deferred to any year during the ten years following their incurral. In the absence of substantial profit tax progressivity and MNC expectations that they will incur losses on their local investments, however, this investment incentive probably has little impact on MNC decision making and on the LDCs' public revenue take.

Viewed in the aggregate, special profit tax deductions apparently constitute a substantial incentive to MNCs considering investment opportunities in Asian LDCs. In comparative terms, this incentive is probably more significant than indirect tax exemptions but certainly less so than profit tax exemptions. As implicit financial subsidies to eligible MNCs they entail an undefinable public revenue burden to the extent that such investments would have been undertaken in the absence of incentives treatment. In addition, they tend to distort the structure of MNC investment decisions in favour of capital-intensive projects since in most cases it is capital that receives the subsidy, and they tend to accelerate investment turnover as the subsidy is generally concentrated in the early years of operation.

SOME ISSUES AND IMPLICATIONS

Without extending the preceding comparative analysis of tax policies further to include such additional issues as tariff structures in respect of MNC materials imports and protecting locally produced MNC goods on domestic markets, packaging of tax incentives to heighten their combined impact on promoted MNC projects, personal income taxes and exemptions on MNC expatriate personnel, and tax-sparing provisions and double-taxation treaties to harmonize MNC tax treatment between home and host countries, it is apparent that tax policy toward MNCs in Asian LDCs ranges from the highly "attractive" to the highly "repellent." Particularly striking is the dissimilarity in orientation between South and West Asia (SWA), on the one hand, and Southeast and East Asia (SEA), on the other. The impact of these subregions' profit and dividend tax structures on MNCs is quite different. Ranging from 15 to about 50 percent and averaging about 40 percent, total effective tax rates in SEA would appear to have a generally stimulative impact on MNC investment decisions when compared with prevailing rates in the major developed countries. In contrast, total effective tax rates in SWA, which range from above 50 to about 70 percent and average about 65 percent, would appear to be inhibitory of MNC investment decisions.

This subregional distinction is accentuated when major tax modifications are introduced into the analysis. Profit tax exemption during the first ten years of an MNC project's operations raises average annual posttax profits to about 90 percent of pretax profits in SEA as against only about 70 percent in SWA. Indirect tax exemption is also of greater consequence in SEA than SWA; for instance, full exemption from customs duties is widely available on capital goods or material-input imports in SEA but available to only a limited degree in a few cases in SWA. Subregional differences in the application of special deductions are readily apparent in the case of "extras," which are far more prevalent in SEA, and in deferrals, which are available only in SEA. When these subregional differences are amplified by the higher frequency with which all types of MNC tax incentives are awarded in SEA than in SWA, the contrast in tax policy attains considerable significance for MNC investment decisions.

These tax policy differences imply common interests among countries within each subregion. The SWA countries pursue a common aim in inhibiting MNC entry with exceptionally high tax rates except in selected cases where tax incentives are provided. Similarly, the SEA countries share an interest in facilitating MNC entry through the imposition of relatively light tax rates supplemented by incentives for MNC projects in preferred fields. These consensual tax policy orientations set the stage for a consideration by the countries concerned of the possibilities of subregional resolution of shared problems through tax policy harmonization.

There is general agreement among tax experts that MNC investment decisions are seldom decisively influenced by the tax policy environment prevailing in the Third World at large, chiefly because the decision to invest in LDCs is dominated by such considerations as the availability of cheap labour, natural resources, local markets, and political stability in the host countries. In conjunction with the recognition that LDCs differ widely in their development strategies and objectives, this condition has been taken by some critics of the concept of subregional MNC tax policy harmonization as justification for continuation of the prevailing pattern of divergent SEA and SWA tax policy orientations. This perception, however, ignores the fact that MNC investment decisions may be significantly affected in the selection of a specific host country as a result of differing LDC tax policy environments. In other words, MNCs seem to be far more responsive to tax policy differences among Asian LDCs than to tax policy differences between these LDCs and their home countries.

The tax regimes prevailing in the Asian LDCs thus tend to generate externalities influencing the distribution of MNC investment within the region along unintended lines. To the extent that this process of interplay among tax systems distorts MNC investment in individual countries away from planned levels, it clearly works against the best interests of the Asian LDCs. Thus, despite the well-known inward versus outward directed development strategy distinction between SWA and SEA, the tax differentials between these two subregions may actually be redirecting MNC investment flows from the former to the latter country group more forcefully than initially planned by the individual countries' policy makers. Within SEA, furthermore, the impulse to improve competitive positions appears to have induced planners to engage in a virtual investment-incentive "price war" permitting MNCs to reap sizable windfall gains.

While the Asian LDCs are not entirely unaware of the counterdevelopmental effects of their region's existing tax policies toward the MNCs, they are caught in a prisoner's dilemma. Tax policy adjustments by any individual country would generate competitive responses from among its neighbors if aimed at increasing MNC investment inflows and would draw no response from neighbors if aimed at reducing MNC windfall gains. In both cases the total MNC presence in the Asian LDCs would remain unaffected; yet in both cases the country initiating action would be punished with the loss of tax revenues or MNC projects.

An appropriate solution would be collective action at the subregional — and subsequently, perhaps, at the regional — level. Useful initial steps might be intergovernmental consultations on reductions in the range of tax policy instruments applied to MNCs, followed by formal consideration of possible reductions in the size differentials of individual MNC-responsive tax policy instruments. While it is recognized that differences in domestic economic conditions and development strategies and objectives bring forth different tax policy environments, such steps toward subregional and eventually regional tax harmonization with respect to MNCs would initiate a process of policy rationalization in a field whose perverse features are impeding, at least in some degree, the development of Asia's LDCs.

ENDNOTES

1.   All data are as of 1975. The major sources consulted include Hong Kong: Inland Revenue Department, *Synopsis of Taxes Administered by the Inland Revenue Department of Hong Kong* (1975); India: Indian Investment Centre, *Taxes and Incentives: A Guide for Investors* (1974) and *Supplement to Taxes and Incentives* (1975); Indonesia: S. Hadikusumo and

S. Budiadji, *A Guide to the Indonesia Taxation* (1975); Iran: Coopers and Lybrand, Chartered Accountants, "Tax and Related Legislation in Iran," mimeographed (1975); Malaysia: Federal Industrial Development Authority, *Malaysia: A Basic Guidebook for Potential Investors* (1973), and supplementary data; Pakistan: Department of Investment Promotion and Supplies, *Incentives to Industries* (1975); Philippines: National Tax Research Center, personal correspondence; Republic of Korea: Economic Planning Board, *Tax Guide for Foreign Investors* (1975); Singapore: Singapore International Chamber of Commerce (in collaboration with Economic Development Board), *Investor's Guide* (1975); Sri Lanka: *Inland Revenue Act, No. 4 of 1963* (as amended through 1974), and supplementary data; Thailand: Kirkwood, Kaplan, Russin, and Vecchi (for Board of Investment), *Thailand Business-Legal Handbook* (1973), and supplementary data.

2.   From the MNCs' viewpoint these surtaxes and surcharges appear simply as increases in the effective tax rate; to the governments concerned, however, such juridical distinctions permit revenue earmarking for budgetary purposes and also permit certain predetermined tax components to be exempted or otherwise specially treated under special circumstances.

3.   Partial integration of the business and personal income tax systems in Iran, Malaysia, and Singapore via a profit tax credit against personal income tax liabilities on distributed dividends is not available to MNC parents (as nonresident shareholders), which thus bear an implicit dividend tax insofar as they are excluded from the tax credit.

4.   Computational details are available from the author upon request.

5.   Each of these assumptions is realistic in the context of conditions prevailing in Asian LDCs and has been entered here solely as a means of clarifying taxable status and specifying the pertinent range of tax incentives and administrative restrictions. Two items, however, deserve a further word of clarification. First *local incorporation* identifies the MNC project as "resident" for tax purposes, making it liable for taxes on total net profits in each of the countries examined, except Hong Kong (and with less certainty because of legal ambiguities — Iran), which limits the tax liability to domestically earned profits irrespective of residency. "Nonresident" firms in the other countries examined are taxed only on net profits from domestic sources, except the Philippines, which taxes gross profits from domestic sources. Secondly, the assumption of a *uniform pre-tax profit rate* is necessarily somewhat arbitrary. Aside from the influence of differing factor endowments and competitive conditions on economic profits, there is also the issue of the impact of differing accounting rules and regulations on taxable profits. Of particular concern here is variation in permitted depreciation expensing conventions, which can have an especially significant effect on comparative taxable profits in the case of capital-intensive MNC projects.

6.   Tax liabilities are also significantly modified by various means of avoiding and evading taxes. Among the more important tax-avoidance techniques applied by MNCs in LDCs are tax shifting (raising local selling prices and/or reducing local factor costs to offset tax liabilities) and transfer pricing (manipulating accounting prices on international intrafirm transactions to alter taxable profits). The extent to which these techniques can be applied in the countries here being examined is largely a function of domestic market structure and the efficiency of local tax administrations, subjects beyond the scope of this essay.

7.   As in the preceding example, the discussion here and in ensuing factual surveys is restricted to resident industrial joint-venture projects.

8.   Among the assumptions underlying this exercise, perhaps the least plausible is the constancy of the pretax profit rate over the entire period being considered. In most cases industrial projects reap low profits or none at all in the first several years, with profits gradually rising as operations come fully on stream and markets are developed. The incentive effect of profit tax exemption concentrated in the early years may therefore be somewhat lower than that suggested in Table 16-4.

9. Mention should also be made of the tax exemption on foreign-earned interest income in Pakistan, Korea, Singapore, and in certain cases, Indonesia. Though technically a direct tax exemption on the foreign income recipient (in the present case frequently the MNC parent), the incidence of this tax exemption is probably shifted largely to the local debtor (the MNC subsidiary), as is the interest income tax in the first place. This reduces the cost of borrowing just as exemption from, say, tariffs can lower the local cost of capital goods imports. An important side effect of this investment incentive is the increased debt leverage that it induces in MNC projects.

10. It is important to distinguish between the application of tariff *reductions* and tariff *increases* as MNC investment incentives. While tariff reductions assist in raising MNC profits by reducing the cost of imported inputs, tariff increases seek to raise profits by raising the domestic prices of competitive imported outputs. Such investment protection is offered as an explicit MNC investment incentive in Malaysia, the Philippines, Thailand, and Iran and is apparently negotiable in certain other Asian LDCs as well.

11. As a direct "rebate" against profit tax liabilities the investment credit may be argued to be more closely akin to profit tax exemptions than special deductions. Its fixed asset base, however, makes it more directly comparable with extra depreciation allowances, and it can be translated into the equivalent of that tax incentives by dividing the value of the credit by the applicable profit tax rate.

16 ECONOMIC POLICY MAKING AND THE STRUCTURES OF CORPORATISM IN LATIN AMERICA

William Glade

Quite unmistakably, we have in recent times been witnessing an intellectual Parousia of corporatism, corresponding apparently to the renewed flourishing in objective reality of this system of economic organization. In its earlier incarnation, the distinguishing attributes of the phenomenon were widely discussed and debated, most often under the rubric of fascism. Even then, many observed, as did von Beckerath in the *Encyclopedia of the Social Sciences,* that "it is difficult to isolate by abstract analysis the distinctive feature of fascism. Viewed either negatively or positively, it has elements in common with other systems of national organization."[1] There were, for instance, clear corporatist traits in the structural configuration that Keynes felt, in the mid-twenties, would eventually come to characterize advanced western capitalism, even in the liberal democracies.[2] Nevertheless, taking a particularistic view, von Beckerath went on to say that

> it is only when viewed as a peculiarly Italian phenomenon that the essence of Fascism becomes clearly delineated. In its philosophy, its origins and development, its political structure and cultural aspirations, it is . . . a particular fusion of syn-

Institutionalism, Allan Gruchy has said on many occasions, is the study of economic systems. This is a look at one such system.

dicalist theory and doctrines of Italian nationalism. While the former has gradually receded into the background, the latter has supplied the movement with its central intellectual pillar, the idea of the nation state . . . transfigured into a *corpus mysticum* . . . armed with a mission which is realized in the course of the historical process . . . . [The citizen] has individual rights only in so far as they do not conflict with the needs of the nation state.[3]

The last phrases are not trivial in meaning — quite the contrary. They point to a key structural characteristic of the system, one that establishes a family linkage between the Italian case and other corporatist economies, both then and now. We shall return to it later for it provides, along with certain other structural characteristics, an understanding of why corporatism tends to be a portmanteau term that is usually rather loosely applied.

HALLMARKS OF PALEOCORPORATISM

Idiosyncratic details of social architecture displayed in the Italian prototype need not detain us. Suffice it to remark several of the major institutional features that help in specifying the corporatist principle of internal organization: the arrangements by which the various units of society were induced to cooperate in the production, distribution, and use of the aggregate product.[4]

To begin with, the concept of social leadership was elitist, based in that instance on a one-party state. Although the fascist party recruited its membership from nearly all strata of society, cutting vertically through the Italian social structure with the appeal of nationalism, it was hierarchically patterned and its leadership was nominated from above. While the haute bourgeoisie retained a privileged place in the distribution of income, it would be simplistic to view the corporatist order as a mere instrument of this class's domination; there, as in Germany, the business class was organizationally disunited and enfeebled by depression, a condition that eventually worked to the benefit of a political elite that both emerged from and controlled the party and government bureaucracies. If any one class was in the driver's seat, it was the middle class, broadly defined as contrasted with the more narrowly and traditionally defined bourgeoisie, although the latter was occasionally able to turn the system to its advantage.[5] Notwithstanding their actual antagonism in the division of the social product, public policy formally insisted on the solidarity of capital and labor in the production process, and in practice relations between these two major functional interest groups were increasingly subordinated to a politically based public authority. "According to Fascist theory," von Beckerath stressed, "the corporative, or guild, state is the visible expression of the supremacy of the state over the economic and social groups within the nation."[6] A planners' preference function, in other words, gradually gained importance in the process of social preference ordering relative to market-generated social preference functions.

Through associational channels, a certain interpenetration of private corporate and governmental bureaucracies characterized the system of decision making and resource allocation. This aspect was, in fact, part of the explicit design of corporatism, for in principle it promised to establish a semistable system of interbureaucratic coordination for jointly determining the goal function for various parts of the economy. Interest groups were formally incorporated into the decisional processes of the system through officially recognized vocationally based corporations, and these became the organizational channels for expressing various group preferences in the formation of the community's effective aggregate preferences.

The foregoing elements, in turn, were combined with commitment to an economically active state.[7] Although private initiative and the capitalistic order were preserved (at least to the extent that capitalism be equated with a regime of private enterprise), there was a virtual identification of the economic system with the state; the state could, and did, intervene in the processes of production whenever private initiative was judged inadequate for the task at hand or when priority political interests were at stake. Owing to depressed economic conditions, in fact, a very considerable portion of the Italian economy passed directly into state management: the I.R.I. complex, the Big Three firms of Italian banking, the Azienda Generale Italiana Petroli, and so on. Since distributive questions were, in the last analysis, also determined by the state, the type of capitalism with which the government administration — with its concentrated power in the executive branch — was allied itself was not one organized primarily by the free play of market forces. Rather, decisional power was fundamentally administrative, albeit supplemented by market-guided decisions.

For all its ambiguities and a consequent problem of boundary definition, the fascist mode of organization came to be recognized as a fairly distinct type of economic system, one that had clear counterparts outside the Italian peninsula. Stripped of pasta, authoritarian capitalism appeared in several European guises: e.g., German National Socialism, pre-Anschluss Austria, Falangist Spain, and Salazar's Portugal.[8] A Romanian enthusiast was even moved to write of the present century as "the century of corporatism."[9] In all cases, a regime of private property was maintained in most of the means of production but was combined with varying degrees of guidance and planning from the central administration of government, reflecting the common corporatist belief in the inefficacy of the market as an organizing principle at the macrosocietal or systemic level. A generalized characteristic of the system, therefore, was subordination of the market to state policy as the mechanism for allocating resources and rewards ("a planned provision of labor, a planned regulation of the market, a planned control of prices and wages," to quote Hitler).

With conscious substitution of a bureaucratic-technical integration of production processes for the price system's automatic allocation, authoritarian capitalism differed conspicuously in both political and economic modalities from the ideal type of the democratic market economies of the West. Neither self-regulating markets nor political parties operating in a pluralistic parliamentary context served as the decisive information-processing and interest-articulating mechanisms. Citizen sovereignty and consumer sovereignty, in other words, were similarly circumscribed, and, for the most part, a distinctive system of interest representation was employed. Official or quasi-official associationally organized interests were accorded special access to the decisional arenas of the state and served, in turn, partly as vehicles for the implementation of policy. In essence, economic associations played largely a facilitating function, i.e., the simplification of administrative contacts with the economic interests subject to state regulation.

The particular institutions of economic organization differed somewhat from case to case, there being, for instance, much more state ownership of industry in Italy than in Germany, more rigorous central planning and more explicit cartelization in the latter than in the former.[10] The accompanying ideological and ritual baggage varied as well. Yet, certain of the foregoing structural features appeared sufficiently evolved that a sort of ultimate reality test was met by these economic arrangements: they became enshrined and differentiated from capitalism as a standard component of textbooks on comparative economic systems.[11]

Granted that the emergence of corporatism rested on a vast complex of antecedent causes, rarely, outside of Marxian discussions, was any effort made to present a genetic accounting of the phenomenon or to elucidate its systemic dynamics. In retrospect, however, it seems more than mere happenstance that the defining characteristics of corporatism were closely associated with special situational exigencies, e.g., with draconian antidepression measures, recovery from civil war, or resource mobilization to place the economy on a wartime footing. Such circumstances displaced the market mechanism as the principal basis for defining the social preference function and provided social justification for the control-enhancing measures by means of which private property interests could be subordinated to public authority.

To the extent that corporatism was a function of the transcendence of macrosocietal ends over individual and enterprise objectives expressed through markets — albeit with a continued reliance on regulated private firms for much microeconomic management — the timing and location of corporatism's first coming seem particularly revealing. Amid the stresses and economic disturbances of the interwar period, it appeared as a dominant mode of organization in Italy, Spain, and Portugal — with Balkan parallels, i.e., in a southern European zone that was clearly marginal to the mainstream of European capitalism, in countries in which the capitalist system was, for a variety of reasons, much more weakly developed than elsewhere. While Germany had, compared with these countries, experienced a much more advanced degree of capitalist evolution, there the system had been gravely undermined by military defeat, territorial loss, governmental change, political conflicts, onerous economic burdens imposed by the Versailles Treaty, and hyperinflation. The case of Austria, too, is similarly instructive in that corporatism appears to have taken root in a setting in which a still emergent capitalist order had been severely dislocated by dismemberment of the empire.[12]

There were, additionally, some New World parallels to these European corporatist systems, discernable by their ideological garb as by their systemic features: the Estado Novo of Vargas's Brazil and, especially, the Justicialismo of Peron's Argentina. For that matter, Mexico, too, displayed corporatist features but was less frequently characterized as corporatist, doubtless because its political allegiance, like Brazil's, lay with the liberal democracies and its political language employed the vocabulary of socialism. All this was of concern mainly to area specialists, however, and in any case these Latin American echoes were scarcely significant enough, on the world scene, to merit more than a mention in comparative systems texts.[13] Nevertheless, for present purposes it is relevant to remark that these three countries, while industrially advanced for Latin America, were still in an incipient level of capitalist development, with private economic institutions relatively feeble and older class structure partially undermined by depression-generated dislocations, wartime disruptions, and (in the case of Mexico) politically inspired social reform programs. In all three cases, too, for somewhat different reasons, there was governmental commitment to accelerated change: to revamping the whole production pattern, more rapidly than the market mechanism could effect it, in accordance with a substantially altered scheme of social priorities.

THE ARRIVAL OF NEOCORPORATISM

It is worth noting that in time four particularly interesting developments came to pass, clarifying considerably the essential features of corporatist socioeconomic structure.

In the first place, after the Götterdämmerung of the forties the customary sections on fascism or authoritarian capitalism were eventually dropped from most textbooks on comparative economic systems, having been consigned to history and displaced by discussions of market socialism, Chinese communism, and similar new styles of macroeconomic organization. By the eighth edition of *Comparative Economic Systems* by Loucks and Whitney, neither corporatism nor fascism even appeared in the index.[14] Germany and Italy had been converted from their former ways, and Peron, too, had been vanquished — for the time being. Spain and Portugal evidently held scant interest except insofar as the Iberian peninsula was viewed as a museum of archaic social technology, and so to all intents and purposes corporatism passed from the scene.[15] Gruchy concluded in the mid-sixties, for instance, that fascism-corporatism was no longer in the running as a competing type of economic system, a view shared by many at the time.

Not long afterwards, however, there were increasingly frequent scholarly reports that corporatism, or at least something closely resembling it, had been sighted in Latin America, notwithstanding the demise of Vargas and the exiling of Peron and his sundry companions. Indeed, the corporatist examples the region afforded were perceived to be rather more numerous than before. As early as the late 1950s, Scott had begun to reinterpret Mexican experience as a case of corporative centralism, and in the outpouring of analysis since that time, corporatism of one stripe or another has been ascribed to the national systems of post-Peron Argentina, post-Vargas Brazil (especially Brazil after April 1964), Peru (after 1968), Chile (under Frei and after Allende, with some seeing it present during the Allende administration), Bolivia, Ecuador, Uruguay, and the Dominican Republic.[16] And a number of corporatist institutions have been detected in Colombia and Venezuela as well. (This institutional convergence of countries otherwise so diverse in their civic traditions and levels of per capita income may well represent the demise of the concept of political development.)

The third development of note is that, meanwhile, corporatist or at least quasi-corporatist traits were being detected, sometimes retrospectively, in the most unlikely places — back, as Keynes had foreseen, in the democratic market-based economies whose pluralistic liberalism and pragmatic policy approach would seem to have set them worlds apart from anything like the doctrinal and institutional eccentricities of fascism. The United States (with the advent of the New Deal), Sweden, the Netherlands, postwar Austria, Denmark, Norway, Greece, France, the United Kingdom, even Switzerland — have all been observed to harbor at least some dimensions of corporatism. The idea spread that corporatism and modern liberal capitalism were not without significant similarities.[17]

Long before, of course, others besides Keynes had reached this conclusion. Brady had said as much in the landmark book, *Business as a System of Power:*

> Thus a comparative study of attempts to expand business controls within the several capitalistic systems becomes a prime necessity for both business and the public. . . . Second, along every significant line the parallelisms in the evolution of business centralization within the several national systems, including those within countries still functioning on a liberal-capitalistic basis, are so close as to make them appear the common product of a single plan. . . . And finally, the implications of power in such wide-spreading business controls, together with the popular challenge to business leaders, cause all economic issues to take on a political meaning, and thereby cause the role of the government to grow in importance in a sort of geometric ratio.[18]

In Brady's reading of the record, there was a correlative rise and universalization of a tendency for "the normal course of business as usual [to lean] even more heavily upon a generalized system of state aid."[19] The point was, in effect, later confirmed and carried further by Galbraith and Shonfield.[20] Recognizing intercountry variations, Shonfield went on to observe that the widespread western commitment to full employment and the accelerated pace of technological progress has tended to produce at least four common features among the advanced industrial countries:

1. a great increase in public sector expenditures and vastly increased reliance on public authority's management of the economic system;
2. a rise in social welfare programs;
3. increasing regulation and control of the market (by both public and private authorities); and
4. the occupation by large corporations of a position of substantial authority and influence.

Moreover, as Weidenbaum demonstrated, public investment via quasi-public enterprises or outright state enterprise had also come to be a mainstay of the contemporary institutional order, even in the United States.[21] Taking these and other observable trends into account, Fusfeld concluded that "the United States has moved well down the path toward a corporate state" in spite of its long historical significance as a bastion of liberal capitalism.[22]

A fourth noteworthy development has been an extention of the concept of corporatism, not only spatially but also temporally, pushing it back to historical antecedents far earlier than the 1920s or 1930s.[23] From this perspective, the corporatist characteristics of Iberian social organization began to emerge even before the late-medieval phase of nation building. Although a chief expositor of this line of inquiry, Wiarda, has interpreted corporatism as the product of a particular evolution, constrained by the embedded norms and Weltanschauung of the Catholic and Roman cultural tradition, there are in this explanatory vein the seeds of another, more structural type of genetic accounting, one built on bureaucratization.

FUNCTIONAL EQUIVALENCIES IN THE STRUCTURAL BASIS OF CORPORATIST ECONOMIES

For present purposes it is useful to prescind from the sometimes bizarre and often internally inconsistent ideological trappings that have adorned corporatism. These normative prescriptions for societal organizations have already attracted much scholarly attention and tend mainly, in varying degrees of elaboration, to depict corporatism as a benevolent, hierarchically structured society based on noblesse oblige when, in practice, control of society's material assets has generally served less generously defined ends.[24]

Shorn of ideological formulations, which seem to be both epiphenomenal and highly variable, corporatism can more profitably be examined as a politicoeconomic modus operandi, though this dimension, too, appears to be variable over time and place. The striking feature of the problématique, in this regard, is the remarkable parallelism in organizational forms and processes that links otherwise differing social contexts. This parallelism between the corporatist dimensions of contemporary Latin American economic systems — or, for that matter, of other developing economies such as that of Turkey — and prewar European corporatist relations of production derives, it is postulated here, from the existence of a series of functional equivalencies in the institutional matrix of corporatism in the two settings.

In exploring these functional equivalents, it is well to keep in mind that a binary conceptualization of corporatism is neither particularly fruitful nor readily squared with observable reality. If one follows Schmitter and others in defining corporatism as "an institutional arrangement for linking the associationally organized interests of civil society with the decisional structures of the state," corporatism seems, judging from the available evidence, to be combinable with gradations of political openness that range, as Brady and Schmitter have indicated, from one-party totalitarian regimes to those characterized by pluralistic competition.[25] Clearly, too, from an historical point of view, there are variations in the degree to which the distinctly corporatist forms of interest representation range from implicit and only partially institutionalized (latent) patterns to explicit and fully institutionalized (manifest) patterns. For our purposes, moreover, corporatist traits may be exhibited in both advanced industrial and newly industrializing economies.

The characteristics of the corporatist process of decision making and policy formation lead, first of all, to the observation that a necessary, though not sufficient, condition for corporatism is the evolution of a certain degree of structural differentiation and complexity in the socioeconomic system. Through industrialization and urbanization, diverse organized secondary groups — sectorially or occupationally defined — appear on the institutional scene to mediate relations between firms and the state, developed through categorical governmental programs and policies (as contrasted, say, with direct bargaining between individual firms and the sovereign). For this reason corporatism is seldom, if ever, found in the similar LDC economies. In these, the political system rests in the hands of a relatively few vested interests and the functions of the state, beside that of consolidating the position of the dominant interests and distributing concessionary favors to individual households and firms, tend to be minimal (as does the state apparatus itself). In simple economies, moreover, the internal cohesion of the dominant class or functional interest group ordinarily enables it to exercise a hegemonic power over the state, rather than entering, along with other interests, into an interactive relationship with it. "Delayed entry" cases of development, then, tend not to be corporatist at their outset, there being absent the array of varied economic or functional interests on the associational expression (and balancing) of which a corporatist order depends. For reasons of administrative convenience and efficacy, however, once a political commitment has been made to accelerated development, the state may well sponsor on a tutelary basis embryonic organizations of a sectorial, industrial, or occupational sort, nurturing the growth of an organized structure of interests that eventually assumes a corporatist character. Examples of this associational cultivation as a facet of development policy abound, from the case of revolutionary Mexico to modern Brazil. In both cases, the state became involved in the process of building up group interests in a system which could eventually function to sustain its prevailing configuration, an anticipatory type of corporatism as it were. The structures of articulation that in paleocorporatism function for defense and control become, in the Latin American context, structures for promotion and control.

Extensive documentation of this point — an aspect of the organization-intensive nature of modern economic growth — can be found in the works of Tannenbaum, Mosk, Kling, Bradenburg, Shafer, Hansen, and others on

Mexico, or in, say, the studies made of Brazil by such specialists as Leff, Schmitter, Roett, Stepan, and Baer, to mention only a few. The eventual maturation of anticipatory corporatism into administrative instrumentalities very much like those mediating European government-business relations is exemplified particularly well by the role that the Lopez Portillo administration in Mexico has assigned the so-called Alianza para la Producción in its recovery and development strategy. The dialogue of CORDIPLAN with various interest groups helped strengthen the successful relationships on which Venezuelan planning has rested and provides yet another case in point.

In the anticipatory corporatism of delayed-entry cases, where state intervention is, for reasons that have been examined by Gerschenkron and Eckstein, prevalent, corporatist methods of social control appear to have another function to play: as a restraint on the growth of consumption in order to expedite the capital accumulation process and direct new investment into areas judged to promote structural transformation. In such cases, the enforced restraint of consumption may be especially critical, given the demonstration effect and the high marginal propensities to consume that prevail in societies now embarking on the industrialization process at per capita income levels lower than those enjoyed by the older developed countries at the time of their entry into modern economic growth. In the developmental context, for example, Brazilian public authority has been able in recent years to employ its control over organized labor to hold down real wage levels, while subordination of the officially endorsed campesino confederation of Mexico to the government's policy objectives has long been used to contain the consumption aspirations of much of the rural populace — a practice taken up more recently by the Peruvian regime as well. Social control mechanisms in these instances serve as functional equivalents of the consumption-restricting institutions that, in the European contexts, have released resources for diversion to military preparedness — as in Nazi Germany — or simply for the maintenance of the state itself and the consumption standards of privileged strata. As the Spanish and Portuguese instances, among others, demonstrate, accelerated capital formation is not necessarily part of either the vindicating ideology or practical accomplishments of corporatism in respect of its restrictive policies on popular consumption.

What seems to be a further common thread among the varieties of corporatism is another salient structural feature of system organization: namely, that Latin American corporatist economic arrangements invariably involve the same amalgamation of statist and capitalist elements that we have noted earlier in discussion of the classic European cases. Whether European or Latin American, the system is one in which capitalist forms of enterprise coexist with extensive state intervention, giving rise to a species of state-supported but also state-regulated, even state-directed, capitalism. The well-known "third-positionism" of a multitude of Latin American governments, in fact, has dwelt on construction of a mode of national economic organization that is intermediate between liberal market capitalism (with private interests dominant) and a full-blown command economy (with socialization of all means of production). In Latin American cases, no less than in the European ones observed previously, the emergence of corporatism has sprung from a social decision to superimpose a preference ordering substantially different from that yielded by the interplay of market forces — but, in contradistinction to a Soviet-style economy, with retention of private ownership of a significant portion of the means of production.

Once again, the matter of apparent commonalities and functional equivalents comes into view. Von Beckerath spoke, it will be recalled, of the historical mission of the state — of certain national needs to which individual rights had to be subordinated in Italian corporatism. For analytical purposes, however, the notion of a national historical mission can be reconceptualized, less grandiosely, as an overriding social priority for which there might be a number of functional equivalents: accelerated economic development, construction of a national security system, mobilization for territorial expansion, and so on. These or any others may be transmitted to the macrosocietal pattern of resource allocation through public policy, directly in the revealed preferences of the public sector's own resource deployment and indirectly by means of constraints imposed by the state on the behavior of private sector firms and households. In Latin American corporatism, desarrollismo was — until recently joined by national security — the prevailing social justification for extensive direct and indirect intervention by the state. Both national development strategy, as influenced by the United Nations Economic Commission for Latin America, and external institutional constraints on development, as identified by Mark,[26] have operated to make the public sector the centerpiece of the economic growth process throughout much of Latin America — to the growing dismay, in recent decades, of important private sector interests.[27]

At the core of the corporatist system, one seems invariably to find private economic power blocks interacting in a transactional mode with the apparatus of state, with neither party altogether subordinated to the other. The suggestion here is that the state is not simply a creature of superordinate segments in the structure of private power (as it is, for instance, in

Nicaragua), nor does it enjoy uncontested dominance over them as, say, in Poland or Yugoslavia. The relation is, rather, an interactive one, one in which it may well be possible to observe what Marx so presciently remarked in *The Eighteenth Brumaire:* the "process whereby state executive power becomes progressively more independent" from the structure of private interests. This is not to say that the loose constraints imposed on state policy by class and other interest groups and the relative autonomy of the state that results are a function of the same set of circumstances in all corporatist systems. Manifestly they are not.

In advanced industrial societies, the relative autonomy of the state sector may be a function of many factors: the rise of countervailing private power blocs, the weakening of once dominant economic interests by wars or depression, regional rivalries, the role of internal contradictions in eroding both the legitimacy and the autonomous strength of the private sector, the fragmentation of private interests by the sheer complexity of the industrial, financial, and commercial structure, and so on. Indeed the very scale and intricacy of the state's administrative machinery and the enhanced importance of public investment activity to the post-Depression operations of western industrial economies have underscored the systemic salience of the regulatory, supportive, and directive roles of government.

In less developed societies, on the other hand, the failure of key private interests to achieve, or preserve, full ruling class status may reside, instead, in a process of historical evolution in which the state apparatus emerged as the paramount social interest well in advance of local private power constellations, in respect of which the state has played a tutelary role.[28] In these cases, Latin American experience suggests that the function, if not the purpose of the broad panoply of interventionary measures has, in effect, often been that of *divide et empera,* the orchestration of interventionary policies being such as to maintain the divisions among the groups and classes of society. Be that as it may, the critical feature in the evolution of authoritarian bureaucratic centralism in late developing countries would seem to be the set of historical circumstances that produces a consolidation of political power antecedent to the gathering of economic forces and interests in the private sector — a phenomenon that has come about through a variety of historical permutations. In these instances, varied though they may be in other respects, the paramount role of the state's initiative and unfolding power leads to a comprehensive bureaucratic surveillance of business and industrial processes not altogether different from the system of bureaucratic guidance that has sprung out of other conditions in the case of the industrially advanced societies.

For this structural reason too, it can be repeated that corporatism is partially a function of growing social complexity and segmentation and is virtually unimaginable in the least developed economies. With economic development come both the proliferation of secondary groups necessary to expand the ambit of political participation and diversify and fragment the polity on the one hand and, on the other, the expansion of the resource base available for enlargement of a centralizing, bureaucratic state apparatus. In Latin America no more than in Europe has the resulting transformation in the relation of social forces produced the polarization of classes anticipated by Marx, although this is not to deny the class character of state power. Instead, profound growth-induced changes in the occupational structure, continued increase in the numbers of the middle class, the uncertain and fluctuating political role of different classes under the peculiar conditions of peripheral capitalist development, and the enhanced role of the state in economic management have altered considerably the institutional support systems for the exercise of public power. Moreover, as Brazilian scholars especially have pointed out in discussions of the concept of the "cartorial state," the growth of a class of public functionaries has for some time been impelled by the swelling ranks of the university trained — i.e., the growth of an educated professional class and "service class," in Renner's terms — at a rate exceeding the capacity of the private sector to absorb them.

As in European corporatism, Latin American social leadership tends to be elitist, but not always does its elite character stem from a monopoly of influence by a dominant party such as Mexico's P.R.I., much less on an uncontested control of the machinery of government by an industrial, mercantile, or financial bourgeoisie (using that term in the orthodox Marxian sense). On account of the extensive social reorganization that major Latin American countries have undergone, the once useful notion of an oligarchic power system has long since ceased to have very much explanatory value. With the passage of time, the relation of the class structure of society to state power has become far more complicated, owing particularly to the growth of a new political elite that some Latin American social scientists — in a creative use of class categories of analysis — have called a state bourgeoisie. Largely middle-class (in the broader sense) in origin, this technocratic bureaucracy has emerged as something resembling a mandarin class, its meritocratic nature related to its control of scarce organizational and technical skills as well as to its commanding position astride the flow of information in a setting in which information is both scarce and organized by an exceedingly imperfect market.

While the concept of a state bourgeoisie may at first appear contradictory, it actually sheds a great deal of light on the structure of the particular social formation that composes corporatism in Latin America today. Further, it does so in two important respects besides merely indicating a category of persons who may, as the technocratic elite of the public sector often do, enjoy real incomes and a style of life virtually indistinguishable from that of private sector capitalists. The state bourgeoisie does not, in other words, merely resemble the bourgeoisie. Rather, the term identifies a class of persons whose members possess a similar power position vis-à-vis other social aggregates and who, indeed, occupy roughly similar positions in the prevailing relations of production.

In the first place, the concept of a state bourgeoisie enables one to correct the widespread misspecification of the production function that has resulted from a rather mechanical transposition to Latin American analysis of the notion of factor mix that has proved useful in understanding the mode of production of market capitalism. Nothing could be clearer about the present epoch in the economic formation of society than that, to specify fully the systemic production function, one must take into account the organization-intensive mode of production that prevails. In a very real sense, the administrative class made up by the professional-bureaucratic intelligentsia controls key forms of intangible property that have high scarcity value in the social process of production: the ability to perform vital services and functions by virtue of its "ownership" of technical and administrative skills. More is involved than simply the talent and education that make up human capital as a critical factor of production. Also central to the production process as it is organized in the highly interventionist systems that predominate in Latin America are the networks of contacts and connections through which information and influence flow and can be mobilized, as well as access to the government policy "inputs" that serve as indispensable external resources for the firm. When all of these resources are specified in the production function in order to make that concept operational for the Latin American social matrix, it becomes obvious that the so-called state bourgeoisie does in fact hold "bourgeois" status by virtue of "owning" major inputs in the dominant mode of production, i.e., controlling significant means of production.

Beyond the foregoing, in the major Latin American economies there exists a considerable parastatal sector in which public managers and bureaucratic entrepreneurs enjoy at least as much de facto control over the means of production entrusted to their charge as do the private-sector managers of whom Berle and Means wrote in their analysis of the large modern corporation. Autonomous or semiautonomous in many instances by virtue of their legal charter, the state enterprises commonly enjoy a further measure of independence owing to the comparative laxity of systems of governmental supervision and coordination. Often, they are no more closely constrained in their operations by the core legislative and administrative structures of the state than the management-controlled corporations of the private sector are by their private shareholders and the market. For all practical purposes, then, since the bureaucratic managers of the public sector frequently sit in effective control of even the conventionally defined means of production, the concept of a state bourgeoisie seems doubly validated.

CORPORATISM AND DEVELOPMENT PATHS

In all of the foregoing, there is no implication that corporatism stands in any fixed evolutionary sequence to other forms of macroeconomic organization, nor that it derives from only one set of historical circumstances. Indeed, the record would seem to negate any theory of unilinear systemic evolution although it does suggest a certain degree of institutional affinity between the corporatist policy configuration and various sets of circumstances that put capitalism under stress. Just as liberal market capitalism, the product of aggressive statism in its embryonic days, has tended, once past its days of ascendence, in some places to move into the more corporatist mode that Shonfield, Brady, Galbraith, and others have described, by way of contrast much of the recent literature on Mexico and Brazil suggests that there the practical result of extensive state entrepreneurship and regulatory intervention has been to initiate and cultivate a constellation of private interests that, at the outset almost wholly dependent on state power for their nurture, later attain sufficient strength to enter into a bargaining relationship with the bureaucratic leadership of the public sector.[29] In these and similar cases, however, there seems to be no basis whatever for anticipating that this type of neomercantilist corporatism will be supplanted by the liberal market capitalism that eventually held sway in the advanced industrial societies after the original period of mercantilism. On the contrary, in some respects these societies appear to offer a quite different prospect: namely, that with accelerated urbanization and the introduction of a welfare public sector the problems of an incipient capitalist and industrial order become confounded with — if not superseded by — the peculiar problems of postindustrial society, without the society's experiencing mature industrial capitalism of a liberal market sort in the interim.

Proximately, then, the structural sources of present-day corporatism appear to be identifiable in two sets of functionally equivalent circumstances summarized by the expression:

$$C = f[(a^1, b^1) \text{ or } (a^2, b^2)]$$

Where C = Corporatism

a = Δ associational agglomeration of private sector interests by:

(a^1) the evolutionary process described by Brady, Galbraith, Fusfeld, and others for advanced industrial societies, or

(a^2) government tutelage of new interests in the LDC's;

b = Δ bureaucratic macrosocietal management via the public sector and the regulatory powers of the positive state as a result of:

(b^1) countervailing power (the use of citizen sovereignty contains large capitalistic interests) in industrial societies, a growing preference for systemic stabilization, growing systemic complexity, and so on, or

(b^2) the quasi-autonomous role of the "Bonapartist" state in LDCs in the management of accelerated economic development and social change.

MAINTENANCE MECHANISMS IN THE CORPORATIST SYSTEM

If corporatism appears as a feature of both mature capitalism and early capitalist development, closer analysis of the phenomenon draws attention to other common attributes of the interface between the state and the private sector of the economy in both sets of circumstances.

On the state side, the critical variables appear to be the growth of administrative bureaucracy and its acquisition of a considerable armamentarium of interventionary techniques. Together these factors have eroded the distinction between policy and administration and have tended de facto to transpose regulatory authority and managerial policy determination from legislatures (with their roots in political parties) to the executive branch of government. The increasing complexity of issues and relationships — and growing awareness of the externalities and ramifications involved — have aided and abetted this process. Further, with increasing structural differentiation of the economic and social systems, the need has grown to encourage development of more specialized mechanisms for aggregating and articulating group interests than are afforded by political parties.

A major corollary of the rise of bureaucratic interventionism has been a growth in the utility of interest grouping or categorization in all manner of extrabureacratic relationships: e.g., for economy in information gathering and communication, for efficiency in interest aggregation, for institutionalized policy dialogue, for defining classes of regulated relationships and regularization in the application of policies, and for the administrative convenience of analyzing and dealing with categories of cases rather than possibly idiosyncratic individual instances. For the executive branch of the United States government to negotiate "orderly marketing" pacts with shoe exporting nations, for instance, it is necessary for the bureaucracy to take an industry-wide view and act on an industry-wide basis both at home and abroad. For Latin American governments to press ahead on regional integration, planning authorities must of necessity invite increased associational (rather than individual firm) participation in discussions and policy formation in order to negotiate appropriate industrial and sectorial complementation agreements.

In short, a major element involved in corporatism is the very rationality of bureaucratization of which Weber wrote. But there is yet another important bureaucratic use of corporative categorization: namely, constituency identification and the mobilization of clientelistic support for agency advantage in bureaucratic politics. In this regard, it is important to keep in mind that the administrative apparatus of the state, especially when it has reached the proportions it has in recent times, is by no means a monolithic, homogenous unit. Rather, the assorted bureaucracies come to have divergent objectives and perceptions, become involved in interagency jurisdictional disputes, attempt to enlarge (and prevent extraagency encroachment on) their own domains, and compete with each other for the allocation of scarce resources. The enormous problems that have been encountered in effecting interagency coordination in Latin American agrarian reform and regional development programs attest to the heterogeneity of interests within the public sector. Not infrequently, in pursuit of their objectives, public sector entities employ techniques of social control and demand management in order to build alliances outside the public sector just as they seek alliances within the state bureaucracy. And for constituency building purposes, establishing relations with groups or associations of firms is far more advantageous than a more atomistic approach to the problem.

On the private sector side, a variety of evolutionary trends — the rise of large-scale private bureaucratic enterprise and business associations with a stake in maintaining orderly conditions in the macroeconomic environment, the aggregation of industry interests to lobby for beneficial policies and policy interpretations, the growth of new interest groups out of development-oriented intervention — have tended to create intermediate associations that bypass the sometimes weak political parties and legislatures. Even where corporatist forms of interest representation are not legally and formally structured into the policy-making process, disproportionalities of power and experientially based adroitness in the management of political influence and manipulation of the media may confer on quasi-corporatist secondary associations such advantages that they enjoy, for all practical purposes, the functional equivalent of the de jure monopolization of communications channels held by, say, the corporations of Italian fascism. Here, too, however, it is essential to keep in mind that the previously mentioned heterogeneity of the public sector is easily matched by the hetereogeneity of the private sector interests — a heterogeneity that can be to some extent amplified and orchestrated by skillful deployment of the interventionary powers of the state. The amplitude of available interventionary techniques, for its part, gives the state a singular ability to distribute advantages in which the incidence of benefits is much more visible than the incidence of net costs. Private actors, then, may have as much need for alliances with segments of the bureaucratic apparatus of government as they have for concerted action with other private groups — sometimes, indeed, even more.

From what has been said, one may glimpse some of the general mechanisms in corporatism that tend towards system maintenance, for the very nature of the interface defines an interpenetration of sectors. Two mutually reinforcing processes are at work: the socialization of the private sector and the privatization of the public sector. Both establish transactional relations that work to enhance the stake of the major actors in the system. Given this symbiosis, we may briefly conclude by suggesting that there are today a number of trends that tend to sustain the equilibrium of a corporatist political economy in Latin America:

1. There is the growing social importance of areas in which public decision making of a politicized character is customarily involved, e.g., expansion of educational and health care systems, urban planning and development, extension of the transport infrastructure, energy development, and formulation of national science policy to support scientific and technological research, in addition to the conventional macroeconomic management responsibilities. To the extent that the "basic needs" approach becomes incorporated into Latin American development policy, the emphasis on public sector investment

activity — in public housing, in provisioning schemes such as that operated by Mexico's CONASUPO, and the like — is likely to be increased even more. The growth of this means of resource allocation, through the political "market" rather than the economic market, almost inevitably evokes as an organizational response the formation and strengthening of associational groups through which claims can be pressed and social demand competition be pursued.

2. There is the observable thrust towards a type of consultative indicative planning based on collaborative guidance of the economy, a collaborative guidance that was largely absent from the "decorative" planning efforts of the Decade of Development and the Alliance for Progress. With greater attention being given to the process of implementation, there is correspondingly greater interest among planning agencies in employing corporatistic associational devices as a means for gathering informational inputs and gaining increased assent for policy outputs.

3. There is the widespread revival of interest in incomes policies to deal with chronic inflationary pressures and manage social conflict and dissensus.

4. There is the gradual movement towards a form of regional integration that incorporates industry-based negotiations and sectorial agreements on a transnational scale, substituting industry-wide organizations for discussions among individual firms in the process of determining national industrial policies in harmony with regional schemes.

5. There is the likelihood of stronger defensive measures being taken through collective action on the part of national industry in response to perceived competitive threats from multinational corporations.

6. There is the continued growth of the parastatal sector through which are created still more intimate linkages for bonding the public sector to the private sector and for forestalling the appearance of private sector solidarity in opposition to the state. With parastatal enterprises serving as both supplier firms and customer firms for private sector enterprises, an increasing number of dependency relations come into being.

7. There is the continuing important role of the state in capital supply and the repercussions, during economic crises, of the traditional disinclination of private firms to dilute control by bringing in more shareholders through equity financing. Because these firms customarily have relied heavily on debt financing, including loans provided on concessionary terms and/or a longer term basis by government

banks, financial setbacks in times of adversity have often tended to push Latin American private enterprises into receivership, transforming debt obligations into equity shares held by state financing institutions. Accustomed to managing equity holdings in state and mixed enterprises initiated by development agencies, state lending institutions have thereby enlarged their shareholding portfolios and increased further that interpenetration of public and private sectors that is one of the hallmarks of corporatism.

In short, for a considerable number of reasons, both general and specific to Latin America, one may expect the corporatist type of economic system to be around for a long time. This being the case, it behooves students of development in that region to familiarize themselves with the methods by which the corporatist system organizes its economic processes. To be sure, there is still some argument over the appropriateness of using the prism of corporatism to refract the components of Latin American economic life, but considering what has become of expectations for the pluralistic liberalism and market-organized economy that development and modernization were once thought to produce, one can conclude that at this time the opportunity costs of using corporatism as an explanatory model are not very high.

ENDNOTES

1.   Erwin von Beckerath, "Fascism," *Encyclopedia of the Social Sciences,* Vol. 5 (New York: Macmillan, 1948), pp. 133–139.

2.   John Maynard Keynes, *Essays in Persuasion* (London: Rupert Hart-Davis, 1952). See the two essays titled "The End of Laissez-Faire" and "Am I a Liberal?" For corporatism in the United States, see John A. Garraty, "The New Deal, National Socialism, and the Great Depression," *American Historical Review* 78 (1973): 914–15.

3.   von Beckerath, "Fascism," p. 134.

4.   The synthesis that follows is derived from George Lowell Field, *The Syndical and Corporative Institutions of Italian Fascism* (New York: Columbia University Press, 1938); Roland Sarti, *Fascism and Industrial Leadership in Italy* (Berkeley: University of California Press, 1971); and Renzo de Felice, *Fascism: An Informal Introduction to its Theory and Practice* (New Brunswick, N. J.: Transaction Books, 1976). These works indicate plainly that macroeconomic management and industrial policy did not always operate in practice as the theory of corporatism envisaged.

5.   The contradictions between the doctrine and practice of corporatism, as well as its ideological untidiness, are illustrated particularly well in Diamant's study of the Austrian case. There, varied professional interests and rural and urban lower middle classes were manipulated by the higher bourgeoisie with which, in principle, they were in opposition. Alfred Diamant, *Austrian Catholics and the First Republic* (Princeton, N.J.: Princeton University Press, 1960).

6.   von Beckerath, "Fascism," p. 137.

7. Diamant, *Austrian Catholics and the First Republic,* pp. 66–69, 283–85, also calls attention to the strong statist tradition in Austrian corporatism, which conferred on the state an omnicompetence that was decidedly at variance with other doctrinal elements of corporatism.

8. Curiously, the pre-World War II Japanese version of authoritarian capitalism was widely neglected by comparative systems scholars, although not by the handful of area specialists (mostly economic historians) who wrote on the economy of Japan.

9. Mihaïl Manoïlesco, *Le Siècle de Corporatisme* (Paris: F. Alcan, 1934).

10. For useful descriptions of the German case, see Robert A. Brady, *The Spirit and Structure of German Fascism* (New York: Viking Press, 1937); Claude W. Guillebaud, *The Economic Recovery of Germany* (London: Macmillan, 1939); and Arthur Schweitzer, *Big Business in the Third Reich* (Bloomington: Indiana University Press, 1964). Brady's book points out similarities in economic and political behavior between Germany and other capitalist economies and shows how limited, in Germany, was the actual application of pure or formal corporatist principles.

11. William N. Loucks and J. Weldon Hout, *Comparative Economic Systems,* 3rd ed. (New York: Harper and Brothers, 1948), for example, devoted the four separate chapters of Part VII to a discussion of "The Doctrines of Fascism," "Fascist Italy," "National Socialist Germany," and "Evaluating the Fascist System." A few years later, the fifth edition of the same book—William N. Loucks, *Comparative Economic Systems* (New York: Harper and Brothers, 1957) still carried a separate section on fascism, but three of the chapters of the third edition had by then been collapsed into one. George P. Adams, Jr., *Competitive Economic Systems* (New York: Thomas Y. Cowell Company, 1955) had, meanwhile, also allotted four chapters to fascism. The treatment in these popular textbooks was typical of the day.

12. The situational-structural basis of Austrian corporatism is made plain in the ponderously partisan work of Charles Gulick, *Austria from Habsburg to Hitler,* vol. 2 (Berkeley: University of California Press, 1948), see esp. pp. 1143–48, 1423–56.

13. Loucks and Hout, *Comparative Economic Systems,* viewed with evident alarm the "transplantation of fascist ideas and personnel from Germany, Spain, and Italy to Argentina" (p. 627), referring explicitly to the Peron government, but was altogether silent on the Brazilian (or any other Latin American) case. In Loucks, *Comparative Economic Systems,* the mention of the Argentine, while still in the same vein, was brief. In Adams, *Competitive Economic Systems,* the reference to Latin America was even more marginal and confined to a single question: "Should Peron's Argentina or Salazar's Portugal properly be called fascist?"

14. William N. Loucks and William G. Whitney, *Comparative Economic Systems,* 8th ed. (New York: Harper & Row, 1969).

15. In Allan G. Gruchy, *Comparative Economic Systems* (Boston: Houghton Mifflin, 1966) fascism and corporatism rated only parts of two pages (pp. 881–82) as a type of capitalism found in Spain and Portugal although Gruchy called attention to the fact that elements of the fascist type of system are found in a number of developing nations.

16. An extensive bibliography may be gleaned from Frederick B. Pike and Thomas Stritch, eds., *The New Corporatism, Social-Political Structures in the Iberian World* (Notre Dame: University of Notre Dame Press, 1974). See also the useful collection of essays in James Malloy, ed., *Authoritarianism and Corporatism in Latin America* (Pittsburgh: Pittsburgh University Press, 1977).

17. See, for example, Charles W. Anderson, *The Political Economy of Modern Spain: Policy-Making in an Authoritarian System* (Madison: University of Wisconsin Press, 1970).

18. Robert A. Brady, *Business as a System of Power* (New York: Columbia University Press, 1943), pp. 5–6.

19. Ibid., p. 246.

20.   John K. Galbraith, *The New Industrial State* (Boston: Houghton Mifflin, 1967); Andrew Shonfield, *Modern Capitalism: The Changing Balance of Public and Private Power* (New York: Oxford University Press, 1965), esp. pp. 230-33.

21.   Murray Weidenbaum, *The Modern Public Sector* (New York: Basic Books, 1969).

22.   Daniel R. Fusfeld, "The Rise of the Corporate State in America," *Journal of Economic Issues* 6 (March 1972). Note also the interpretation of Andreas G. Papandreou, *Paternalistic Capitalism* (Minneapolis: University of Minnesota Press, 1972).

23.   See Howard J. Wiarda, "Corporatism and Development in the Iberic-Latin World: Persistent Strains and New Variations," and Ronald C. Newton, "Natural Corporatism and the Passing of Populism in Latin America," both in Pike and Stritch, eds., *The New Corporatism, Social-Political Structures in the Iberian World*. See also Diamant, *Austrian Catholics and the First Republic*.

24.   On the Christian Democratic version of corporatist ideology see Francisco José Moreno, "The Breakdown of Chilean Democracy," *World Affairs* (Summer 1975): 15-25.

25.   Philippe C. Schmitter, "Still the Century of Corporatism?" *Review of Politics* (January 1974): 86.

26.   Louis J. Mark, "The Favored Status of the State Entrepreneur in Economic Development Programs," *Economic Development and Cultural Change* 7 (July 1959): 422-30.

27.   See William Glade, *The Latin American Economies* (New York: American Book Company, 1969) for a fuller account of this development style.

28.   On this matter, see William Glade, "The State and Economic Development in Mediterranean Polities," Paper presented at the 1973 Annual Meeting of the American Political Science Association, New Orleans, September 4-8. This point, the primacy of bureaucratized political power over commercial and industrial interests, was illuminatingly dealt with by Veblen in his studies of the German and Japanese experiences with industrialization. T. Veblen, *Imperial Germany and the Industrial Revolution* (New York: Viking Press, 1942), esp. Chapters 5 and 7; and "The Opportunity of Japan," in T. Veblen, *Essays in Our Changing Order* (New York: Viking Press, 1954).

29.   Immanuel Wallerstein, *The Modern World-System* (New York: Academic Press, 1974), ch. 3.

17 A HOLISTIC APPROACH TO UNDERDEVELOPMENT

James H. Street

When Gruchy three decades ago sought a more descriptive adjective for the distinctive American contribution to economic science then known as institutionalism, he chose "holistic." "The term 'holistic' " he wrote, "has been selected because it calls attention to what is most characteristic of the new economics: its interest in studying the economic system as an evolving, unified whole or synthesis, in the light of which the system's parts take on their full meaning."[1] The holistic approach to economics Gruchy defined as embracing two basic conceptions, one relating to the nature of the economic system as a whole and the other to the nature of human behavior. These were the most distinguishing elements that he found in common in the works of Veblen, Commons, Mitchell, Clark, and others in the heterodox American movement.

The first conception is that the economic system is "a cultural process or going concern, rather than a mechanism or equilibrium of stable economic relations."[2] The second is that human behavior is characterized by a constant readjustment to a world of ever-changing realities, as distinguished from the standard economic view that human behavior is primarily devoted to utilitarian deliberation and pecuniary calculation in a static system of markets.

239

These conceptions are now much less novel than they were in the early period of controversy. Yet in countless offshoots and proliferations they continue to support sharply divergent approaches to the study of advanced economies, the central subject matter of the discipline. As new heterodoxies emerge, both at home and abroad, it is becoming clear that the perceptions of holistic economics have equal force when applied to less developed countries. This is particularly true of those undergoing accelerated change, as in the case of many in Latin America and Africa. While they have diverse roots, the heterodoxies, including the Latin American Structuralist School, The Dependency School, and the radical economics of the New Left, share a common dissatisfaction with standard economics and tend in some respects to converge with institutionalism in their respective conceptions of economic development. This paper will focus on some relations between the Dependency School and current institutional theory as applied to developing countries.[3]

UNDERDEVELOPMENT AS A PROCESS

In the 1950s, a group of Latin American economists, which included Prebisch, Sunkel, and Pinto Santa Cruz, began to analyze the problems of their region as reflections of a distorted growth process that could not be understood in terms of the standard economic models relied upon by European and North American economists who had come to their countries as teachers and policy advisors.[4] Almost wholly unaware of the work of the North American institutionalists, this group, which came to be known as the Structuralist School, reached conclusions already set out by Gruchy:

> The economy, when viewed as a going system, is quite unlike the monistic, classical view of a static, competitive economy. It is instead a pluralistic economicro-cultural scheme of things which divides into a number of different types of economic activity ranging from the purely competitive to the purely monopolistic. This pluralistic economy possesses a cultural rather than a mechanical balance or equilibrium, which is the result of the working of a number of factors such as social habit, self-interest, and communal controls of various sorts. These various factors combine to give order to, and to provide a continuing basis for, the total complex of economic relations. It should be pointed out, however, that there is nothing permanent about the balance which the going economic system possesses; at times this balance is quite precariously established, as in the recent half-century of great technological change.[5]

The structuralists indeed thought of their national economies as having become gravely unbalanced in the historical process of growth, with some sectors, such as manufacturing, showing great dynamism, while others, such as agriculture and the traditional export sectors, severely lagged. The remedies urged upon Latin American governments by such authorities as the International Monetary Fund "experts" seemed only to aggravate these disequilibrium tendencies and indeed threatened to stop the growth process itself while achieving only limited forms of stability.[6]

In the celebrated monetarist-structuralist controversy, the structuralists argued that chronic inflation of the type then persistent in Argentina, Brazil, Chile, and Uruguay could not be attributed solely to irresponsible monetary and fiscal policies, as the IMF representatives and Chicago School economists insisted.[7] Hence inflation would not be curbed by a simple return to austerity conditions and the rule of the market. The structuralists believed that secular inflation was a result of underlying structural imbalances, and that without attention to such causes and a deliberate stimulus to growth, the inflationary pressure would persist. They argued that unless certain blockages or "bottlenecks" were eliminated, the growth process would become even more distorted.

In studying these bottlenecks, the structuralists made important advances in the holistic approach to understanding the development process. They examined empirically the structural shifts that had taken place in their economies, with particular attention to patterns of demographic growth and internal geographic, occupational, and social movements that had been almost wholly neglected by standard economists in their analyses. The bottlenecks they identified often turned out to be precisely the kind of institutional obstructions that had been described in other cultural contexts by Veblen, Commons, and Ayres and emphasized in Gruchy's description of holistic analysis. The structuralists showed that, given the peculiar cultural background of Latin America, reliance on market forces often contributed in exaggerated ways to conspicuous and wasteful consumption, as well as to speculative and superficial investment decisions inconsistent with the requirements of orderly growth.

This view was not only consistent with that of Veblen and Ayres, but of the general neo-institutionalist conception as summarized by Gruchy.

> The economic system of the neo-institutionalists is an open system whereas the economic system of the conventional economists is a closed system. When the neoinstitutionalists developed their concept of the economic system as a process they constructed it in such a way as to leave this process open to change and development and a lack of harmony between private firm efficiency and overall social efficiency. Their concept of the economic system as a dynamic evolving process is not built on the assumption that self-correcting market forces will always maintain the equilibrium of the economic system, or on the assumption that optimal efficiency of the micro-economic unit will necessarily lead automatically to the optimal efficiency of the total economic system. In this manner the

neo-institutionalists have kept the economic system, when viewed as a process, an open system into which disequilibrating forces can be introduced as an integral feature of economic activity.[8]

Not having the benefit of the North American institutionalist background, the Latin American structuralists were slower to recognize the critical importance of technological behavior as a motor force in the growth process. In their earlier writings, the structuralists tended to treat technological innovation as something available exclusively to the industrially advanced — or "center" — countries, as something to be withheld from the less developed or "periphery" countries or to be employed only as an instrument of neocolonial exploitation.[9] (This view persists in much of the current analysis of the technological gap by members of the Dependency School.)

Later, Prebisch and some of his associates realized that indigenous technological effort can and, indeed, must be stimulated in order to promote the growth process as well as the other social goals of a comprehensive development program. By this time the principal work of Ayres had been more widely disseminated and the empirical studies of Kuznets had corroborated the basic historical finding that a country's economic growth is "based on advancing technology and the institutional and ideological adjustments that it demands."[10]

Much of the extensive statistical investigation of comparative development carried out by Kuznets over the past quarter century has reinforced the structuralist view of the growth process and extended its application far beyond the Latin American region to a global range.[11] It is now quite common to read in the writings of development economists such as Rosenberg that "technological change serves as a mechanism of *adaptation* to a world in flux."[12] Raj says, "The most important of the factors internal to these [less developed] countries which determine their success in facing and overcoming the barriers to development are the economic and political power structure, the interests and values it upholds, and the choices that can (and cannot) be effectively made within such a framework."[13] The relation between technology and institutions in an evolving international economy is now a matter of world concern.

CONTRIBUTIONS OF THE DEPENDENCY SCHOOL

Economists loosely grouped as members of the Dependency School have carried Latin American structuralism a step further and given it a special emphasis. Dependency theory, it should be noted, takes a number of forms related to their respective intellectual derivations.[14] In its most limited form it is little more than a restatement of the colonial-neocolonial thesis long sustained by many historians of Latin America: "By dependence we mean a situation in which the economy of certain countries is conditioned by the development and expansion of another country to which the former is subjected."[15]

In a more expanded form, it is an extension of the regional structuralist analysis to incorporate a world economic structure that has grown increasingly maladjusted as its units have become inextricably more interdependent. In one way or another this is the interpretation accepted by Prebisch, Sunkel, and Pinto as they have moved from structuralism to dependency, and by others associated with this moderate form of dependency theory, among them Wionczek, Furtado, and Dos Santos.[16]

As a structuralist, Prebisch directed his attention to the foreign trade sector and developed a distinctive analysis of the secular terms of trade between the center and the periphery countries. He believed that a long-term deterioration in the terms of trade could be demonstrated empirically and explained by differing elasticities of demand, degrees of competition in resource versus finished good markets, and other factors peculiar to the respective cultural characteristics of the trading regions.[17] Although the analysis was much controverted, it was refined by Myrdal and has had a strong influence on policies later adopted by the International Monetary Fund with respect to shortfalls in foreign exchange earnings and by the World Bank with respect to nations' capacities to plan and repay long-term investments.

Prebisch concluded that a secular deterioration in the terms of trade and the consequent increased burden of debt repayment leads to increasing dependency by the developing countries, and that this trend requires new domestic and international institutional arrangements. These include countercyclical import substitution measures, increased regional market integration, international commodity agreements to reduce price fluctuations, and arrangements for transfers of income or loans to compensate for the gains to the center as a result of unjustifiably favorable terms of trade.

Prebisch's dependency analysis was reinforced by an independent study made by Singer, which showed that the early industrialization of a number of less developed countries had had few spread effects within their economies and had, in fact, tied them closer to foreign markets.[18]

Sunkel sees underdevelopment of the periphery and development of the center countries as "simply the two faces of a single universal process." Underdevelopment and development have been simultaneous historical occurrences that have interacted in ways that have permitted development of the advanced countries to take place at the expense of the underdevelopment of countries that have fed the process.[19]

In the earlier colonial and neocolonial periods, political and financial means of domination prevailed. Sunkel has concluded, however, that since World War II, international capitalism has become much more highly organized in the hands of multinational corporations, and governments work hand-in-glove with them to dominate weaker economies. Research and development are centralized in the home country, and foreign users are obliged to buy complete packages of entrepreneurship, management, skills, design, technology, financing, and market organization at oligopoly or monopoly prices. Even domestic brainpower, government credit agencies, import substitution policies, and other preferential arrangements are co-opted for the benefit of foreign firms. The result is increasing dependency and a widening of the technological gap.[20] Most other dependency theorists would share this conclusion.

Some dependency writers, taking their inspiration from Marxist-Leninist sources, would go even further.[21] They interpret underdevelopment as a deliberate form of international exploitation, by which the dominant capitalist countries extract the surpluses and even the potential surpluses of the periphery to increase their own power and wealth. Foreign investment and foreign aid alike are means of appropriating income, and the native capitalist classes — "lumpenbourgeoisie" — of the less developed countries are merely the agents of their overlords in the imperialist countries.[22] In the absence of international capitalist exploitation, the less developed countries would have developed their own industrial systems along more egalitarian lines, but these inherent countries established exclusive control over the relevant technology. A potential investible surplus that would have been created within the developing countries is drained by luxury consumption or aborted by monopoly control.

In this, the radical and most pessimistic view, dependency is a persistent historical condition from which there is no escape short of social revolution.

DEPENDENCY AND INSTITUTIONALISM

As heterodox explanations of economic development and underdevelopment, dependency and institutionalist theory share certain characteristics. Both are holistic, in Gruchy's sense. They do not conceive of development narrowly in conventional terms, but look upon it as "an evolving, unified whole or synthesis, in the light of which the system's parts take on their full meaning." The approach is interdisciplinary, drawing on anthropology, history, politics, and sociology, as well as economics, for an understanding of development. Historical evolution, shifting class structures, and modes of political control are central to the economic analysis, not extraneous to it, as in much standard economics. Moreover, neither institutionalists nor dependency theorists are reluctant to make explicit normative judgments, in contrast with economists who still assert a preference for positivism and eschew explicit value judgments, while at the same time implicitly upholding the accepted values of a market system.

Both institutionalism and dependency theory are deeply critical of orthodox economic doctrine on the grounds that it fails to provide an adequate historical explanation of the development process and that it is too narrowly based, in its preoccupation with the market, to serve as a useful guide for development policy. In yet another aspect they are similar. Both institutionalism and dependency theory recognize the importance of long-term trends and are more concerned with their explanation than with that of short-term crises, which often spring from immediate and particularistic political dilemmas. Yet, while institutionalism and dependency theory have much in common, the former provides a more comprehensive explanation of the development process, and there are significant differences in its interpretation. In concentrating solely on the exogenous factors influencing the development process, the Dependency School has granted scant importance to domestic, and often deeply cultural, factors that have also contributed to economic retardation.

There is little doubt that the present control of most high technology and the means of its propagation by multinational corporations poses difficulties in the international transfer and acquisition of useful knowledge, and thus reinforces existing dependency relationships. However, in focusing attention on this comparatively recent development, dependency theory has neglected to explain the relative paucity of indigenous scientific and technological activity within the underdeveloped world, or to suggest means by which such activity could be stimulated as a way to overcome continued dependency. In Latin America, institutionalists would investigate the reasons for the disappearance in the colonial period of the native innovative spirit characteristic of the Aztec and Inca civilizations and the subsequent failure to revive it in modern times. They question whether, without concrete efforts to implant an indigenous scientific and technological strategy to cope with the region's problems, the widening development gap can be overcome.

Moreover, institutionalists would not abandon the promising study of domestic bottlenecks undertaken by the structuralists in favor of a recent exclusive concern with outside influences. They find that many of the obstacles to economic development remain in the repressive features of local institutions, in which military intervention, reverence for the caudillo, or charismatic leader, and a preference for ceremonial over functional behavior in many levels of society play a large part.

Institutionalists are less ideologically committed than the more radical dependency theorists to a Marxist view of historical inevitability, class struggle, and the probability or desirability of a violent solution. While they recognize the powerful force of institutions and the social conflicts they engender, they rarely take a doomsday view of the necessity for an ultimate breakdown of the social structure. They are more inclined to think that the historical process can be altered through the application of collective intelligence, or the conscious search for useful innovations and alternatives.

Bath and James have noted the lack of conceptual clarity and consistency among dependency theorists when they utilize such terms as "social class," "ruling class," "elite," and "peasants and workers" in relation to class struggle analysis.[23] As these authors observe, "the rather mechanistic employment of the concept of class may underrate the role played by individualism and personalismo in Latin American political culture." In a fluid society, the shifting composition of groups may interfere with the development of class solidarity and make it difficult for the social analyst to establish clearly where the dependency relationships reside.

Institutionalists note that coercive and exploitative behavior may be observed among the lower classes as well as among dominant elites, and among Third World countries as well as among capitalist. Thus, the recent pricing decisions of the Organization of Petroleum Exporting Countries, in their impact on other underdeveloped countries that must import oil, created new dependency relationships and showed little to distinguish their actions from other forms of monopolistic behavior originating in industrial countries.

The prediction that dependency must ultimately lead to the violent overthrow of the dominant classes and that this outcome will insure a regime of social progress is met with skepticism by most institutionalists. A number of major social upheavals have occurred in Latin America without establishing a model for the alleviation of high infant mortality, widespread hunger, rampant inflation, mass unemployment, urban overcrowding, and political repression.

Much of the dependency analysis tends to reinforce the fatalistic mood traditionally present in Latin American society. In contrast, institutionalism seeks to discover ways in which social effort may be redirected constructively and formal institutions reshaped to become functionally useful. This is more than a preference for optimism over pessimism; it stems from a stronger belief in the efficacy of technology in all its forms and in the progressive evolutionary character of society.

The efficacy of technology rests upon two principles elaborated by Ayres: that technology is essentially an autonomous, self-sustaining process, and that the potential for fruitful discoveries will be enhanced in a receptive environment.[24] Ayres rejected the conventional notion that invention and discovery are best explained in market terms: i.e., that they depend chiefly on consumer demand or on financial investment. Instead, technology is an independent continuum of interrelated discoveries and applications whose extension depends on a preexisting milieu filled with artifacts and with informed investigators who constantly manipulate and recombine them and examine the results. Thus the greater the stock of existing technological devices, the greater the number of permutations and recombinations in the form of new inventions that are likely to occur.

In addition, such an environment of widespread research and development increases the chances of serendipity — the faculty of making desirable but unsought-for discoveries by accident. Ayres has cited many such instances of "accidental" discoveries rendered virtually predictable by the facilitating conditions of the cultural environment. A survey of the technological history of Latin America and sub-Saharan Africa would reveal that such an environment has existed in few places in the respective regions and, in modern times, over only relatively short periods. This cultural hiatus helps to explain the paucity of technological creativity, with a few notable exceptions.

A third principle laid down by Ayres suggests that Latin America and Africa may benefit from the circumstance that growth is now taking place under frontier conditions.[25] Ayres has shown that the possibilities for cross-fertilization of techniques is increased when a new frontier is penetrated. A frontier is a region that offers the space for expansion of population in movement, for a rupture with old institutions, and for the application of techniques brought from other regions to achieve an accelerated rate of development. Given the increased cultural contact and the special challenges posed by frontier conditions, new combinations and adaptations of useful knowledge are almost certain to occur. There is mounting evidence that such inventions and adaptations, particularly in agricultural biology and in industrial techniques, are occurring with increasing frequency in Latin America.[26] The Dependency School has tended to overlook or to minimize the significance of these achievements.

CONCLUSION

A holistic approach to underdevelopment has proved abundantly fruitful in understanding the growth process as it occurs in a variety of geographic and cultural settings. Yet, as we have seen, holism is a general framework that embraces a number of alternative interpretations. Institutionalists believe that their approach is not only more comprehensive than that of the Dependency School, but that it offers much greater promise for a strategy of progress.

In view of the widening technological gap between the advanced and the less developed countries and the inadequacy of existing institutions to cope with the problems of unbalanced growth, it is clear that forms of social planning that Gruchy and other institutionalists have long advocated are urgently needed. For developing countries, such planning must include both a comprehensive strategy for fostering domestic scientific and technological activity and a major effort to substitute functional for ceremonial objectives in the operation of basic social institutions. For social science, the task is to continue to investigate the most feasible means to achieve such a social transformation.

ENDNOTES

1. Allen G. Gruchy, *Modern Economic Thought: The American Contribution* (New York: Prentice-Hall, 1947), p. viii.

2. Ibid., pp. 557–58.

3. As the writer's experience has been derived chiefly in Latin America, he relies on the work of other institutionalists for applications to Africa. See, for example, Thomas R. de Gregori, *Technology and the Economic Development of the Tropical African Frontier* (Cleveland: Western Reserve University, 1969); and Jacob Oser, *Promoting Economic Development; with Illustrations from Kenya* (Evanston Ill.: Northwestern University Press, 1967).

4. For references to the literature of the formative period of the structuralist movement, see Joseph Grunwald, "The 'Structuralist' School on Price Stability and Development: The Chilean Case," in Albert O. Hirschman, ed., *Latin American Issues: Essays and Comments* (New York: Twentieth Century Fund, 1961), pp. 95–123; and James H. Street, "The Latin American 'Structuralists' and the Institutionalists: Convergence in Development Theory," *Journal of Economic Issues* 1 (June 1967): 44–62.

5. Gruchy, *Modern Economic Thought*, p. 558.

6. Aníbal Pinto Santa Cruz, *Ni estabilidad ni desarrollo — La politica del Fondo Monetario Internacional* (Santiago, Chile: Editorial Universitaria, 1960).

7. Osvaldo Sunkel, "Chilean Inflation — a Heterodox Approach," *International Economic Papers,* No. 10 (London: Macmillan, 1960); and Werner Baer, "The Inflation Controversy in Latin America: A Survey," *Latin American Research Review* 2 (Spring 1967): 3–25.

8. Allan G. Gruchy, *Contemporary Economic Thought: The Contribution of Neo-Institutional Economics* (Clifton, N.J.: Augustus M. Kelley, 1974), pp. 294–95.

9. Street, "The Latin American 'Structuralists' and the Institutionalists," pp. 56–59.

10. Clarence E. Ayres, *The Theory of Economic Progress,* 2d ed. (New York: Schocken Books, 1962); Simon Kuznets, "Modern Economic Growth: Findings and Reflections," *American Economic Review* 63 (June 1973): 247.

11. Simon Kuznets, *Modern Economic Growth: Rate, Structure, and Spread* (New Haven: Yale University Press, 1966). Kuznets's contribution to economic development theory extends to many other works.

12. Nathan Rosenberg, "Technology, Natural Resources and Economic Growth" (Paper presented at the Fifth World Congress of the International Economic Association, Tokyo, 29 August-3 September 1977, p. 7. (Mimeograph)

13. K. N. Raj. "Barriers to Development" (Paper presented at the Fifth World Congress of the International Economic Association, Tokyo, 29 August-3 September 1977, p. 10. (Mimeograph)

14. For a comprehensive bibliography and critique of the Dependency School, see C. Richard Bath and Dilmus D. James, "Dependency Analysis of Latin America: Some Criticisms, Some Suggestions," *Latin American Research Review* 11 (Fall 1976): 3-54.

15. Theotonio Dos Santos, "The Structure of Dependence," *American Economic Review* 60 (May 1970): 231; Stanley J. Stein and Barbara Stein, *The Colonial Heritage: Essays on Economic Dependence in Perspective* (New York: Oxford University Press, 1970).

16. Bath and James, "Dependency Analysis," pp. 6-10.

17. Raúl Prebisch, "Commercial Policy in the Underdeveloped Countries," *American Economic Review* 49 (May 1959): 251-73; and "The Economic Development of Latin America and Its Principal Problems," *Economic Bulletin for Latin America* 7 (February 1962): 1-22. Gunnar Myrdal, *Rich Lands and Poor* (New York: Harper and Bros. 1957), chs. 5, 8.

18. Hans Singer, "The Distribution of Gains between Investing and Borrowing Countries," *American Economic Review* 40 (May 1950): 473-85.

19. Osvaldo Sunkel, "Transnational Capitalism and National Disintegration in Latin America," *Social and Economic Studies* 22 (1973): 132-76.

20. Sunkel, "The Pattern of Latin American Dependence," in Victor L. Urquidi and Rosemary Thorp, eds., *Latin America in the International Economy*, (London: Macmillan, 1973), pp. 3-25.

21. André Gunder Frank, *Capitalism and Underdevelopment in Latin America: Historical Studies of Chile and Brazil* (New York: Monthly Review Press, 1967). See also James Petras, ed., *Latin America: From Dependence to Revolution* (New York: John Wiley and Sons, 1973).

22. Frank, *Lumpenbourgeoisie: Lumpendevelopment, Dependence, Class and Politics in Latin America* (New York: Monthly Review Press, 1972).

23. Bath and James, "Dependency Analysis," pp. 14-19. The quotation is on p. 19.

24. Ayres, *The Theory of Economic Progress*, pp. 125-54.

25. James H. Street, "The Technological Frontier in Latin America: Creativity and Productivity," *Journal of Economic Issues* 10 (September 1976): 538-58.

26. Dilmus D. James and James H. Street, eds., *Technological Progress in Latin America: The Prospects for Overcoming Dependency* (forthcoming).